CADOGAN
island guides

THE NORTH
CARI

CW00499041

Cadogan Books plc
London House, Parkgate Road, London SW11 4NQ

Distributed in the USA by
The Globe Pequot Press
6 Business Park Road, PO Box 833, Old Saybrook,
Connecticut 06475-0833

Copyright © James Henderson 1994
Illustrations © Charles Shearer 1994

Book and cover design by Animage
Cover illustrations by Sue Dray
Maps © Cadogan Guides, drawn by Thames Cartographic Ltd

Series Editors: Rachel Fielding and Vicki Ingle
Editing: Dominique Shead
Indexing: Isobel McLean
Production: Rupert Wheeler Book Production Services
Macintosh: Jacqueline Lewin

ISBN 0-94-7754-82-2

A catalogue record for this book is available from the British Library
US Library of Congress Cataloging-in-Publication-Data available

The author and publishers have made every effort to ensure the accuracy of the information in this book at the time of going to press. However, they cannot accept any responsibility for any loss, injury or inconvenience resulting from the use of information contained in this guide.

Printed and bound in Great Britain by Redwood Books Ltd, Trowbridge, Wiltshire on Jordan Opaque supplied by McNaughton Publishing Papers Ltd.

About the Author

For the past six years, James Henderson has studied the Caribbean from a top-floor flat in London, from the window of tiny island-hopping planes and through scuba-diving masks. He travels there as much as possible, braving flash tropical downpours and droughts, *coups d'état*, 'jerk', drunken bus drivers and posses of mad Californians; dodging safari buses of cruise-ship passengers and the attentions of over-zealous aloe masseuses, jumbies and machete-flourishing coconut salesmen. Half English and half Scots, he has lived in the UK, USA, Cyprus and the Arabian Gulf, and has wandered Europe, Pakistan and Afghanistan.

He has lingered longest in the Caribbean, still watching for the Green Flash and writing features for the *Financial Times*.

Acknowledgements

For the third time, my thanks go to all West Indians, native and adoptive, who make travelling in the islands such fun; for all the lifts (cars, bikes, boats and planes), beers, beds for the night; to all the voluble taxi-drivers, limers and tourism officials who responded so kindly to hours of questions, and then replied to urgent and demanding faxes. I'd like to thank, in particular: in Antigua, Irma Tomlinson, Mrs Tongue and family; in Montserrat, Leona Midgette and the Osbornes; in Nevis Lauren Griffin; Goldwyn Caines in St Kitts and in Anguilla, Amelia Vanterpool; in the Dutch Windwards, William Bell, Maxine Suares and Roland Lopes and Glen Holm; in Saint Martin, Maryse Romney for amazing footwork, and Elise Magras in St Barts. For a tour of the Virgin Islands Russel Harrigan, Keith Dawson and the crowd at Soper's Hole; in the USVI Bob Kirkpatrick and particularly Gail and Jared for joining me in at Christmas.

Back in London, thanks go to all tourist board members and others who sat through a further bombardment of questions and to those who took the trouble to write with Caribbean tales of joy (and sometimes woe).

Please help us to keep this guide up to date

Keeping a guide to the Caribbean up to date is a daunting task—you need to start again as soon as you've reached the end. We need your thoughts to create as complete a picture as possible for each update. If you feel that you have some ideas for the guide, send them in; be as opinionated as you like. Writers of the best letters each year are awarded a complimentary guide of their choice from the series.

Contents

Introduction

The views from island to island in the Caribbean present even seasoned travellers with such heart-stopping moments they wish time would stand still. Each island stands out majestically, etched on the horizon, visible for as much as fifty miles. Some are rainforested volcanic peaks that soar from the waves, so tall that their heights are permanently wreathed with clouds; elsewhere there are islands with gentler slopes, scrub-covered coral caps set in absurdly bright turquoise shallows.

Even in the days of quick and convenient air travel, the islands are best approached by sea. You can get the measure of them as they grow from a grey stain on the horizon to a green mountain towering above you; typically, a line of waterfront houses ahead, standing among the palm trees and the masts of yachts at anchor. You glide into harbour, tie up and take a leisurely walk ashore. For centuries people have arrived in the Caribbean this way. It makes flying in seem brutal by comparison.

With so many islands packed close, many linked by ferry, the north-eastern Caribbean is particularly suited to island-hopping; and it's surprising just how different from one another the islands can be. Just a few miles separate a busy port like St Thomas, now a cruise-ship stop and almost a far-flung American shopping precinct, from the isolated cruising grounds of the pirates in the British Virgin Islands; and the enigmatic British Crown colony of Anguilla from one of the most chic parts of France, the equally enigmatic St Barts.

The landmasses themselves are all quite small. (Antigua is the largest at about a hundred square miles, and has a population of 65,000.) Life is slow and gentle, with plenty of opportunity for sitting around in waterfront bars admiring the sea or the sunset. Until recently most of the islands were poor, but with tourist development some have become quite prosperous. Building is threatening to overwhelm a few; in places island life is almost invisible beneath a fabric of international glitz.

As a general rule the northeastern islands are more expensive than others in the Caribbean, and you can usually expect to pay as much for food and lodging as you would at home. A few islands have gone in for package tourism in a big way, particularly St Thomas, Sint Maarten and lately Antigua. These islands offer a complete and typically hedonistic Caribbean break—with sun, sea, sand, sports, restaurants, casinos and nightlife.

But, if it's more of an escape that you crave, scattered among even the major developments you can still find some Caribbean gems: delightful waterfront restaurants where the waves wash gently beneath you, super-luxurious hotels in incomparable tropical settings and, of course, an easy island life, spiced by the ever-present liveliness of the West Indians themselves.

Guide to the Guide

Each island is organized according to the same format. The **Introduction** sets the scene and brings out the island's unique characteristics. This is followed by a **History** of the island, and unique '**Topics**' of interest including a section on **Flora and Fauna**. Next come the practical details: **Getting There and Around**, with details of services by boat; **Tourist Information**, including facts about local **currency and exchange**. Next come the all-important sections on beach-bound Caribbean life: a round-up of the best **Beaches**, **Beach bars** and **Watersports**. A **Sailing Guide** recommends favourite anchorages and the liveliest marinas. Where applicable, **land-based sports** are mentioned too, including tennis, horse-riding and golf. Next is the **gazetteer**, a round-up of sights, starting with each capital city and followed by a tour or worthwhile places to visit. Each island section or chapter concludes with a list of **Festivals**, and a list of recommendations on **Where to Stay**, **Eating Out**, **Nightlife**, **Shopping** and **Further Reading**.

Essential Geography

The islands of the northeastern Caribbean make up the northern half of the Lesser Antilles. They stand in two arcs, running essentially southeast to northwest. An inner ring of relatively young volcanoes (about 15 million years old) comprises the islands from Montserrat up to Saba. Farther out in the Atlantic, another, much older string of islands (about 100 million years old) runs from Antigua to Anguilla. Here you will find the best sand, because the coral reefs have been ground down into granules by wave action and then washed up on the tide. Geographically speaking, the Virgin Islands are really in the Greater Antilles (they are attached to the same mass as Puerto Rico), but in history and culture they are more similar to the Leeward Islands to their east.

The area has a variety of names: Caribbean comes from the indigenous tribe of American Indians, the Caribs, who inhabited the Lesser Antilles until the arrival of the Europeans. The origin of the term West Indies lies with Columbus himself—he discovered the islands while trying to find a route via the west to India—and 'Antilles' derives from Antillia, supposedly a corruption of Atlantis, the lost continent that was presumed to lie beyond the Azores.

The region is made up of independent nations (formerly British colonies), current British and Dutch Crown colonies, overseas *départements* of France and a Territory of the United States. This guide approaches them from Antigua and Barbuda in the south, tracks north along the island chain through the old British Leeward Islands, Montserrat, St Kitts and Nevis and to Anguilla, then collects the three Dutch Windward Islands of Sint Maarten, Sint Eustatius and Saba (the Dutch Leewards are 600 miles downwind). Then we deal with the two French *communes* of Saint Martin and Saint Barthélémy. Finally there are the British and US Virgin Islands.

The Northeastern Caribbean at a Glance

Anguilla: Laid back and uncrowded, Anguilla is slowly developing It is still known for its enclaves of high luxury, but there are cheaper places to stay. Eating out is quite pricey, but there are good restaurants and bars on beaches of superb sand.

Antigua: This is the chosen retreat of many wealthy expatriates, with the hotels and restaurants to serve them, alongside a large package-tourism industry. It is fairly expensive, but is easy to reach and has active beaches with watersports as well as countless miles of undisturbed, superb sand. Antigua is known for its sailing, out of English Harbour and Falmouth Harbour in the south.

Barbuda: Attached to Antigua, tiny Barbuda is one of the least-known islands in the Caribbean. It has superb sand, a couple of outrageously expensive hotels and a lazy Caribbean life that has not changed in about fifty years.

The British Virgin Islands: The BVI are easy-going, sophisticated and pretty expensive. There are good restaurants and bars on Tortola (the main island) and a nautical feel with all the passing yachts—the islands have excellent sailing. Across Francis Drake Channel are the nearly deserted Norman Island, Cooper Island (nothing but a beach bar) and the second island, Virgin Gorda, with a string of excellent hotels and beaches. Jost van Dyke and Anegada are low-key.

Montserrat: Slow and sedate, Montserrat has just a few comfortable hotels and villas. There is not much nightlife, and few beaches in the typical Caribbean mould.

Nevis: Undeveloped Nevis has slow and gentle small-island life, a few bars and restaurants, some excellent beaches and several classic Caribbean plantation hotels.

Saba: Saba is a tiny outcrop with gentle, easy-going islanders, a quiet and trusty retreat with excellent diving. It is developing slowly, but retains its old charm.

Saint Barthélémy (St Barts): St Barts is a champagne playground, as only the French would conceive. It has some charming hotels and fine restaurants, and is very expensive. There is barely any West Indian culture to distract you from the essentials of gourmet dining, sunning and posing.

St Kitts: The larger and marginally more developed partner of Nevis in the Leeward Islands, St Kitts has an easy-going West Indian atmosphere. Its beaches and the traditional Caribbean resort hotels are in the south; the north has some of the Caribbean's best plantation hotels.

Saint Martin: Saint Martin is the larger and (marginally) less developed French half of the island, shared with Dutch Sint Maarten. It has good beaches, some smart hotels, a number of nice (if expensive) guest houses and excellent restaurants, all with a Gallic atmosphere that is quite expensive.

Sint Eustatius: A tiny outcrop, whose heyday was really two centuries ago, Sint Eustatius is a very peaceful writer's retreat.

Sint Maarten: Sint Maarten is the more developed (Dutch) half of an island shared with French Saint Martin with a large tourist industry. It has excellent beaches and good sports facilities, casinos and shops. There are also great restaurants (with an endless choice of others in the French half) and bars. It is strong on package tourism and too developed for some, but the locals swear by the island.

The United States Virgin Islands: St Thomas is highly developed and easily reached from mainland USA. There are big hotels and endless shopping in Charlotte Amalie. The island gets crowded, but it has great restaurants and bars and is a good transit point. St Croix is larger and less developed, but still has some nice hotels and restaurants; it has recovered from Hurricane Hugo. St John is the least developed— much of it is National Park. There are good bars and restaurants on the coasts.

Travel

Getting There

By Air

From the UK

The eastern Caribbean is quite well served from the UK, both by scheduled and charter flights. The transatlantic flight takes around 8 hours and so with the time change (chasing the sun around the earth) you usually arrive in good time to catch onward flights to almost all the Caribbean islands or just to settle down and watch the sunset. Peak fares are charged in the weeks around Christmas, and between July and September. This is slightly curious because it does not coincide with the Caribbean's own high season (the winter in the northern hemisphere), which runs from about mid-January to mid-April.

British Airways has the widest range of services to the eastern Caribbean from the UK, with direct flights to Antigua, Barbados, Puerto Rico and St Lucia. Concorde flies to Barbados during the winter season, nearly cutting the journey time in half. All BA flights except Concorde depart from Gatwick (*see* individual island sections for regularity of service, reservations © 071 759 5511).

BWIA, the airline of Trinidad and Tobago, also has a number of flights, departing London Heathrow for Port of Spain in Trinidad (occasionally Tobago *en route*), Barbados and Antigua, with easy onward connections to the other eastern Caribbean islands. BWIA reservations in the UK: © 071 839 9333.

Generally speaking, scheduled flights from the UK to the Caribbean are expensive. Peak season fares (a scheduled economy return) cost between £800 and £900 and in the low season they drop to between £700 and £800. Prices do not vary that much between the airlines and they vary little according to your destination. These fares require 21 days' advance booking, and there are penalties for changing reservations. There are slightly more expensive fares available if you want a bit more flexibility. The trip on Concorde will set you back a cool £4500.

Lower fares (than the official published rates above) are almost always on offer, subject to availability, on the scheduled airlines and these can be booked through travel agents. The charter airlines (Caledonian, Air UK and Airtours) also offer seats on a flight-only basis and these are perhaps your best bet for a cheap ticket, but there are very tight restrictions. Contact the Caribbean travel agents mentioned below. With luck, you can find a return fare to the Caribbean for as little as £300.

UK travel agents specializing in flights to the Caribbean, on scheduled and charter airlines, include **Transatlantic Wings**, 70 Pembroke Road, London W8 6NX (© 071 602 4021), **Caribbean Gold**, 7 Albion Court, Albion Place, London

W6 0QT (℗ 081 741 8491), **Caribbean Travel**, 367 Portobello Road, London W10 5SG (℗ 081 969 6230), **New Look Travel**, 111 High Street, London NW10 4TR (℗ 081 965 9657), **Newmont Travel**, 85 Balls Pond Road, London N1 4BL (℗ 071 254 6546) and **Stoke Newington Travel**, 168 Stoke Newington Road, London N16 7UY (℗ 071 254 0136). There are two flights clubs in the UK. You join for a minimal fee and then are sent information about fares at considerable reductions (subject to the usual availability). BWIA's **Sunjet Reunion Club** can be contacted at 48 Leicester Square, London WC2H 7LT (℗ 071 930 1335) and the **Reunion Club** run by tour operator Caribbean Connection can be reached at 93 Newman Street, London W1P 3LE (℗ 071 344 0101).

From Europe

Lufthansa fly from Frankfurt to Antigua, San Juan (both twice weekly) and Sint Maarten (weekly); **BWIA** to Antigua, Barbados and Trinidad from Frankfurt in Germany (reservations ℗ 069 628 025) and Zurich in Switzerland (reservations ℗ 1 312 7373); **Air France** from Paris to Martinique, Guadeloupe and Sint Maarten; and **KLM** from Amsterdam to Sint Maarten. **Iberia**, Spain's national airline, flies to Spanish Caribbean countries, with flights to San Juan (Puerto Rico), Santo Domingo (the Dominican Republic), Havana and Aruba. Scheduled fares are expensive. There is also a number of European charter operators which offer discounted fares.

From the USA

American Airlines have the most extensive service from the States to the eastern Caribbean. They fly to Antigua, Sint Maarten, St Thomas and St Croix, usually in time to catch onward flights. Many services originate in New York (JFK) or Miami (there are often two flights a day), or touch them *en route*. American Airlines also have a hub in the Caribbean island of Puerto Rico, from where their subsidiary American Eagle has onward flights to the British Virgin Islands, Anguilla, Sint Maarten and St Kitts (Vigie airport near Castries). **Continental Airlines** fly from Newark, New Jersey to Antigua and the Virgin Islands. **Delta** flies regularly from Miami and has other services from Orlando to Nassau, San Juan, St Thomas and St Croix (in the USVI) and Sint Maarten. **USA Air** fly from a variety of cities on the east coast (Baltimore, Philadelphia, Charlotte and Tampa) to San Juan, St Thomas and Sint Maarten.

Fares from the USA vary little from one carrier to another. The seasons are strictly observed: mid-December to mid-April is high season, late June to mid-September is the summer peak, and the rest of the year is low season. Sample scheduled midweek round-trip fares from Miami to Jamaica are $250 and to Antigua $400, from New York to Jamaica $350 and to Antigua $450 in low season. From the Midwest add around $100, from the West Coast $200. These fares require advance booking and there is usually a minimum stay of a week; supplements are payable for weekend travel and cancellations. Charter flights are also available through travel agents and this may mean as much as a third off the scheduled price. Check the newspapers and your travel agent.

From Canada

Air Canada flies direct, usually out of Toronto but occasionally Montreal, to a number of destinations in the eastern Caribbean, including Antigua, Guadeloupe, St Lucia and Barbados. Another alternative is to connect with American or Caribbean carriers in New York or Miami. **BWIA** also fly from Toronto in Canada to Port of Spain, stopping over in Antigua and Barbados. Once again, there are plenty of charter flights from Canada servicing the vacation packages. Further details on flights to and between the islands are listed under the 'Getting There' sections for each island.

By Boat

Cruise liner is a popular way of travelling around the Caribbean, and it enables you to visit as many as four or five different islands in a week, without the hassle of delayed flights or even packing your suitcase. Most depart from Miami or Fort Lauderdale and a few are based in San Juan, Puerto Rico. They sail all year round.

Cruise-ship companies include **Celebrity Cruises,** with three liners (UK ✆ 071 412 0290, fax 412 0908, USA toll free ✆ 800 437 3111), **Cunard** (UK ✆ 071 839 1414, fax 839 1837, USA toll free ✆ 800 221 4770), **Kloster Cruise Lines** (UK ✆ 071 493 6041, fax 081 748 4542, USA toll free ✆ 800 327 3090), which has six liners, and **Princess Cruises** (UK ✆ 071 831 1881, USA toll free ✆ 800 421 0880).

A large number of yachts make the Atlantic crossing to the Caribbean towards the end of the year (after spending the summer in the Mediterranean), arriving in time for the winter sailing season. You might be able to pick up a yacht on the south coast of Britain, in the south of France, in Gibraltar, or even in the Canaries any time from September (just after the hurricane season). Try the yacht club noticeboards and yachting magazines. The **Cruising Association**, CA House,

1 Northey Street, Lime House Basin, London E14 8BT (© 071 537 2828), has a crewing service, connecting skippers and crew in a monthly newsletter (£18 to have your name on the list). You negotiate from there with the skipper.

Experience is not necessarily required. Most yachts will charge you just enough to cover food or nothing at all, but there are one or two sharks around who have been making outrageous charges for what can be quite a hard three-week sail. If you are worried about the crossing, catamarans are more comfortable. The return journey across the Atlantic generally takes place at the end of April, fairly soon after Antigua Race week, and the ports of Antigua are the best places to look if you wish to make the eastward crossing.

In the same way the American yachting community migrates down to the Caribbean over the winter. Once again, try yacht club noticeboards, the yachting magazines and the ports on the eastern seaboard.

Entry Requirements and Customs

As a British citizen you do not need a visa to any of the Commonwealth Caribbean countries or the French or Netherlands Antilles. Americans and Canadians travelling as tourists do not need a visa to enter any Caribbean country. Citizens of other countries do not usually need a visa, except sometimes to Puerto Rico and the US Virgin Islands (same regulations as USA). In most of the Caribbean islands, a proof of identity is enough, though a passport is the best document for Europeans. Business visitors should consult the Embassy before departure.

The Caribbean may be known for being laid back. Their immigration authorities, however, are most definitely not so. Invariably they will demand to see an onward ticket and they will hold your passport until you produce one. Some islands may require proof of funds. On the immigration form you will also be asked to give a local address: this is almost a formality as they rarely check up, but it eases entry to put something down. Addresses of hotels and guest houses are at the end of each separate island chapter.

It is worth remembering to keep some change for when you leave, because most countries levy a **departure tax**, usually payable in US dollars, but sometimes demanded in local currency (listed in the separate island sections).

Drugs not issued on prescription are illegal in the Caribbean and people do occasionally end up inside for possession of user quantities. Customs officials operate a strict policy against them and they search bags going in and out of the countries. While on an island you will probably be approached by 'oregano salesman' with an offer of marijuana (weed, ganja etc.) and occasionally cocaine. You will not be popular if you are caught. Alcohol and tobacco allowances vary from island to island.

Most holidays to the Caribbean are sold as scheduled or charter packages, and with these you can get anything from a two-week, two-destination package at two different luxury resorts at opposite ends of the Caribbean Sea, through the proliferation of wedding and honeymoon packages (complete with nuptial underwear if you want), to the charter holidays that take advantage of the low season rates and give you a return flight and two weeks' accommodation for less than the price of a normal scheduled return airfare. Because of the discounts they can get by block-booking airline seats and hotel rooms, tour operators can put together a package more cheaply than an independent traveller. A well-informed travel agent can sift through the multiplicity of packages and find the best one for you. Many of the tour companies include obligatory **insurance** in their packages, but travel agents will always sell you a policy. Check your existing policies—it is worth insuring against medical problems, cancelled flights and lost luggage.

Tour Operators in the UK

The biggest Caribbean tour operator in the UK, and one of the most flexible when it comes to tailor-making a holiday is **Caribbean Connection**, which offers a wide-ranging selection of hotels and villas in many of the Caribbean islands; Concorde House, Forest Street, Chester CH1 1QR (© 0244 341131, fax 0244 310255). **Elegant Resorts**, 24 Nicholas Street, Chester CH1 2ER (© 0244 329671, fax 0244 341084) also offer top of the range packages and have knowledgeable staff; as do **Thomas Cook Holidays**, PO Box 36, Thorpe Wood, Peterborough, Cambridgeshire PE3 6SB (© 0733 332255, fax 0733 505784). Smaller operators include the friendly **Caribtours** at 161 Fulham Road, London SW3 6SN (© 071 581 3517, fax 071 225 2491) who give a personalized service; **Harlequin Worldwide Travel** at 2 North Road, South Ockendon, Essex RM15 6QJ (© 0708 852780, fax 0708 854952), who tailor-make to off-beat hotels in lesser-known island destinations as well as the big Caribbean hotels; and **Silk Cut Faraway Holidays**, Meon House, Petersfield, Hants GU32 3JN (© 0730 265211, fax 0730 260263), a smaller operator which offers tailor-made trips to smaller hotels around the islands. They also have a villa programme through their sister company, Meon Villas. **VFB Holidays** 'Faraway France' arrange trips to the French Caribbean. **BVI Holidays** (© 0279 656111, fax 0279 506616) specialize in the BVI.

If your main desire is to get to the West Indies for as little money as possible, you can travel with one of the charter package companies and the best prices are in summer. Some of the cheapest are offered by **Airtours** at Wavell House, Holcombe Road, Helmshore, Rossendale, Lancs BB4 4NB (© 0706 260000). **Thomson**

Holidays, Greater London House, Hampstead Road, London NW1 7SD (reservations: London © 081 200 8733; Birmingham © 021 632 6282; Manchester © 061 236 3828) reach most of the major Caribbean islands, departing from Heathrow, Gatwick and Manchester.

special-interest holidays

Honeymoon packages (with wedding included if you want) get ever more popular and most of the tour operators above will arrange one for you. Some tour operators are offering twin-destination holidays, perhaps with a week in another Caribbean island or in Florida. If you have specific requirements, most would be happy to tailor-make a holiday for you, though it may cost a fair bit. If you wish to spend less, the specialist Caribbean travel agent **Transatlantic Wings**, 70 Pembroke Road, London W8 6NX (© 071 602 4021, fax 071 603 6101), offer transatlantic flights and bookings in a number of smaller and more off-beat Caribbean hotels. The **Caribbean Centre** (© 081 940 3399) will also book hotels for you (with some considerably discounted rates), either for a full two-week period or for a couple of days before you set off travelling.

Tour Operators in the USA

Many Caribbean hotels have a booking agent in the United States or a dedicated reservation number, so you may choose to arrange your bookings direct and fix your own transport. Tour operators working out of the USA include **Caribbean Concepts**, 575 Underhill Boulevard, Syosset, NY 11791 (© 516 496 9800, fax 516 496 9880, toll free © 800 423 4433), a small operator catering to the upper end of the market, who will arrange flights, car hire and hotel accommodation; **Alken Tours** (© 718 856 7711, fax 718 282 1152); **French Caribbean International**, 5662 Calle Real, Suite 333, Santa Barbara, CA 93117–2317 (©/fax 805 967 9850, US and Canada © 800 373 6246), specialists in the French Caribbean islands; and **Fling Vacations**, 999 Postal Road, Allentown PA 18103 (© 215 266 6110, fax 266 0280, toll free © 800 523 9624). Big Caribbean operators include **American Express Vacations** (toll free © 800 241 1700), **GoGo Tours**, with offices all over the country (head office 201 934 3500 or toll free in New York City © 800 526 0405) and **Travel Impressions** (toll free © 800 284 0044). Most tour companies will arrange a **honeymoon** for you in the Caribbean.

Getting Around

Island hopping is one of the great pleasures of a holiday in the Lesser Antilles. There is a grand variety of islands within a relatively short distance of one another and they are visible one from the next for the 500 miles from Grenada in the south to Anguilla in the north. Twenty minutes' flying can get you from a French over-seas *département* to independent islands that have a strong British heritage, from busy, developed countries to tiny, comatose blips with just a few shacks and palm trees.

Most of the big Caribbean tour operators will arrange an island-hopping itinerary for you, with flights between hotels. If you wish to travel more independently (and less expensively) you can take off on your own with one of the island-hopper tickets issued by the local Caribbean airlines (*see* below). The specialist Caribbean travel agent **Transatlantic Wings** (© 602 4021, address above) is the most know-ledgeable agent in the UK and they will make suggestions and book itineraries for you. If you do not want to arrange an actual island-hopping itinerary, it is perfectly possible to make short day or weekend tours (some by sailboat, others by plane) of the islands near to the one on which you are staying. There are endless trips to the islands around Sint Maarten—Saba, Statia, St Barts and Anguilla. Travel is very easy from the USVI and the BVI and vice-versa.

By Air

Most island hopping nowadays is by **aeroplane** (often Twin Otters or Islanders and increasingly DASH 8s). Some of these planes, which carry about twenty passen-gers, do look a bit like coffins with wings on and when they take off they have so much lift that it feels almost alarming, but they are very safe and reliable. The pilot will stand at the beginning of the runway and run the engines hard until the con-trol panel becomes a blur and the plane thrums like an outsize tuning fork. Then he lets off the brakes and puts the props in drive. Flight can be a bit of a novelty (some people actually pay for rides like this at funfairs). Planes this size tend to bounce off clouds—there are vertical streams of air within them which will leave your stomach a hundred feet above you in a matter of a second or so. If you do find a penetrable cloud, you might find it coming through the overhead blowers. In calmer moments the views of the islands and the sea from 3000ft are fantastic.

Island hoppers are affectionately known as the islands' bus service. They tend to run along the island-chain and will simply miss out a destination if nobody wants to get on or off. The main centres for travel around the eastern Caribbean are San Juan in Puerto Rico, Sint Maarten, Antigua and islands down to Trinidad. Gener-ally, island-hopping by plane is a good and reliable way of travelling. A couple of words of warning, however. Booking can be a little haphazard. Planes are some-times oversold, and those booked in advance may well leave half empty. Travelling standby often works. And it is worth reconfirming obsessively. If you miss one flight you may find that the whole of the rest of the itinerary is cancelled. A dose of judicious anger in the airline office sometimes helps you get what you want. Most airlines are usually quite amenable when it comes to excess luggage, except when the plane is full.

The biggest carrier in the Eastern Caribbean is **LIAT** (officially this is Leeward Islands Air Transport, but it is also known as 'Leave Island Any Time', 'Likeable Interested Attentive Tolerant', 'Lost in Air Transit' or 'Luggage in Another Town'). Many LIAT flights originate in Antigua and they fly as far south (usually at least two a day) as Barbados and Port of Spain, Trinidad, and to Puerto Rico in the north (with some flights to Santiago in the Dominican Republic). There is also a link from St Lucia to Caracas. LIAT has three hopper tickets which are ideal for people travelling around the Caribbean. The *Super Caribbean Explorer* ticket allows you unlimited stops in one direction (though you are permitted to return to a destination to make a connection) for a period of a month, with return to point of start, price US$367. The *Caribbean Explorer* lasts for a 21-day period and allows three stops (none repeated except for connections), with return to point of origin, price US$199. The *Eastern Caribbean Airpass* allows stops in between three and six LIAT destinations over a 21-day period, each leg being charged at US$60. There are some restrictions. Super Explorer tickets may be bought in the Caribbean, but the other two must be bought before departure from your country of residence, in conjunction with a ticket to the Caribbean (any carrier will do, despite what some airlines assure you).

BWIA (pronounced Beewee), the Trinidad and Tobago airline, has the *Intra-Caribbean Airpass* which allows you one stop at any BWIA destination in the Caribbean; connections are allowed (maximum stay 24 hours) over a 30-day period, with return to the original point of departure, price US$356. This is particularly interesting because it includes Jamaica, which is not covered by LIAT. Other BWIA destinations are Antigua, Barbados, Grenada, Guyana, Trinidad and Tobago.

ALM (the airline of the Netherlands Antilles) also has a number of hopper tickets: the *ABC Pass*, which enables you to fly between Aruba, Bonaire and Curaçao, three coupons US$135; the *Sint Maarten Pass*, which includes the return flight to Sint Maarten as well, five coupons US$249; and the *ALM System Pass*, which enables you to fly to all ALM destinations (only one stop on the mainland USA), eight coupons US$695. Some tickets must be issued in conjunction with trans-Atlantic tickets or before leaving the USA.

Many islands have their own individual airline. **Air Guadeloupe** (℡ 590 82 47 00) radiates north and south from Guadeloupe, flying south to Dominica and north to Antigua and Sint Maarten. **Winair** (℡ 599 552002), the airline of the Dutch Windward Islands, is based in Sint Maarten and flies to all the neighbouring islands in that region.

Many airlines link the British Virgin Islands to the US Virgin Islands and to San Juan. For details, *see* the separate island sections. The last option is to **charter** a small plane, which can work out at a good price if there are enough people. All Caribbean airports have a charter company (five-seaters, nine-seaters and sometimes helicopters) on call.

The Caribbean also has some pretty hairy airstrips. Some are very short—you will know about this just after landing when the whole plane shudders because the pilot applies reverse thrust. Others are hairy because there is an obstacle course on approach to landing. At St Barthélémy there are two approaches: from the sea (marginally preferable) where you get a close inspection of some second-degree jungle and the local cemetery just before you land; and over land, for which the traffic stops on the road in case the plane's wheel takes off a driver's hat (and for the view). But the most spectacular of them all is the strip on Saba, just 400 yards long (shorter than any self-respecting aircraft carrier) and with a 100ft drop at either end. Taking off is exciting; landing has a stress quotient. People say: 'they only use half the runway'. Just pray that it is the first half.

By Boat

Until thirty years ago all the islands of the Caribbean were linked by elegant old sloops and schooners once or twice a week. These have mostly gone now, but it is still sometimes possible to hitch a ride on the **freighters** which bring provisions and manufactured goods into the islands. Go to the dock and ask around and they might sign you on as 'crew'. **Ferries** connect all the Virgin Islands and some of the islands around Sint Maarten (*see* separate island sections). Another possibility is to travel by hitching a ride on a **yacht**, which you can catch at the main centres (BVI, USVI, Antigua, Martinique, St Lucia and some of the Grenadines). If you go down to the marina and ask around, you may come up with something: the crews are often happy to take along the occasional passenger who is prepared to help out.

For details of car hire, public transport, taxis, etc., *see* the 'Getting Around' sections at located at the beginning of each island section within the touring chapters of the guide.

Practical A–Z

Beaches

If the 20th century's ultimate quest is the finest sun-drenched, palm-fringed curve of satin-soft, ankle-deep sand, washed by warm waves, gin-clear shadows and an aquamarine sea, all of course with a perfect sunset view, then the Caribbean offers happy hunting grounds. In the northeastern Caribbean the best sands tend to be on the low-lying, coral-clad, outer ring of islands between Antigua and Anguilla. Here you will find long stretches of bright white sand with offshore reefs for snorkelling and perfect aquamarine sea. On the mountainous islands you will find some charming calm, palm-backed coves tucked between the massive headlands. The sand tends to be golden-brown on these islands. The Virgin Islands have the best of both worlds, with white sand in the magnificent secluded coves with a backdrop of huge volcanic peaks. There are few beaches on Montserrat and St Eustatius and none on Saba.

All but the quietest islands have an active beach where you can arrange most watersports and there will also be a number of secluded retreats where you can realistically expect to be alone or nearly alone if you are prepared to get off the beaten track (*see* the individual island sections). Swimming is safe in most places, but do not to swim alone, particularly on an unprotected Atlantic shore.

Bookshops

In the UK, the following London shops have a wide selection of travel books with special sections for the Caribbean: **Daunt's** bookshop at 83 Marylebone High Street, London W1M 4DE (© 071 224 2295)—they will send you a reading list of their material; the **Travel Bookshop** at 13 Blenheim Crescent, London W11 2EE (© 071 229 5260); **Stanfords** at 12–14 Longacre, London WC2E 9LP (© 071 836 1321)—this is also a specialist map shop.

In the USA, try: **British Travel Books**, 40 West 57th Street, New York, NY 10019 (© 212 765 0898); **Rand McNally Map Travel**, 444 North Michigan Avenue, Chicago, IL 60611; **The Complete Traveller**, 4038 Westheimer, Houston, TX 77027; **Traveller's Bookstore**, 22 West 52nd Street, New York, NY 10019 (© 212 664 0995); **Travel Logs**, 222 West 83rd Street, New York, NY 10024 (© 212 799 8761); **Travel Merchandise**, 1425 K Street NW, Washington, DC 20005 (© 202 371 6656).

Calendar of Events

The biggest festivals in the Caribbean are the various Carnivals, usually pre-Lenten, but sometimes held at the end of the sugar harvest. The summer months are a particularly popular time of year for festivities (the West Indians think the weather is better then) and so there are many official celebrations and general blow-outs in the British islands (around Emancipation Day, 1 August) and religious festivals in the Catholic islands. Many islands have slightly more formal events commemorating Independence days and National Memorials (even military parades in some islands). As you would expect in the Caribbean there are many other less formal get-togethers, centred around music and around sports, some tennis and golf competitions sponsored by big international companies, and other events centred around the sea, with local and open sailing regattas and fishing competitions. Finally, there are some island cultural events.

The summer months are the best if you want to see the West Indians at play and there are a number of festivals in June, July and August. Things also get booked up then. Generally speaking you will have no problem joining in the festivities in any Caribbean event: you will find that the islanders make you welcome.

January

January sees the culmination of the St Kitts Carnival with street parades and carnival masquerades. Elsewhere the pre-Lenten **Carnivals** are just warming up, with weekend fêtes and the early stages of calypso and carnival king and queen competitions. St Barts holds a Music Festival.

February

Many Caribbean **Carnivals** culminate in February, in a three-day jump-up, with calypso and steel band competitions and masked parades in the streets on Shrove Tuesday (Mardi Gras) or Ash Wednesday: in the northeastern Caribbean these include Saint Martin and St Barthélémy.

March

Montserrat celebrates **St Patrick's Day** on 17 March and 30 March is the anniversary of the transfer to American ownership of the USVI.

April

The Netherlands Antilles commemorate Queen Beatrix's official birthday with parties on 30 April and there are also local celebrations for **Easter**, with traditional kite-flying all over the area. Many of the **sailing** competitions get underway, including the Spring Regatta in the BVI and Antigua's International Sailing Week.

May

Abolition Day is remembered with fêtes in the French islands on 27 May, and during May St Martin holds a **Food Festival** with jump-ups and classic cooking.

July

A number of islands in the northeastern Caribbean hold festivals and carnivals during July. The USVI remember emancipation on 3 July. In Nevis there is a more Caribbean cultural event in **Culturama**—carnival parades and island-wide festivities. Saba's **Summer Festival** runs for a week with carnival events. Late in the month a number of islands get their carnivals moving—BVI, St Eustatius, Antigua—so that they culminate in the first few days of August.

August

Most of the former British islands have festivities on 1 August, the date of emancipation, or the day closest to it. Anguilla holds its **carnival week**, with a regatta running concurrently, at the start of the month, the **Anegada** race in the BVI late in the month. **St Barts** celebrates its saint's day on 24th.

September

St Kitts and Nevis celebrate **Independence** on 19 September and St John, USVI, holds its **carnival** near the beginning of the month. **Foxy's Wooden Boat Regatta** is held early in the month in tiny Jost van Dyke in the BVI.

November

Sint Eustatius commemorates the first salute to the American flag on 16 November and nearby Saint Martin/Sint Maarten get together and hold joint festivities on **Concordia Day** on 11 November. Late November sees the beginning of the Antigua sailing season with the **Nicholson's boat show**.

December

Saba celebrates its flag day on 7 December. St Kitts starts **Carnival Week** on about 20 December. All Caribbean islands celebrate Christmas.

Children

Despite its reputation as a honeymooners' and couples' destination, travelling with children in the Caribbean is perfectly possible and you will find that in most islands the locals are indulgent and friendly towards them (they might be invited to join the screaming little-persons' posses that chase around the beaches and country-side). Just a few hotels at the top of the range have a policy of not accepting any children below a certain age (usually 12); others have built special playgrounds for them (notably Malliouhana in Anguilla) and provide nannies so that you can sun yourself in peace. The majority of hotels will accept children, though they will have only limited facilities for them. Children are sometimes allowed to stay for free in the same room as their parents and baby-sitters are usually on call in any hotel.

If you have a large family it might be easiest to opt for a two- or three-room flat in an apartment complex. Many of these will have hotel-like facilities including water-sports concessions and a restaurant. If you are happy to look after yourself, then you might take a villa. Children are accepted happily in restaurants.

Climate

Colonists once knew the Bahamas as the 'isles of perpetual June' because of their fair and clement weather. Generally speaking the climate over the whole Caribbean area is impeccable. As islands their temperature is kept constant by the sea and so the climate is far gentler than that in the continent that surrounds them. The sun is hot of course; particularly in winter the edge is taken off the heat by a breeze. For most of the year, air conditioning is not really necessary. The temperature varies just a few degrees across the year and across the geographical area, from the Virgin Islands to Antigua. Temperatures drop at night; in summer there is no need to cover up, but you might need a thin jersey on a winter evening.

Average winter and summer temperatures, °C (°F)

	Antigua	Sint Maarten	St Thomas (USVI)
Winter	24(75)	25(77)	25(76)
Summer	27(80)	28(82)	28(82)

There are just two main seasons in the Caribbean: wet, in which tropical showers pass by, offload thousands of gallons of water in seconds, and then the sun comes out to dry it all up again; and the dry season, in which it still rains but less frequently or heavily. Wet seasons are in May or June and October or November. A tropical shower will drench you (with warm rain) in a matter of seconds. You may consider taking a waterproof, but remember that the sun will dry you out almost as quickly as you got wet. Of more concern are cold fronts which spin off the continental weather system up north, putting a blanket of cloud over the islands for three or four days at a time. They have been a bit more frequent in recent years.

hurricanes

Hurricanes are the severest natural disaster in an area of otherwise benign weather. The worst ones in the last few years were Hurricane Gilbert in 1988, which wasted Jamaica and the Cayman Islands, and Hurricane Hugo in 1989, the worst hurricane this century, which carved a swathe through Guadeloupe and then flattened Montserrat and St Croix. Turning anti-clockwise in the northern hemisphere, hurricanes rise near the coast of Africa. Fed by warm winds over the water, they get a couple of thousand miles run-up before they slice their way through the islands, blowing with winds up to 200mph and at the same time delivering a massive deluge of rain, which causes yet more destruction. They uproot telegraph poles, blow tin roofs around and disturb the sea as much as 200ft below the surface (causing damage to the corals).

If you hear that a hurricane is on the way, find the strongest concrete bunker possible and shelter in it with everybody else. If all goes quiet at the height of the storm, then you are in the eye (the very centre of the hurricane): batten down the hatches because it will start again in a few minutes. If you are in a sailing boat, the best place to head for is a mangrove swamp. The most likely month for hurricanes is September. The traditional rhyme runs: *June too soon, July stand by, September remember, October all over.*

Electricity

In most Caribbean islands the electrical supply is 110 or 120 volts at 60 cycles, and so American electrical appliances need no adaptor (British and French visitors will need to take one). The French islands work to 220 volts and the Dutch islands at 110. The British islands are mixed; those that have developed recently tend to be on the American standard (BVI and Anguilla), but some of the British Caribbean islands have a 230 or 240 volt supply at 50 cycles per second. Even then, some hotels work on the American system, so it may be worth checking before you go. If hotel rooms are not fitted with electrical appliances, ask at the front desk, where they may well keep some stashed away.

Food and Drink

When visiting the Caribbean to write *The Traveller's Tree*, Patrick Leigh Fermor decided that: 'Hotel cooking in the island is so appalling that a stretcher may profitably be ordered at the same time as dinner'. Admittedly this was in the late forties, but Caribbean food, particularly hotel food, is generally pretty unadventurous, and has a lacklustre 'international style'. The former British colonial influence may have something to do with it, and more recently the overwhelming number of American visitors, because a quick trip to the French Antilles will tell a different story. If you're a type for whom food can be heaven, then unless you choose carefully and spend a fair bit of money, the Caribbean is likely to be 'burger-tory'.

On the restaurant circuit things have improved recently, particularly in the northeastern Caribbean, and you will find at least one good and often adventurous restaurant in most islands now. Some chefs and restaurateurs have taken the best of West Indian ingredients and traditions and applied continental techniques to produce a sophisticated and satisfying Caribbean cuisine. Also a number of famous chefs have made their way down to the Caribbean.

Dress codes for dinner have almost entirely died out in the Caribbean and few hotel dining rooms will request that you wear even a jacket or a tie. Service is often a problem, though. Even in quite smart restaurants and hotel dining rooms it can be haphazard. Wine is available in the smarter restaurants; it does not take well to the heat but a few restaurants have cooled cellars.

A week's worth of curry goat or stew fish might be more than any newcomer could take, but it is worth getting out in search of West Indian food. It has its own distinctive flavours, it is cheaper and the restaurants are often more fun. It is also worth seeking out the beach bars, where you can eat barbecued fish and vegetables.

Gastronomes should really head for the French islands, where there is a strong tradition of creole cookery with luxurious sauces, served with meticulous attention to detail both in the preparation and in the service. Like their metropolitan counterparts, the French Antilleans treat their food with a little more ceremony than other West Indians. You will have a surprise in the Dutch Caribbean islands, where there are echoes of Holland in dishes made with Edam cheese, but more curiously Indonesian food (the Dutch West Indies meets the Dutch East Indies) in *rijstafel*. The tastes of India have come through strongest in Trinidad, but curry goat and roti (an envelope of dough with a meat or vegetable filling) have reached everywhere.

Caribbean food is traditionally quite spicy and West Indians can be quite liberal with chilli pepper in their cook-ups. Beware of bottles marked Hot Pepper. Fish is abundant, and often delicious, as are seafoods such as lobster and crab and an island favourite, conch. Other foods that have become popular are made of ingredients that were originally hardship foods, often fed to the slaves, because they were cheap at the time. The Jamaican national dish is ackee and saltfish; now that there is refrigeration and food is no longer salted in order to preserve it, salted cod is expensive and difficult to get hold of. Rice 'n' peas (or peas 'n' rice depending on which island you are in) is another standard meal in the cheaper restaurants in the British islands and is particularly good when served with coconut milk. Callaloo is a traditional West Indian soup made from spinach and oil-dung is a pot of vegetables cooked in coconut oil.

West Indian dishes are usually served with traditional vegetables, many also brought to the Caribbean as slave food from elsewhere in the tropical world (there are many vegetables unknown in the temperate zones). Try breadfruit, fried plantain (like a banana) and cassava (originally an Arawak food) and the delicious christophene. The Caribbean is of course famous for its **fruits**—mango, banana, pineapple, soursop and papaya among others—which taste good in the ice-creams.

It is not usually necessary to make a **reservation** in Caribbean restaurants, except at the most popular in the high season. Some restaurants will close out of season. Under the Eating Out sections in this book, restaurants are divided into three **price categories**: *expensive, moderate* and *cheap*. As some islands are generally more expensive than others, the pricing of these categories will vary a little according to the island. Imported steak, shrimp and lobster tend to be about 30 per cent more expensive than other dishes and so they are not included within the different pricing categories.

The Caribbean is famous for cocktails and many of them were invented here, making the best use of the exotic fruits. The Piña Colada (pineapple and coconut cream and rum) supposedly originated in Puerto Rico and the Daquiri (crushed ice, rum and fruit syrup whisked up like a sorbet) in Havana. The Cuba Libre, mixed after the Cuban Revolution in 1959, is made of rum with lemon and cola, and Hemingway's Mojito is made with white rum, fresh mint and Angostura Bitters. The planter's punch, traditionally drunk all over the Caribbean, is made from rum and water with a twist of lime and sugar, topped with ground nutmeg.

Rum and Red Stripe

Rum is the Caribbean 'national' drink—fifty years ago bars kept their bottles of rum on the counter free of charge and it was the water you had to pay for. Distilled from sugar molasses, rum is produced all over the islands and though it often tastes like rocket fuel, it gives the West Indians their energy for dancing, so it cannot be all bad. The most popular local variety of rum and the quickest to produce is 'white rum', which is drunk in the rum bars and at local dances. Gold rums are a little mellower; their colour comes from caramel which is introduced as they age in wooden barrels; some are blended. In the French islands rums are treated much as brandies and they are laid down to mature for years. There are even vintages. Look out for Appleton from Jamaica, Mountgay from Barbados, Trois Rivières, Rhum Bally and Rhum St James from Martinique. Finally, some rums are flavoured with tropical fruits, either by the producer during the ageing process or by individual restaurants, who then serve them as a digestif.

Far more so than wine, the West Indians prefer a cool beer to combat the heat and nowadays many islands brew their own, often under licence from the major international drinks companies. Some of the best known are Red Stripe from Jamaica, Banks from Barbados and Carib from Trinidad. Cuban beers include Hatuey and there are two new beers from Antigua (Wadadli) and St Lucia (Piton, La Bière Sent Lisi). Perhaps the best of all the Caribbean beers is produced in the Dominican Republic, a light lager called Presidente. Heineken and American beers such as Bud are almost universally available.

Soft Drinks

Life in the Caribbean sun is hot work, and so, besides the bottled drinks available in the shops, the West Indians have an array of drinks on sale in the street. Snow cones and Sky juice are made with crushed ice (scraped off a huge block), water and a dash of fruit concentrate and put into a bag or cup. You swill it around with a straw and the effect is something like a cold ribena. You have to be careful not to drink the water and the concentrate too quickly otherwise you are just left with a mound of ice crystals. In some islands you get weird and wonderful toppings with condensed milk and crushed peanuts.

Tropical fruits make excellent non-alchoholic drinks: fruit punches are ideal if you are not ready for the evening's alchoholic intake. A particularly good drink, which originiates in Trinidad is a Bentley, lemon and lime with a dash of bitters. If in doubt, lime juice is an excellent choice for a soft drink, though not all places have fresh limes in stock all the time. Other popular West Indian drinks are sorrel, the red Christmas drink not unlike Ribena, ginger beer, and mauby juice, a disgusting bitter concoction made of tree bark. The usual international soft drinks, Coke, Fanta, Sprite etc., are sold everywhere, and some more Caribbean ones like Ting.

Another option available in all the islands is coconuts, which are often sold in the street. Do not be alarmed when the vendor pulls out a 2ft machete, because he will deftly top the coconut with a few strokes, leaving just a small hole through which you can drink. Get an older coconut if you can, because the milk will be fuller and sweeter. Once you have drunk the milk, hand it back to the vendor, who will split it for you so that you can eat the delicious coconut slime that lines the inside (it eventually turns into the white coconut flesh). You will also be offered sugar-cane juice, either as a liquid, or in the sticks themselves, which you bite off and chew to a pulp (very sweet).

Health

In the 18th century if you were caught in a cholera epidemic you could have looked forward to a tonic of diluted sulphuric acid and tincture of cardamom or ammoniated tincture of opium as treatment. There are references to 'this fatal climate' on gravestones and memorials throughout the Caribbean. Today, however, the Caribbean is basically a very healthy place and unless you are unlucky there is no reason that you should experience health problems.

You should check that your polio and typhoid inoculations are up to date and you may wish to have yourself immunized or take precautions against the following diseases. **Hepatitis** occurs rarely: you can have an injection giving some cover against Hepatitis A, which is caught mainly from water and food. There has been some incidence of **cholera** in South America over the last few years and there have recently been warnings in Trinidad. If you are travelling to the less developed islands and wish to take sterile needles (and possibly plasma), make sure they are packed up to look official otherwise customs might begin to wonder.

There is quite a high incidence of venereal diseases around the Caribbean, including **HIV**, which some reckon started in Haiti (there is little evidence that this is true, though it is prevalent there). The risks from casual sex are clear.

Warnings

Sun-burn can ruin your holiday and so it is worth taking it easy for the first few days. You are recommended to keep to short stints of about 15–20 minutes in the hottest part of the day (11am–3pm). Take high-protection-factor suncream. Sun-hats are easily found. Be particularly careful if you go snorkelling, because the combination of the sun and the cooling water is lethal. Take sunglasses. Traditional West Indian methods of soothing sun-burn include the application of juice of **aloe**, a fleshy cactus-like plant, which is used a lot in cosmetics anyway. Break a leaf and squeeze out the soothing juice. After-sunburn treatments include calomine lotion.

There are very few poisonous things in the Caribbean, but you may well come across the **manchineel tree**, which often grows on the beach. These are tall, bushy trees with a fruit like a small apple, known by Columbus's men as the apple of death (*manzana* means apple in Spanish). Do not eat them! Steer clear of the tree itself because the sap is poisonous. You should not even shelter under them in the rain because the sap will blister your skin. A **palm tree** may seem the ideal place to shade yourself but beware! People have been killed by falling coconuts.

Mosquitoes are a plague, though many tourist areas are treated to get rid of them. They can cause dengue fever (in the Greater Antilles) and malaria (in Hispaniola only). Burn mosquito coils, and off the beaten track you might consider taking a mosquito net (there will probably already be nails in the walls where others have had the same idea). There are many insect repellents, including Autan, Jungle Formula and *OFF!*. Less potentially harmful, but equally irritating, are the tiny invisible **sand-flies** which plague certain beaches after rain and towards the end of the afternoon. In 1631, Sir Henry Colt wrote: 'First you have such abundance of small knatts by ye sea shore towards ye sun goinge down yt bite so as no rest cann be had without fyers under your Hamaccas'. For a barely visible insect, they pack a big bite. There are one or two poisonous centipedes and only certain islands have poisonous snakes (or snakes at all for that matter).

Swimming holds very few dangers in the Caribbean, though among the reefs and rocks you should look out for fire coral and particularly for spiny sea urchins (little black balls with spines up to 6 inches long radiating in all directions). If you stand on one, the spines break off, and give you a very unpleasant and possibly infectious injury. Sharks are occasionally spotted in Caribbean waters by divers, but have hardly ever been known to attack humans.

The water in most islands in the eastern Caribbean is drinkable from the tap, but to make sure, you might want to drink the water served by the hotel to begin with. There is a shortage of water in many of the flatter islands of the northeastern Caribbean, and so, even in expensive hotels, you may find that nothing comes out when you turn on the tap. You are always asked to conserve water where possible.

Insurance

The islands of the northeastern Caribbean are fairly benign when it comes to personal security and theft, but good travel insurance is essential for your peace of mind and has saved many travellers a lot a heartache. Take great care when choosing your policy and always read the small print. A good travel insurance should always give full cover for your possessions and your health. In case of illness, it should provide for all medical costs, hospital benefits, permanent disabilities and the flight home. In case of loss or theft, it should recompense you for lost luggage, money and valuables, also for travel delay and personal liability. Most important, it should provide you with a 24-hour contact number in the event of medical emergencies. Should anything be stolen, a copy of the police report should be asked for and kept as it will be required by your insurance company.

If your own bank or insurance company hasn't an adequate travel insurance scheme (they usually have), then try the comprehensive schemes offered by **Trailfinders** (℃ 071 938 3939) or **Jardine's** (℃ 061 228 3742), or the 'Centurion Assistance' policy offered by **American Express** (℃ 0444 239900). Tour operators often include insurance, but this is not always adequate.

Language

English is spoken in the tourist industry in most Caribbean countries, partly because many of the islands have a former colonial connection with Britain and partly because of the large number of American visitors. Some islands also have a local *patois*, an everyday language based on the original official colonial language, but these are often incomprehensible to the foreign visitor. **English** is the official language of all the British Commonwealth Caribbean countries—Barbados, Trinidad and Tobago, the Windward Islands (Grenada, St Vincent and the Grenadines, St Lucia, Dominica), the Leeward Islands (Antigua, Montserrat, St Kitts and Nevis and Anguilla), the British and United States Virgin Islands, Jamaica, the Caymans, the Turks and Caicos and the Bahamas. **French** is the official language of the French Antilles, Martinique, Guadeloupe, St Martin and St Barts, but English is widely spoken in the hotels. **Dutch** is the official language of the

Netherlands Antilles, but English is traditionally the language of the Dutch Windwards, St Maarten, Saba and Sint Eustatius.

Living and Working in the Caribbean

Like sailing around the world, setting up in the Caribbean is a lifetime's dream for some. Beware! Things are not necessarily what they seem during a short visit. Battling with bureaucracy and local prejudices is a perennial problem (small island communities are notoriously inward-looking and once you scratch the surface of the West Indies you will find things are no different there) and island inertia can get people down too. There is a heartless expression which says that people arrive with a container full of belongings and (after a year's frustration) leave with a suitcase. Perhaps it is best to rent for six months or a year to learn the ropes and see if you like the way of life before you put money in.

Having said that, many people do adapt to the West Indies and certain islands do encourage investment. Buying rights vary from island to island, but most require that if you buy a plot of land you must build within a certain period, and often that you employ a local person. Details are available from the individual High Commissions and Embassies.

Working in the Caribbean is also not as easy as it might seem because most islands impose strict quotas of foreign workers on businesses, ensuring that the work remains for the locals. Casual work is almost impossible to find. If you are lucky, you might find some work in the bars in islands where there is a large expatriate community or in islands with a large sailing contingent, where crews are sometimes needed. Americans have equal employment rights in the US Virgin Islands of course, and EU members can work (officially at least) in the French islands, but the British have no special rights in the few remaining British Crown colonies.

Maps and Publications

There are just a few general Caribbean maps and they are available from any good bookstore or map store. Really detailed maps of individual islands are not generally available (either on island or in the UK). You might find them at a map specialist, but they are not really needed when on island unless you are walking in remote areas. In most places it is enough to get a photocopied map at the tourist offices.

Most islands have their own newspaper; these tend to be dailies in the larger islands, and perhaps two or three times weekly in the smaller ones. Many American papers and magazines are on sale (usually a day or so late), but not so many papers make it over from Europe. There are just a couple of pan-Caribbean papers, including *Caribbean Week*. The BWIA inflight magazine, *Caribbean Beat*, covers Caribbean-wide affairs and is a good read.

Generally speaking the Caribbean is not cheap. Flights are quite expensive to begin with and if you stay on the tourist circuit you will find yourself paying prices not unlike those in Europe or the USA. However, if you get off the tourist track and stay in local West Indian guest houses and eat local food, you will pay a little less. All the same, do not expect to stay anywhere for much less than US$25.

A few Caribbean countries have their own currency, but many of the smaller islands share a denomination, often according to the past colonial set-up. The US dollar, however, is the currency in universal demand around the area and many countries have pegged their currency to it. At the moment the greenback is permitted to circulate more or less freely in all the islands and so there is not much of a black market. Prices in the tourist industry throughout the Caribbean are also quoted in or fixed to US dollars and it is even possible in places to spend a couple of weeks working exclusively in that currency (in tourist hotels and their watersports concessions, restaurants and shops). However, if you go off the beaten track, it is a good idea to have local currency. It is also sensible to take small denominations.

Hustling is fairly widespread in the Caribbean, though the islands of the northeast tend to have a lower hassle factor than most. All visitors are presumed to have a few dollars that they would not mind releasing (they could afford the airfare after all) and some islands have a band of opportunists who will try to persuade you to do so in return for a variety of services, anything from an errand to collect a box full of different fruits from the local market to drugs, or just as a gift. You are vulnerable particularly in the first 48 hours or until you have a bit of colour. It varies from island to island, but in some island you can expect to be accosted if you go to the downtown area and on any public beach. A firm and polite no to whatever is offered is the easiest way to guarantee your peace.

Official Currencies

You will need to check the exchange rates before you travel, as those not listed as fixed can alter on the exchange:

The Leeward Islands (the former British islands of Antigua and Barbuda, St Kitts and Nevis and the Crown Colonies of Montserrat and Anguilla—the Eastern Caribbean dollar, fixed to US dollar (US$1 = EC$2.65), US currency also accepted.

French Caribbean (French Antilles—St Martin, St Barthélémy and also Martinique and Guadeloupe)—French franc, (US$1 = Fr5.5 approx), US dollar also accepted in tourist areas.

Dutch Caribbean (Netherlands Antilles—Sint Maarten, Saba, Statia, also Curaçao and Bonaire)—Netherlands Antillean florin or guilder, fixed to US dollar (US$1 = NAFl 1.78), US dollar freely accepted.

British and US Virgin Islands—US dollar official currency.

The banks give the best rate of exchange. At hotels you usually receive a lower rate. Exchanges in most islands will accept hard currency **traveller's cheques**—sterling, French franc, Deutschmark and Canadian dollar, but the most popular is the US dollar, particularly if you are going to a country where the dollar is an acceptable alternative currency. You will also get a better rate of exchange. Some banks are beginning to charge for the exchange of traveller's cheques, however. Take some small denomination cheques and remember to record the number so that you can be refunded if you lose them. Generally, banking is quite sophisticated in most islands, but service is often slow. **Credit cards** are widely accepted for anything that is connected with the tourist industry—in hotels, restaurants and tourist shops. You can draw cash on a credit card at the bank—there are AMEX and VISA representatives on all the islands. **Personal cheques** are rarely accepted.

Packing

With such pleasant weather and such an informal air in the Caribbean, you can take a minimalist approach to packing. There are just a couple of restaurants and hotel dining rooms in the whole area which require even a jacket and a tie for men (though most do like trousers and a shirt with a collar). Daytime wear is a skirt or shorts and a light shirt, evening wear about the same, perhaps a longer skirt or trousers. Jeans are too warm in the summer months, so you might consider taking cotton trousers. Also pack a sunhat, sunglasses, suncream and a swimsuit (though they can be bought on arrival).

Photography

You will find that many West Indians either dive for cover or start remonstrating violently at the very sight of a camera. Some will talk about you stealing their soul and others about the money you will have to pay. If you see a good shot and go for it, you can usually talk your way out of trouble, but if you stop and chat first then most people will allow you to photograph them.

In the middle of the day, the brightness of the Caribbean sun bleaches all colour out of the landscape except the strongest tropical shades, but as the afternoon draws in you will find a stunning depth of colour in the reds, golds and greens. The plants of the Caribbean are bright and colourful and particularly good after rain. Film is very expensive in the islands and the heat can be a problem too (you might put it in the hotel fridge).

Post Offices

Post can take anything from 2 days to 3 months to get from the Caribbean to Europe or North America. Don't depend on it. You probably have no need to go anywhere near a post office anyway because hotels usually have postcards and stamps and once you have written them they are happy to post them for you. Opening hours vary from island to island.

Shopping

Shopping is one of the Caribbean's biggest industries, but hardly any of the things that are sold here originate in the area. There are objects of cultural value to be found, particularly in the larger islands, but most of it is shipped in to satisfy the collector passions of long-distance shoppers (some of whom take the same cruise year after year to take advantage of preferential customs allowances). On the shelves of all the air-conditioned boutiques and the newer shopping malls that have begun to infest the area you can find jewels and precious stones, perfumes, photographic equipment, clothes, Cuban cigars etc.

The islands follow roughly speaking the historical patterns of their nation, with the French the leaders in perfumes and designer clothes and the Dutch, always great traders, with well-priced photographic equipment from the Far East. St Thomas (USVI), where almost anything is on sale, is in danger of becoming one outsize emporium. The lure is, of course, the reduced prices (in comparison to the mainland) and every shop announces itself as 'duty-free' or 'in-bond'. The best duty-free shopping-centre islands in the Caribbean are Sint Maarten, St Thomas in the USVI and Nassau and Freeport in the Bahamas.

There is quite an active art scene now in many of the islands: galleries exhibiting work by local and expatriate artists are mentioned in the text. There are occasionally things of interest in the craft markets, but particularly on the bigger islands you will find some highly original work.

Sports

Diving

The Caribbean has some superb corals and fish, the best in the Western hemisphere. The variety is stunning, from the world's third-largest barrier reef a few miles off the coast of Andros in the Bahamas, to the colourful seascapes of Bonaire and the Caymans to warm and cool water springs under the sea off the volcanic islands.

The reefs are incredibly colourful. You will see yellow and pink tube sponges and purple trumpet sponges, sea feathers and seafans (gorgonians) that stand against the current alongside a forest of staghorn, elkhorn and black coral and the more exotic species like the domes of startlingly white brain coral, star corals and yellow pencil coral. Near the surface the corals are multicoloured and tightly bunched as they compete for space; as you descend, the yellows and the reds and whites fade, leaving the purples and blues of the larger corals that catch the last of the sunlight at depth (until you shine a light and see them in their full glory). Many islands have laws to protect their reefs and their fish (there are hardly any places left in the Caribbean where you are allowed to use spearguns). In certain islands you are asked not to buy coral jewellery because it will probably have been taken illegally from the reef. One of the few dangerous things on the reef are fire corals, which will give you a nasty sting if you touch one. Do not annoy Moray eels and watch out for sea urchins.

Other underwater life includes a stunning array of crustaceans and of course tropical fish. On the bottom you will find beautifully camouflaged crabs that stare at you goggle-eyed, starfish, lobsters, sea anemones and pretty pink and white feather-duster worms. Around them swim angelfish, squirrelfish, surgeonfish, striped sergeant majors, grunts and soldierfish. Above them little shoals of wrasses and blue tang shimmy in the bubbles. If you get too close, puffer fish blow themselves up like a spiky football, smiling uncomfortably. And beware the poisonous stonefish. If you hear of lobsters migrating (as many as a hundred following one another in a line across the sea bed), then make sure to go out and look.

At night a whole new seascape opens up as some corals close up for the night and others open up in an array of different colours. While some fish tuck themselves into a crevice in the reef to sleep (eyes kept open or in a sort of sleeping-bag of mucus so that they cannot be detected by their scent), starfish, lobsters and sea urchins scuttle around the seabed on the hunt for food. If you stop breathing for a moment, you will hear the midnight parrotfish crunching on the coral polyps, spitting out the broken-down fragments of reef that eventually turn into sand.

In the northeastern Caribbean the best diving is in Saba, followed by the Virgin Islands. All islands have facilities for scuba divers. Most dive-shops in the Caribbean are affiliated to PADI (many also to NAUI) and they will expect you to present a certificate of competence if you wish to go out on to the reefs straight away, but all islands except the smallest have lessons available in the resorts if you are a novice. An open-water qualifying course (which allows you to dive in a pair with another qualified open-water diver) takes about a week, but with a resort course you can usually get underwater in a morning. You will have a session in the swimming-pool before you are allowed to dive with an instructor in the open sea.

The **snorkelling** is also good off many of the islands and most hotels have equipment for their guests and on hire to non-residents. Beware, if you go snorkelling on a sunny day soon after you arrive, because the water and the sun make a fearsome combination on unprotected skin (wear a shirt, perhaps). In most places you can arrange glass-bottom boat tours and snorkelling trips. For those who would like to see the deeper corals, but who do not dive, there are submarines in St Thomas in the USVI, St Barts and St Martin.

Fishing

A sport that is traditionally renowned in the Gulf Stream (between Key West and Havana, and between Florida and the Bahamas), but which is now possible in all islands is **deep-sea** or **big game fishing**. Docked at the yachting marina, the deep-sea boats are huge, gleaming cruisers, slightly top-heavy because of their tall spotting towers, usually equipped with tackle and bait and 'fighting chair'. Beer in hand, you trawl the line behind the boat, waiting for a bite and then watch the beast surface and fight as you cruise along, giving line and steadily hauling it in.

The magnificent creatures that you are out to kill are fish such as the blue marlin, which inhabits the deepest waters and can weigh anything up to 1100lb and measure 10ft in length. Giant or bluefin tuna can weigh up to 1000lb. Wahoo, around 100lb, is a racer and a fighter and the white marlin can weigh up to 150lb. Perhaps the most beautiful of them all is the sailfish, with a huge spiny fan on its back, which will jump clean out of the water and 'tail' (literally stand upright on its tail) in its desperate attempts to get free. Smaller fish include blackfin and allison tuna, bonito, dorado and barracuda.

Sailing

See **A Sailing Guide**, pp.33–40.

Windsurfing

Because of the warmth and the constant winds off the Atlantic Ocean, the Caribbean offers superb windsurfing, particularly when the winds are at their highest in the early months of the year. The sport is well developed—a number of championship competitions have been held in the Caribbean—and you can hire a board on any island. Instruction is usually available. The best places to go are the northeast coasts of Sint Maarten, St Barts and Antigua.

Miscellaneous Watersports

On the smaller islands there is usually at least one beach where you will find all the **watersports**: anything from a windsurfer and a few minutes on waterskis to a parasail flight, a trip on a pedalo or a high-speed trip around the bay on an inflated sausage (it'll keep the kids quiet anyway). Glass-bottom boat tours are usually available and in most hotels you are able to hire small sailboats such as hobie cats and sunfish. Jetskis (standing up) and wetbikes (sitting) have made their mark in the West Indies and are available for hire at most major centres (though some islands have banned them recently) and a recent arrival are kayaks, which are fun on waves and good for reaching remoter snorkelling areas around a rocky coastline. Hotels set on their own beach will invariably have a selection of watersports, though not usually as complete as above. Prices vary considerably across the Caribbean. Most things can be booked through the hotels or their beach concessionaires. There is not really that much beach culture in the Caribbean islands, but there are some beach bars where you can hang out. Rum cruises and sunset tours aboard a resurrected galleon complete with boozatorium and lots of walking the plank are available on the larger and more touristed islands.

Other Sports

Sports based on land include **tennis**, which is well served all over the Caribbean. There are courts in many of the hotels and in island clubs. There are occasional pro-am competitions. If there is no court at your hotel, arrange with another through the front desk, or simply wander in and ask. Hotels generally charge a small fee and they usually have racquets and balls for hire. **Riding** is also offered on the majority of the islands and this is a good way to see the rainforest and the sugar flats if you think that your calves might not be up to the hike.

On the larger islands and those with a developed tourist industry there are **golf** courses open to visitors on payment of a green fee (except in some hotels where it is included in the package). If you decide to play, be flexible because the courses will often give priority to hotel guests. Most courses have equipment for hire.

There is good **walking** in the Caribbean islands, which are cut and crossed with traditional trails originally used by farmers. The rainforest is fascinating to walk in because the growth is so incredibly lush. The heat will be most bearable between dawn, usually at around 6am, and 10am, before the sun gets too high and then between 4pm and dusk. However, the higher you go, the cooler it gets, and the temperature in the forest is not bad anyway. It gets dark quickly in the Caribbean, so be careful to be back by 6pm otherwise you may find yourself stranded, at the mercy of such fearsome spirits of the Caribbean night as the *Soucouyant* and *La Diablesse*. It often rains in the rainforests, of course, so take a waterproof coat and high up in the hills you will need a jersey underneath because the winds can make it cold. Gym-shoes or sneakers are usually enough, unless you are headed into very steep and slippery country, when you should have some ankle support—perhaps a pair of light tropical boots. Tour companies on all the larger islands will transport you to and from your hotel and provide a guide.

Telephones

Communications in the Caribbean are quite good. Many hotel rooms are fitted with direct dial phones as standard, though in both the less developed and the larger countries getting through can be a bit haphazard. Public phones are not that dependable, but there are usually booths at the marinas and in the towns. Calls seem to cost a quarter in almost every Caribbean currency and many islands have a system of phonecards. The former British islands and remaining British Crown colonies have an extensive network run mainly by Cable and Wireless (with the advantage that a cardphone bought in an EC$ country can be used all the way along the chain between Grenada and the BVI). There are no coin phones on the French islands, where you will need a *télécarte*, which is also valid on all other French islands. If you are having trouble placing a call you can always wander into the nearest hotel, where they will help you out for a fee.

Time Zones

Apart from Club Med enclaves (which have their own time schedule for some reason), the whole of the eastern Caribbean (Barbados up to the Virgin Islands) is 4 hours behind GMT. 'Caribbean Time' is an expression you will hear all over the islands and it refers to the West Indians' elastic and entirely unpredictable schedules. Businesses can be punctual, but in restaurants and shops they will have little sympathy with a slave to the second hand.

Tourist Information

The Caribbean tourist industry generates a huge volume of paper, from sleek, advertising-driven glossies found in hotel rooms down to humble leaflets left at strategic points for yachties and other passers by. There is usually a tourist information office at the airport, and they are happy to help out with accommodation, directions and pertinent local advice and gossip. There is usually an information office in the main town and on larger islands there will be tourist offices in the major tourist spots. For those who want more detail there is usually an information department in the Department of Tourism. Opening hours vary across the islands; basically they follow island business hours, with respect for local traditions (such as a two-hour lunch break in some places).

All the Caribbean islands publish some sort of tourism magazine to help with orientation when you arrive on island. These usually include lists of accommodation, restaurants and shops (listed even-handed without selection or recommendation) and some feature articles as well as general advice about how not to get sunburned. Tourist boards often put out leaflets about 'sights' of local interest and if you do visit a local museum there is usually printed material on sale.

Local Tourist Offices: Antigua: PO Box 363, St John's; **Montserrat**: PO Box 7, Plymouth; **St Kitts**: PO Box 132, Basseterre; **Nevis**: Main Street, Charlestown; **Anguilla**: Dept of Tourism, The Valley; **Sint Maarten**: Imperial Building, 23 Walter Misbett's Road; **St Eustatius**: Tourist Office, Upper Town; **Saba**: Tourist Office, Windwardside; **St Martin**: Office du Tourisme, Marigot; **St Barts**: Office du Tourisme, Quai Gén. de Gaulle, Gustavia; **BVI**: PO Box 134, Road Town, Tortola; **USVI**: PO Box 6400, Charlotte Amalie, St Thomas.

Where to Stay

 The West Indies have some of the finest and most luxurious hotels in the world. You can stay at island resorts where you communicate by flag, on endless beaches which are deserted at dawn, in 18th-century plantation splendour with a view across the canefields, and in high-pastel luxury in the Caribbean's newest resorts. Many of the islands offer top-notch hotels, but try the Virgin Islands for isolated island settings, St Kitts and Nevis for plantation estate elegance, St Barts for chic, and Anguilla for distinctive style and sumptuous, small-island charm.

The ultimate Caribbean setting, perhaps a private beachfront cabin with a personal hammock hanging between two nearby palm trees, can be found all over the area, but there are many other styles of Caribbean hotel, from the huge skyscrapers of Aruba to the old plantation house hotels of St Kitts and Nevis with the luxury of the planters' world of two centuries ago. The most recent Caribbean hotels tend to be large, humming palaces with blocks of rooms decorated in a symphony of bright pastel colours set against white tile floors.

Choosing Where to Stay

You are quite likely to select your holiday for the hotel, perhaps because of its reputation, or because of a deal on offer through the tour operator. It is worth asking around and listening to what others say about it. Hotels are selected for this book on grounds of value (within their price category), but also for other reasons such as setting, service, friendliness and general management. Many of the big names in Caribbean hotels are included, but smaller, more off-beat places are included too. Hotels and guest houses are listed in the following five categories:

luxury	—	US$500 and above for a double per night
very expensive	—	US$300–500
expensive	—	US$150–300
moderate	—	US$75–150
cheap	—	US$30–75
very cheap	—	under US$30

In almost every Caribbean island the hotels will add an obligatory government tax (usually between 3% and 7%) and a service charge, usually 10%. **Note: All prices quoted in this book are for a double room in the peak winter season unless otherwise stated**.

Plans and Seasons

MAP means Modified American Plan (with breakfast and dinner included in the price) and **EP** means European Plan (no meals). You may also come across **CP**, Continental Plan, with room and breakfast and **FAP**, or Full American Plan, with a room and all meals. See also **all-inclusive**. The Caribbean high season is mid-December or January until mid-April and prices will be highest then. 'Off-season' travel will bring reductions of as much as 30% in some cases, making some of the idyllic places suddenly affordable. One serious problem with the Caribbean is that holidays invariably seem to revolve around the couple and so single travellers will often find themselves paying the same as a couple for a room. You can try bargaining, but it is unlikely to do any good.

All-inclusive Hotels

The all-inclusive hotel plan has become increasingly popular in recent years and has spread to most Caribbean islands now. As the name implies, the rate is all-inclusive, and once you have paid the initial bill you do not have to pull out your wallet again. It is easier to budget of course, but it may discourage you from leaving the hotel and exploring, or going out to try the restaurants for dinner. There is now quite a wide variety of standards and prices within the all-inclusives and some have gone up-market, offering champagne and *à la carte* dining instead of the traditional buffet-style meals. Originally the concept was a Caribbean version of Club Med, with a permanently ongoing diet of sports and entertainment for those who wanted it. This has altered in some cases recently, with some hotels offering a straight all-inclusive plan (all meals and drinks paid for) and less of the activities. It is worth checking what facilities are included in the package.

Inns

Dotted sporadically around the Caribbean are some magnificent old gingerbread-style homes, often former plantation houses, that have been converted into inns, ideal for the independent traveller with a bit of cash. Usually they will offer a more personal style than the bigger hotels. Some of the best are the inns tucked into the hillsides of Charlotte Amalie on St Thomas.

Villas, Apartments and Condominiums

In addition to the many hotels there are also **villas** all over the islands, most of them relatively modern and well equipped. You can cater for yourself, or arrange for a cook. Contact them through the individual island villa rentals organizations or the tourist boards. The Caribbean now copes reasonably well with self-catering or efficiency holidays and so there are a large number of **apartments** on all the islands, some built in one building like a hotel, others scattered in landscaped grounds. Finally, **condominiums** are also springing up in many islands, answering to those who wish to invest in their vacation.

Guest Houses

These are the cheapest option and they are more fun, cheaper, and have far more character than bottom of the range tourist hotels. They are usually presided over by an ample and generous mother figure and staying in them can be a good way to be introduced to local West Indian life in just a few days. In some you may notice a remarkable turnover of guests as these guest houses often rent rooms out by the hour as well as by the night.

In the major yachting centres you can sometimes persuade the yachties to give you a berth on the charter boats while they are in dock. Simply go down to the marina and ask around and you may come up with something.

Camping

Rules vary throughout the islands and although it is generally not encouraged, particularly on the beaches, there are camp sites on the larger islands (the French Antilles are quite well organized for camping). As a general rule, permission should be obtained from the police before camping, but you will probably get away with it.

Women

West Indian men are quite macho by nature, so visiting women can expect a fair amount of public attention—in the British islands the *soots* (soups, tss!), a sort of sharp hiss between the teeth. Advances of this sort are usually laughed off or ignored by local women and visitors can do the same; they are often quite public and loud, but they are not usually persistent and are verbal rather than physical.

There is quite a big thing going between local lads and visiting women in the Caribbean. West Indians are quite forthright about sex anyway. Male staff in some surprisingly smart hotels will make a pass at a single woman, or one whose man happens to be absent.

West Indian women are quite modest when it comes to showing their bodies in public. It is almost unknown except in the French islands for a West Indian to go topless on the beach (though they do often go naked when washing in rivers, so be careful when out walking). They expect foreigners to observe the same rules. They also expect women to wear more than a swimsuit when out and about or in town, so you might take a cotton wrap.

A Sailing Guide

Sailing in the Eastern Caribbean

With its many islands so close to one another, the eastern Caribbean has endless cruising grounds, some of the best in the world. Over the 500-mile length of the Lesser Antilles there are perhaps a hundred or so islands and cays, some highly developed, with busy marinas and strings of waterfront restaurants, others no more than isolated sand-spits with a just a few palm trees and a rickety shack of a bar.

At moments, as you cruise under full sail, you can be completely surrounded by islands, crouched on the horizon like animals ready to pounce. As you carve through the water, dolphins dance at your prow, and at night, in certain places, you will leave a trail of phosphorescence in your wake. You can coast the massive volcanic Windwards where headlands and inlets gradually glide by, until you find your cove and anchorage for the night, then buy your supper from local fishermen, or you can head for an isolated bay, drop anchor and listen for the noise of a party from a nearby beach bar.

For many, sailing off into the sunset is a lifetime's dream. It restores a sense of independence and self-reliance lost to most people in the hectic business of modern life. For some it is escapism in its finest form: your most important decisions revolve around what to have for dinner and when to up-anchor and move on to another harbour. But the Caribbean is not only for the world's seaborne gypsies. Caribbean sailing is relatively easy and forgiving, particularly if you have cut your teeth in the cold northern hemisphere. Caribbean winds are fairly constant, gentle and reliable (there is the great advantage that the trade winds blow perpendicular to the chain of islands) and you can usually expect to put up a full configuration of sails without the yacht becoming unmanageable. A fully provisioned yacht can be waiting on your arrival and you can sail as much or as little as you want. You don't even have to put up a sail if you don't want to (just switch on the motor).

With dependable sun and warmth and a magnificently beautiful setting, an island-hopping trip on a yacht can offer the best of the Caribbean to many travellers. Fly-in visitors who stay on land will rhapsodize about their time in the islands, but as far as sailors are concerned they simply have no idea what the Caribbean is about.

Planning Your Trip

There is a huge variety of yachts on offer in the Caribbean: sailing yachts can vary from compact fibreglass 30-footers for two, through to custom-built wooden craft contructed to a classic design. And then there are motor cruisers, gleaming white with four-storey superstructures, golf-ball radar navigation and onboard Renoirs and clay-pigeon traps.

With regard to hire, essentially there are two options: bare-boats and crewed yachts. If you take a **bare-boat** then you basically look after yourself, though the charter company will help with briefing and provisioning in advance, and often will support you in case of emergencies. **Crewed yachts** come with a skipper at least, often a cook as well, and you will be looked after during the trip. If you so require, you can be waited on by a whole retinue of flunkies all apparelled in neatly pressed white uniforms.

Bare-boats

As a general rule, bare-boats can be booked direct through the established companies (*see* below) and some of these have offices in the metropolitan countries. If not, you can go through a broker (*see* below). Some companies will allow you to take a yacht from one island and leave it at the next.

Worldwide Charter Companies with Caribbean Fleets

The Moorings: in the UK, 188 Northdown Road, Cliftonville, Kent CT9 2QN (© 0843 227140, fax 0843 228784); **in the USA**, 19345 US 19 North, Suite 402, Clearwater, Florida 34624-3193 (© 800 535 72 89, fax 813 530 97 47); **in France**, 20 rue des Pyramides, 75001 Paris (© 42 61 66 77, fax 42 97 43 58); **in Germany**, Kaiser Ludwig Strasse 17, D-82027 Gruenwald (© 89 64 15 90, fax 89 64 15 917).

Sunsail: in the UK, The Port House, Port Solent, Portsmouth, Hampshire PO6 4TH (© 0705 210345, fax 0705 219827); **in the USA**, 115 E. Broward Blvd, Fort Lauderdale FL33301 (© 305 524 7553, fax 305 524 6312; **in France**, 3, rue de Paradis, 75010 Paris (© 44 79 01 10, fax 42 46 39 90).

Crewed Yachts

For crewed yachts a system has developed in which you contact a broker in your own country; they in turn contact a management company in the islands which has a number of yachts on their books and will make the arrangements at that end. In this case, it is usually up to you to arrange your own flights and transfers, though of course the crew will look after everything once you have arrived at the yacht. If you are taking a skippered yacht it is worth making sure that you have a suitable crew (there are husband-and-wife teams who would prefer a family to a crowd of of rowdy lads on a stag-week). Of course the skipper of a crewed yacht is usually happy to pick you up and drop you wherever you wish.

Brokers in the UK

Yacht Connections, The Hames, Church Road, South Ascot, Berks SL5 9DP (© 0344 24987, fax 0344 26849).

Tenrag, Bramling House, Bramling, New Canterbury, Kent CT3 1NB (℃ 0227 721874, fax 0227 721617).

Camper and Nicholsons, 25 Brixton Street, London W1X 7DB (℃ 071 491 2950, fax 071 629 2068). A company that specialises in a large selection of luxurious yachts for those who would prefer a motor vessel (gin palace).

Brokers in the USA

Yacht Connections, PO Box 3160, Coos Bay, Oregon 97420 (℃ 503 888 4482, fax 503 888 5582), toll free 800 238 6912.

Interpack, 1050 Anchorage Lane, San Diego, California 92106, (℃ 619 222 0327, fax 619 222 0326).

Whitney Yacht Charters, 4065 Crockers Lake Blvd, 2722 Sarasota, Florida 34238, (℃ 813 927 0108, fax 813 9227819, toll free 800 223 1426).

Camper and Nicholsons, 450 Royal Palm Way, Palm Beach, Florida 33480 (℃ 407 655 2121, fax 407 655 2202).

Some of the big Caribbean tour operators (who usually offer hotel-based holidays) will arrange a week aboard and a week ashore packages. *See* the listing in **Travel**, p.6). There are also a number of hotels around the Caribbean with a yacht on call which you can take in exchange for nights ashore. Finally you might also consider a holiday on one of the Caribbean's many tall ships—classic-style four-masted sailing yachts done up in 20th-century comfort. They work like cruise ships except that they take 50–150 passengers and so are more personal (you can even operate the computerized sails). Contact **Windstar Cruises** (℃ 071 628 7711) and the **Windjammer Company** (℃ 0272 272273).

Arrival

If you are chartering a bare-boat, the charter company will brief you on the area. This will include a recommended itinerary (according to whether you are looking for isolation or a lively, bar-hopping trip); the best places to stay overnight; good spots for swimming and snorkelling; recommended bars and restaurants; and the best bets for an isolated beach. You can arrange to have your yacht provisioned (packed with food and drink) in advance of your arrival.

You will also be asked to prove that you can sail. At least one person within the group should be an experienced sailor who understands navigation. This is particularly important in the Windward Islands, where the sailing is more complex and the distances between anchorages greater.

Life on board a yacht can be quite intimate. If you don't know your fellow travellers well already, by the end of a week on board together you certainly will. It is worth choosing the other members of the charter with a certain care. Perhaps those with a certain easy-going tolerance and general self-reliance are the best bet.

Life on Board

Of course yachts are very compact. It seems admirable somehow that all the requisites for cooking and washing-up can fit into an average galley a tiny fraction of the size of a normal kitchen, all carefully designed so that they work just as well when the yacht is bounding along at a tilt of 45 degrees.

Usually the hatchway leads straight down into the saloon or main cabin and galley (kitchen), and this is the main living area. Because of the Caribbean heat and the American influence, there tend to be huge coolers (fridges) on even the smallest yachts. Many yachts will have a small library and some have videos (there are video stores on most islands). Cabins tend to be small. They can also be quite hot (though most are fitted with fans, and are designed to benefit from any breeze). A good alternative is to sleep up on deck (though you might easily be woken by a rain-shower in the cool of the early morning). Bathrooms are also tiny, and fresh water becomes a precious commodity; the water for washing and flushing the 'head' (a slightly technical process which must be performed correctly or you will sink the boat) has to be piped aboard, so yachtsmen are usually manic about not wasting it.

Most on-board life takes place on deck. The cockpit is ideally suited for general sitting about, or waiting until the sun goes over the yardarm (if you know which bit that is). There is usually a sunshade and a fold-away table so that you can eat there. Otherwise, there is deck space where you can sunbathe and generally lounge around. A word of warning: with little shelter and strong tropical sun reflected off the sea, and the many white surfaces, you can be seriously burned in a short time. When you feel like cooling off, just slither over the side. Most yachts have snorkelling gear and some of the larger yachts also carry a windsurfer.

The VHF radio is a novel addition to life on a sailing holiday. As well being useful for emergencies, it can be used for co-ordinating beach picnics and chatting to friends. You may even find yourself using it to order dinner in advance at the local beach restaurant: 'Marina Cay, this is Amberjack; that'll be two lobsters in lime butter, a creole shrimp and a kingfish, please; eight o'clock OK? Over.' 'Marina Cay, copy that, dinner at eight, over and out.' Frequencies vary from island to island, but there is usually an open channel (often VHF 16 or 68) on which people make contact. Then they switch to a different channel to have their conversation. Taxi-drivers and shopkeepers will also listen out on these frequencies. Another novelty for those who generally live in a house is the yacht's dinghy, usually an inflatable with an outboard motor attached, used to take you to the nearby snorkelling spot or beach or out to dinner in the evening.

Days tend to start quite slowly. Yachts begin to scatter from the night's anchorage in the late morning (if passengers can bear the idea of any activity in the heat), making their way to a lunchtime stop on a beach or at a snorkelling area. Many don't move at all until the late afternoon, heading off to a new anchorage by dusk. (Beware, though: in the busier areas in high season you will find that the more popular anchorages fill up quite early in the day.) However, if you are sailing into a difficult anchorage it is a good idea to have the sun overhead as it will enable you to read the reefs more easily.

Evenings can be lively, and in the Virgin Islands particularly you will find that you come across the same crowd as you move from anchorage to anchorage. There is a certain feeling of camaraderie among yacht-borne travellers and many of the bars are run by sailors, who are usually sympathetic to visitors. If there is a good crowd then it can get very active and noisy. In some bars jam sessions will materialise spontaneously as the night's drinkers pick up any instrument lying around and start to play. However, if you are not feeling up to making whoopee you can always stay on board, where you will be left alone. A yacht is a person's castle.

Sailing A–Z

Anchorages in the Islands

There is a good variety of sailing in the eastern Caribbean. As a very general rule it is easiest in the Virgin Islands and becomes more demanding as you head further south through the Leeward Islands down to the Windwards, where the distances between the island are greater and you are more exposed. The northerly islands are also more developed: there are more restaurants, marinas and general facilities like chandleries and boatyards in the Virgin Islands and in Sint Maarten and Antigua than in the Windward Islands. All the French islands are highly developed.

The **Virgin Islands** serve their sailors well. Anchorages are close together, usually not more than a couple of hours' sailing from each other, and there are few reefs (except around Anegada, where many companies ask you not to go). And in many of the anchorages there are beach bars, which provide nightly entertainment as you move from bar to bar; there is even a sort of circuit in high season. Though the Virgin Islands can become quite crowded in winter, there are still plenty of isolated anchorages where you can expect to be alone.

Sint Maarten/Saint Martin is also a very popular centre. It is the hub of the Leeward Islands and acts as a convenient stopover for yachts travelling further south. There are plenty of marinas and restaurants, and excellent repair facilities. From here it is easy to make short trips to Anguilla and St Barts.

Antigua is another centre, with excellent all-round sailing, secluded anchorages off the beaches and the island of the northeast, as well as a lively shoreside life, particularly around Race Week in April. The great gathering point is English Harbour in the southeast.

Guadeloupe has excellent variety in its combination of volcanic and the coral-based land, and also because of its offshore islands Marie Galante and the Saints. Both Guadeloupe and **Martinique** are similarly developed, with good facilities and excellent provisioning.

Further south, **St Lucia** has a steadily growing reputation for sailing, particularly as a starting point for the Grenadines.

The **Grenadines** are another classic sailing centre. The many islands are close to one another and have excellent beaches and coves. They have a slightly raw, more West Indian quality about them than the Virgin Islands, with more accessible local life as well as pretty tourist spots.

Immigration and Customs

You are required to clear with immigration on arrival, and sometimes again on departure from each island (or country in certain cases like the Virgin Islands and the Grenadines). It may not be vital to complete the formalities first thing, but check with official publications or with other sailors. Outside office hours you may have to pay an overtime fee for registration; you can also usually expect to pay a departure tax when you leave. In some islands a cruising fee is charged.

Ports of entry are mentioned in the separate island chapters. Customs procedures are less formal, and are usually located along with immigration.

Marinas and Chandleries

Facilities vary considerably across the islands and they are generally more comprehensive in the islands mentioned above as sailing 'centres'. The smallest islands may not have a marina, but there is usually a place where you can get the most important sailing requisites like fuel, water and ice. Most marinas have a laundry, postal facilities and showers; where there is no marina, there is usually a hotel which will help out. Some smaller islands may have a chandlery, but don't count on it. When it comes to technical work on your yacht, you will be dependent on the main centres: Antigua, Guadeloupe, Martinique, St Lucia, St Thomas in the USVI, Tortola in the BVI, and Sint Maarten/St Martin.

Provisioning and Rubbish

In all the major centres there is a supermarket within walking distance of the dock, usually strategically positioned to catch sailors. They will also have ice for sale. In less developed islands you will have to go to the local supermarket or to the market, though you can get water at most docks. There are usually video stores on shore too, and some marinas have cable TV on-line. It is worth asking around because fishermen may well be happy to sell you fish they have caught. In some of the islands (mostly the Windwards) you will be approached by lads who will offer to fetch food from the market and to act as general fixer for you. If you decide to use them, it is best to choose just one and stick with him.

Rubbish should be bagged and sealed and then dropped at a marina. Biodegradeable items can be thrown overboard, but never any plastic items; these have caused problems with the fishlife around the islands.

Security

This is generally not a problem, but it is sensible to take the few simple precautions. Lock your yacht if you leave it alone and go ashore. Also lock your dinghy to the dock and the outboard motor to the dinghy. You can usually arrange for someone to watch over it for you.

Telephones

There will often be a telephone in the marina. Details of telephones are given in the 'Tourist Information' sections of the separate island chapters.

Winds and Weather

The **trade winds** (*Alizés* in French and *Passaatwinden* in Dutch) are well known with land-based Caribbean travellers for taking the edge off the tropical heat, but for sailors they provide the perfect means to make their way around the islands. They are equatorial winds, northeasterlies and easterlies, and they blow fairly reliably across the year at between 10 and 25 knots. They vary in strength a little, at their strongest over the winter and gentler in August and September, and in direction: in winter they are northeasterly, but with the tilting of the earth they verge towards southeasterlies over the summer. Sometimes the winds are a little fluky around dusk, when there are offshore breezes as the islands cool down.

The weather in the islands is also pretty benign, though over the winter the occasional swell will be set off by the weather systems in the north, making the sea uncomfortable in certain anchorages. Westerly winds are very unusual. The other major consideration is the hurricane season (July to September). There is usually ample warning over the radio as well as on the grapevine. You are advised to head for a 'hurricane hole', as the most protected harbours have become known, or an area of mangroves.

Topics

Columbus greeted by Arawak Indians on San Salvador 41

Columbus is famous as the discoverer of America. One Caribbean calypso singer objected that this view was Eurocentric arrogance, as American Indians clearly beat him to it by forty thousand years. However, his voyages were to have an importance that changed the world. Certainly he gave the West Indies their name. He was sailing for the Indies via the west, trying to reopen the spice trade with the East recently cut off by the Arabs. Discovery of new lands was secondary.

Cristoforo Colombo (or Cristobal Colon in Spanish) was born in the 1450s in Genoa, son of a weaver, but he chose his career as a sailor while still a young man. Columbus was largely self-taught. He was obviously intelligent and forceful, but he was domineering in authority and this was his downfall; he was also inflexible and jumped to illogical geographical conclusions, deciding at one stage that the world was pear-shaped. All the same, he was a bold and accomplished explorer and a fine navigator. He was persuasive and even charismatic in court, impressing Queen Isabella so much that she helped him despite the advice of her courtiers.

If he was a visionary, and he stuck to his plan for years before he was granted the opportunity to carry it out, his dreams also tipped into self-delusion. He considered himself chosen by God to bring Christianity to the New World, and he was paranoid about others encroaching on what he considered his domain. He insisted on huge public honour as reward for his service to the Crown of Spain: he was granted the titles of 'Admiral of the Ocean Sea' and 'Viceroy of India'. But he fulfilled the dreams of the age. The world was outgrowing its Mediterranean confines and tColumbus was a master mariner who was acquainted with all available maps. Slowly the plan evolved. He would try to reach the east by sailing west.

On 3 August 1492 Columbus set off from Palos, touching the Canaries and then navigating due west. He expected to come to Japan or China after about 2500 miles (about where America is). They sailed with the wind behind for over a month, through the Sargasso Sea, into the unknown. But steadily the crew became more rebellious (fearing they might not get home). On 12 October 1492, they sighted land, one of the Bahamian islands. Columbus called the island San Salvador in honour of the Saviour, but clearly he had not found Japan, so after a few days he set off in search of it. He touched Cuba and then his flagship was wrecked off Hispaniola and he was forced to leave about forty men behind when he sailed for Spain, where he announced that he had reached Asia. A second expedition was sent the same year, with 1500 settlers to colonize the island of Hispaniola. Administrative problems began almost at once and were compounded when Columbus left his brother Diego in charge during his exploration of Cuba and Jamaica.

Columbus led a third voyage in 1498, arriving in Trinidad, narrowly missing the continent of South America. From here he sailed to Hispaniola by dead reckoning, no mean feat. He found the colony in disarray and was forced to treat with the rebels. Eventually his viceregal authority was revoked and he was shipped back to Spain in chains. He was treated kindly by Ferdinand and Isabella and permitted to return to the New World on a fourth journey in 1502, on the express understanding that he was not to set foot on Hispaniola. In some ways his last trip was the most successful; however he was shipwrecked on the coast of Jamaica and had to wait a year before he was rescued and made it back to Spain.

Columbus died in Spain in 1506, faintly ridiculed because of all his problems in the Indies, his eccentric behaviour and his excessive claims against the Crown. Though his experience as a seaman had probably told him otherwise, he maintained to his death that he had arrived in the Far East.

The Dutch Influence in the Caribbean

The six islands that make up the Netherlands Antilles are split into two groups of three, separated by some 500 miles of the Caribbean Sea. The ABC islands (Aruba, Bonaire and Curaçao, or the Dutch Leewards) are positioned just off the coast of South America, and the three Ss (Sint Maarten, St Eustatius and Saba or the Dutch Windwards) are found in the northeastern Caribbean, scattered among the British Leeward Islands. The reason for the confusion of the names resides in now obscure sailing terminology.

The Netherlands Antilles may be within the Dutch Kingdom, but they are by no means a tropical version of Holland. The Dutch were never great colonizers and what influence they had has been creolized. Post-boxes are painted Royal Dutch red, the currency is guilders and florins and Dutch is spoken in the schools and in the Post Office, but the drivers here are much more akin to their fellow West Indians than the good burghers of the Netherlands, and the traditional shapes of Dutch architecture look distinctly different painted in Caribbean colours. In addition, the Dutch Windward Islands have been strongly influenced by the English-speaking islands around them—most inhabitants speak English as well as Dutch.

The heart of Dutch influence in the Caribbean is really Curaçao, the largest island in the Dutch Leewards, and it is here that the Dutch creole effect is most clearly visible. It is home to the *Staten*, the Dutch Antillean Parliament and to the extraordinary indigenous Dutch Antillean language, Papiamento, which has an almost mystical heritage of Spanish, Portuguese, English and African languages. You will hear this spoken very occasionally in the Windwards. In the trio of the Dutch Windward Islands the Dutch culture is less pronounced, even in its creole form.

The Dutch came to the Caribbean with a different agenda from the other European nations. Instead of planting, they came to trade. They had the fleets and so they shipped out machinery for the planters and returned to Europe loaded up with tobacco and sugar. Rather than eyeing the fertile lands taken by the English and French, the Dutch headed for good harbours. St Eustatius was the most important port in the Caribbean in its time, so successful that it became known as the Golden Rock.

And it is strange how the patterns of history repeat themselves: the Dutch islands still have a reputation as trading ports. Nowadays it is cruise ship passengers who come to Philipsburg in Sint Maarten (and to Aruba and Curaçao in the Dutch Leewards) to take advantage of the duty-free status and the goods that have been shipped in from all over the world.

French Caribbean Culture

French colonization was a more thorough-going affair than that of the British. Where British planters mostly hoped to 'return' to England with a fortune (many were West Indian born and bred, but still thought of England as home), the French installed themselves in the islands and made their lives there.

The familiar verve of the French is ever-present in the French Caribbean islands. Chic customers glide by shops filled with Christian Lacroix and Yves St Laurent, and lovers linger over a meal under coloured awnings while citizens play *boules* in the dusty town squares. In Fort de France, the capital of Martinique, there is even a Parisian haste, a *je m'en foutisme* untypical of the Caribbean. The illusion of being in France is only spiked by the bristle of palm trees and the variety of skin tones.

But for those who know France it is the departures from French culture, not these similarities, which are most fascinating: the steep rainforested slopes and the flatlands blanketed with sugarcane or bananas, where the islanders walk at a relaxed and graceful pace, the rivers where the *blanchisseuses* have laid out washing on the rocks, the markets that are mercantile mayhem. Like all the Caribbean islands, the French Caribbean islands have developed their own unique creole culture. The air pulses to the sound of the relentless French Caribbean rhythm, zouk (as it did in times past to the famous rhythms, the béguine and the mazurka).

It is often said how beautiful the people of Martinique and Guadeloupe are. Though the French islands always had a slightly higher proportion of whites, the old settlers were clearly also less prudish about taking an African mistress and so the mix of racial strains is more thorough. It has created some striking faces; a hundred years ago the creole beauties of Martinique were renowned all over the Caribbean. These 'doudous' (from *douce chérie*) presented themselves with characteristic Gallic flair, bedecked in reams of brightly coloured cotton and yards of lace petticoat, with a foulard thrown over one shoulder. (You can still see the chequered madras material in the islands.) But the focal point of the outfit was the hat. This too was fashioned of bright silk material, often yellow and checked, and there was supposedly a code in its design—*tête à un bout* (one point): my heart is for the taking; *tête à deux bouts*: my heart is taken; *tête à trois bouts*: my heart is spoken for, but you can try your luck.

The official language of the islands is French, the language of the people is *créole*, that curious mix of French and African which has crystallized into a new language. Each of the Caribbean islands which has seen a French presence has a version of its own. You will hear it spoken in Dominica, St Lucia and occasionally Grenada, which the French have owned at one time or other, and even as far away as Trinidad, taken there by French Royalists fleeing the *patriotes* in revolutionary times. The eastern Caribbean *créoles* are not, however, interchangeable with the *kweyol* of the Haitians, once also French subjects.

Some of the leading figures of the French black consciousness and literary movement of the 1930s, the Négritude, were from Martinique. Etienne Lero and Aimé Césaire, together with Léopold Senghor of Senegal, re-examined the position of the black man, formerly the slave, and his relation to the white man, the colonial master. Aimé Césaire became famous with his *Cahier d'un retour au pays natal* in 1939 and a later play *La Tragédie du roi Christophe*. He has only recently retired from Martiniquan politics after nearly fifty years as mayor of Fort de France.

More recent French Caribbean authors (most of whom write in French) worth looking out for include, from Martinique, Edouard Glissant, recent winner of the Prix Goncourt with *Texaco*, Aimé Césaire, Patrick Chamoiseau (*Solibo Magnifique*, which is set in Fort de France), Joseph Zobel (*Rue Cases-Nègres*), Rafaël Confiant (*Eau de café*, winner of the 1991 Prix Novembre), Boukman and Xavier Orville. Guadeloupean writers include Maryse Condé, whose finest book is probably *La Vie scélérate*, Simone Schwarz-Bart (known for her *Un Plat de porc aux bananes vertes* and *Ti Jean l'Horizon*), Max Jeanne and Daniel Maximin.

Politically, France has taken a radically different approach to the Caribbean from Britain. Instead of encouraging a gradual move to independence, France has embraced her islands, taking them into the *république* and giving them the status of overseas *départements*, equal to that of Savoie or Lot-et-Garonne. Martinique and Guadeloupe are *régions* in their own right, possessing the extra powers and responsibilities brought by decentralization in 1985. They are administered by a *préfet* appointed by the French government. Their people vote in French elections and they each send three deputies and two senators to the National Assembly in Paris. Milk costs the same as it does in the *métropole*, as continental France is called, and so does a car. There is National Service. Rumour has it that they even fly in croissants. In standard of living alone, the contrast with neighbouring islands is striking, and it could never be maintained without direct support from Paris.

There are some who envy the other islands their autonomy—independence movements have expressed themselves in graffiti campaigns and have occasionally erupted into violence, with bomb attacks—but most French Antilleans appreciate the benefits and would not change their situation, except to gain the maximum self-government while under the French umbrella.

Music

People joke that the West Indians change the roll of their gait as they walk along the street, switching rhythm to each successive stereo system that they pass. Music has been central to Caribbean life since slave days when it was a principal form of recreation, and you will hear it everywhere, all day. At Carnival they dance for days.

There are almost as many beats as there are islands in the Caribbean and they go on changing and developing over time. The roots are audible in many cases—you will see marching bands dressed in their red tunics playing 'O, when the Saints' **reggae**-style, Indian flourishes appear in Trinidadian **calypso**, the Latin beat is so clear in Cuban and Puerto Rican **salsa** and the vocals of rap appear in calypso and Jamaican **dancehall**. But in all the Caribbean sounds, the rhythm is relentlessly fast and the beat is as solid as the African drums from which it is derived.

The West Indians will use anything to make music. At carnival the crowds shuffle along to the sound of a couple of drums, a car wheel-rim, a cheese-grater and a cowbell. Even garden forks have been tuned up in Curaçao. But the best example of them all is the steel drum in Trinidad, which was invented in the yards of Port of Spain after the last war. Discarded biscuit tins and oil drums were bashed out and then tuned up and an orchestra was created.

As you travel around the islands, you will see speakers set up in the street just for the hell of it. Cars practically bulge with the beat and they can often be heard before they can be seen coming along the road. If you are invited to a *fête*, go, because they are a wild side of West Indian life. Dance is all lower carriage movement, shuffle-stepping and swaying hips, and is incredibly energetic.

The rhythms of one island often spread to another. The main popular rhythms and their countries of origin are as follows:

Soca (soul-calypso)—Trinidad, where calypso itself started. Barbados and other islands nearby also produce their own calypsonians, some of them very good.

Zouk—Martinique and Guadeloupe, with a bustling double beat.

Salsa—two different sorts, one each from Cuba and Puerto Rico, the latter influenced by the 'Neo-Riceñans' (Puerto Ricans in New York).

Merengue—the Dominican Republic, also a strongly Latin sound. Another local rhythm, *bachata*, has recently been revived and become popular.

Compas—Haiti, a bit rougher, but not dissimilar to the zouk of the French Antilles, also echoes of West Africa.

Any of the Caribbean **carnivals** is worth attending if you happen to be on the island. You can often join in if you do go by asking around (usually for a small fee to cover the cost of the costume). It is worth crossing half the world to get to the **Trinidad Carnival** (many Trinidadians do), which takes place at the beginning of Lent. Also there are steel band and calypso competitions.

The Volcanic Origins of the Islands

The Lesser Antilles are made up of two distinct types of land. The islands are the partly submerged peaks of two mountain ranges which run more or less north to south; their lines are easily visible on the map. The islands of the inner chain, which runs from Grenada in the south to Saba in the north, are vast, in many cases active, volcanoes. They soar from the water to thousands of feet and they are immensely lush, covered in rainforest. The outer islands, which are lower and therefore less fertile, touch the volcanic chain at Guadeloupe and run north through Barbuda, St Barts, St Martin and Anguilla.

The volcanic islands have sprouted at the fault line of the Caribbean and Atlantic tectonic plates. As the Atlantic crust gradually forces its way under the Caribbean plate, lava escapes from the magma beneath and explodes through the volcanoes. Though the eruptions have calmed down somewhat over the last few million years, the main soufrières do blow about once a century and cause earthquakes that reverberate along the whole chain of the Lesser Antilles. On one day in 1867, weird happenings on Grenada in the far south, where the harbour water swelled and contracted as though the underworld were breathing, were echoed by seismic activity as far north as the Virgin Island of St Thomas.

Strictly speaking, the outer chain of islands is volcanic in origin as well. These volcanoes were active about a hundred million years ago (the inner chain is only about 15 million years old), when the rift between the tectonic plates was further east.

Now the outer islands stand on a shelf under which the Atlantic plate has moved. Over millions of years their old volcanic peaks have subsided and been repeatedly submerged in the sea and then exposed by the Ice Ages. As the water rose and receded around them they became encrusted with generations of coral growth, and this left them with a coral limestone cap.

Each one of the Windwards has its soufrière, a sulphurous volcanic vent, and if you go exploring you will be greeted by its smell (soufrière means sulphur, so it smells like a stink-bomb). The St Vincent volcano and those on nearby Martinique and Guadeloupe are the most violent, tending to blast out volumes of lava and super-heated gases that collapse mountains and destroy anything in their path, as well as belching plumes of gas and a showers of pumice stones. On the other islands, including the northerly islands inthe chain, things are a little less extreme. Here there are fumaroles which constantly vent, letting off pressure which might other-wise build up and cause an explosion. In the Grenadines there is an underwater volcano (Kick 'em Jenny), now quite close to the surface, whose activity has been spotted by pilots and yachtsmen passing over the area. Elsewhere, release of gases underwater makes for interesting dive-sites.

An American seer has predicted that the 1990s are to be an active time for the Windward Islands. According to her, one island will appear during the decade—presumably Kick 'em Jenny—but, more worryingly, she has also predicted that another island will disappear.

Antigua and Barbuda

rocky coastline / Antigua

The graceful and welcoming contours of Antigua inspired Columbus to name the island in honour of a statue of the Virgin in Seville Cathedral, Santa Maria de la Antigua. Its rolling yellow-green hills and the sweeping curves of its bays are soft on the eye after the towering volcanic violence of the Windwards. Barbuda, Antigua's smaller sister island 30 miles to the north, is even gentler and more laid back, not making it above 130ft.

Antigua (pronounced more as in 'beleaguer' than in 'ambiguou(s)') has a population of 65,000 and is the largest of the Leeward Islands (108 square miles). For years it was the linchpin of British influence in the area—St John's was the seat of government and the principal military and naval fortifications were here. Perhaps this past has given Antigua its feel of stability. The island has a long-standing following and it attracts a large number of the five-star tourists that every Caribbean island favours. There is a certain air of confidence as it faces the future, having become fully independent from Britain only in 1981.

Antigua's shape has something of a confused amoeba about it, with pseudopodia heading off in every direction. These headlands enclose the bays used so successfully by navies and by smugglers over the centuries. Except for one corner of ancient volcanic outflow in the southwest, the island is made entirely of limestone coral. The Atlantic coast, beaten by the waves over the millennia, looks pitted and scarred like a neolithic cake-mix, but on the protected shores of the Caribbean side the gentler wave action on the reefs has pushed up miles of blinding white sand.

Antigua lies lower in the water than its southerly volcanic neighbours and its climate is gentler and drier. The same northeast trade winds blow in from the Atlantic, but Antigua does not collect the rain-clouds that linger above the Windwards. The early settlements were plagued by a lack of water and in 1731 a bucketful of it was even sold for three shillings. This is not to say that Antigua does not experience tropical rainstorms, however: they can catch you unawares and the proverbial bucketful will soak you in seconds.

For much of its history, Antigua's coastline bristled with forts and the land was covered to the last inch with canefields, dotted occasionally with a windmill and estate house. But now the 160 plantations have gone and their fields have turned into rolling

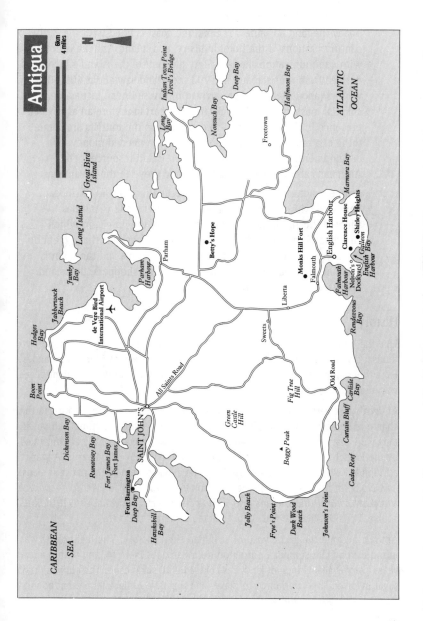

Antigua

6km
4 miles

N

CARIBBEAN
SEA

Boom Point
Hodges Bay
Dickenson Bay
Runaway Bay
Fort James Bay
Fort James
Fort Barrington
Deep Bay
Hawksbill Bay
Jabberrock Beach
de Vere Bird International Airport
SAINT JOHN'S
All Saints Road
Green Castle Hill
Boggy Peak
Fig Tree Hill
Old Road
Jolly Beach
Frye's Point
Dark Wood Beach
Johnson's Point
Cades Reef
Curtain Bluff
Carlisle Bay
Sweets
Liberta
Falmouth
Monks Hill Fort
Parham
Parham Harbour
Betty's Hope
Jumby Bay
Long Island
Great Bird Island
Long Bay
Indian Town Point
Devil's Bridge
Nonsuch Bay
Deep Bay
Freetown
Halfmoon Bay
Marmora Bay
English Harbour
Clarence House
Shirley Heights
Galleon Bay
Falmouth Harbour
Nelson's Dockyard
English Harbour
Rendezvous Bay
ATLANTIC OCEAN

51

scrubland, where the dilapidated conical shells of the windmills stand silent without their sails.

Today the land has a new regime; the coast is lined with the 20th-century bastions of the hotel industry, and inland Antigua is dotted with communications aerials. Sixty per cent of the island's income is derived from tourists, and in 1993 the island saw about 400,000 visitors (about half of whom arrived by cruise-liner). Just as the colonial masters in their dockyards and barracks were an ambivalent presence in the 18th and 19th centuries, so the tourists are something of a mixed blessing. They bring much-needed money for development, but they are a burden on island resources. The Antiguans are pretty cool, however, and they see the advantages.

Antigua is one of the most popular destinations in the Caribbean. Recently, with an increase of package tourists, the island has adopted the all-inclusive format in many of the hotels, in which guests tend to stay in the hotel property. This means that except on the days when the cruise ships put into St John's and the town is overrun with marauding bands of lobster-red shoppers, the island holds the tourist invasion remarkably well.

History

Like the other Leeward Islands, Antigua saw its first island-hoppers around two thousand years ago, when Arawaks from South America arrived in their canoes. For a thousand years they fished and tended small plots of cassava until their peace was interrupted by the intrusion of the Caribs.

Antigua's first permanent European settlement arrived from nearby St Kitts in the charge of Philip Warner in 1632. Like earlier settlers whose attempts had failed, they were plagued by a lack of water and by the Caribs, occasionally accompanied by the French, who nipped over on raids from the nearby Windwards. A war of attrition followed, with the colonists determined to exterminate the native Indians. Law No.88 in the old Antiguan Statute Book for 1693 reads *'An Act to encourage the destroying of the Indians and Taking their Periagoes (canoes)'*. It took its course. By 1805, the law was simply marked down as *'Obsolete'*.

Antigua became the archetypal West Indian sugar factory. The technology was introduced by Christopher Codrington from Barbados in 1674, and within a few years every available inch of land was covered with sugar-cane. The cultivation of sugar involved large workforces of slaves and this gave Antigua its present population of mainly African descent.

As the Caribbean empires flourished in the 18th century and the wars for territory hotted up, the British chose Antigua as their main military and naval base in the Leeward Islands, creating a link between their other defences in Barbados to the south and in Jamaica in the Greater Antilles. The fortifications at Shirley Heights above English Harbour on the south coast proved so formidable that the French and Spanish navies simply avoided them. In the 19th century the wars came to an end and the empires crystallized. The abolition movement managed to outlaw slavery in 1834, but the freed slaves had no choice but to continue working the plantations. There was no other source of employment. The slaves were free, but their situation hardly improved. As sugar declined in the late 19th century (the price of West Indian cane sugar could not compete with subsidized European beet sugar), Antigua waned and the island became another poor and quiet outcrop in the Caribbean backwater. It was not until this century that things began to pick up again. The latest empire to make itself felt is of course tourism, which Antigua has developed for the past forty years.

A wartime agreement granting the United States bases on the island brought a large influx of Americans during the Second World War, and this put the island on the map. The agreements are still retained and the US Air Force and Navy still have bases in Antigua.

Antiguan politics have a similar heritage to those of other British islands. Trade unions sprang up all over the Caribbean in the thirties and the islanders rallied to them, first as a way to organize political power in the face of colonial rule and later to develop into the movement for self-determination and eventually Independence. Vere Bird, a President of the Antigua Trades and Labour Union in the 1940s, became the leading light in Antiguan politics, becoming Chief Minister, and later Prime Minister under 'Associated Statehood' in 1967. He became the first leader of independent Antigua and Barbuda on 1 November 1981 and continued as Prime Minister until 1994, when his Antigua Labour Party was taken over by his son, the Hon. Lester Bird. They were re-elected with a majority of eleven out of seventeen seats over the United People's Party led by the Hon. Baldwin Spence. The Governor of Antigua is Sir James Carlisle.

Flora and Fauna

Set in the yellow-green expanses of scrub, Antiguan gardens are splendid with the bright pinks and purples of hibiscus and bougainvillea. There is one pocket of lusher vegetation, Fig Tree Hill in the southwest, and here you will see slopes covered in elephant ears and of course fig trees (the local name for the banana). Flitting in its foliage you can find Antigua's two hummingbirds and several doves. On the plains you are bound to see the ever-present mournful cattle egret, standing sentinel by the cattle that give it its name. In the coastal ponds (there are many, behind the hotels on Dickenson Bay, in the creeks on the east coast and by Jolly Beach) you will see boobies, terns and sandpipers as well as the ubiquitous pelican. You can also visit the offshore islands, including Great Bird Island, which is particularly known as home to the red-billed tropicbird.

✆ (809)–   ***Getting There***

Antigua's Vere Cornwall Bird International Airport has excellent connections around the Caribbean and from Europe (about eight hours) and North America. It is a hub for the northeastern Caribbean. Departure tax of EC$25 (US$10) is payable except by those who have spent less than 24 hours in the country.

By Air from Europe: There are usually daily flights from Britain: British Airways from Gatwick (local ✆ 462 3219) and BWIA (✆ 462 0262) from Heathrow and charter operators Caledonian and Airtours. Lufthansa (✆ 462 0983) has two flights each week from Frankfurt and BWIA flies weekly from Zurich.

By Air from North America: BWIA fly in non-stop from Miami every day and regularly from New York, and American Airlines (✆ 462 0950) have direct flights from JFK New York and easy connections via Miami and San Juan. Continental fly from Newark, New Jersey. BWIA also fly from Toronto in Canada, as does Air Canada (✆ 462 1147).

By Air from other Caribbean Islands: Antigua is the headquarters of LIAT (✆ 462 3142), so there are more flights to and from here on the airline's services than anywhere else. On LIAT and other carriers (Air Guadeloupe, Air St Kitts Nevis, ✆ 465 8571) there are daily direct flights or easy connections to all the islands between San Juan, Puerto Rico in the north and Trinidad and Barbados in the south. There are two daily flights to Barbuda and about six to Montserrat. If you need to charter a plane, contact Carib Aviation (✆ 462 3147, fax 462 3125).

By Boat: There are no scheduled boat services to Antigua. You might persuade a freighter captain to let you aboard for the ride, but your best bet is to get a passage on a yacht—there are lots based in English Harbour.

Getting Around

The **bus service** in Antigua is scant. It tends to run early in the morning, bringing workers into town from the outlying areas, and it finishes around 6pm. You will have difficulty finding public transport after dark or on

Sundays. There is a fairly regular service (leaving either when the bus is full or when the urge takes the driver) between St John's and **English Harbour** in the southeast of the island. Getting back at night is a problem, though the All Saint's–St John's run continues until late. Other roads are run less frequently. No buses at all run either to the airport or to the northern tourist area, leaving you dependent on taxis, but a number of the hotels run buses for their workers, so you might be lucky enough to catch a ride with them. The **East Bus Station**, on Independence Avenue on the outskirts of St John's, serves the north and east of the island. Opposite the St John's market is the **West Bus Station**, from which buses leave for villages in the southern part of the island. Travelling on the buses is cheap, and the longest fare across the island costs around EC$3. Hitch-hiking around the island works adequately. To signal to both car and bus drivers, the traditional Caribbean sign is to point rapidly at the ground.

Good tourists, of course, go by **taxi**, and there is a superabundance of them in St John's and at the airport. They can also be ordered through the hotels. The government fixes taxi rates and it is worth establishing the price (and currency) before setting off. The ride from the airport into St John's costs US$8 and from St John's to Nelson's Dockyard US$35. Many of the taxi-drivers are knowledgeable about Antiguan lore and so you will often get an impromptu tour if you wish, but any taxi-driver would be happy to take you on a more formal tour of the island, which will cover many of the island sights. A day's tour costs around US$60 and is easily fixed through any hotel foyer. Companies offering tours include: **Antours** (© 462 4788) and **Bryson's Travel** (© 462 0223). **Tropikelly Tours** (© 461 0383) offers off-road tours in four-wheel-drive vehicles to less-explored island sights.

Hiring a car is probably the best way to get around the island, and there are plenty of rental firms. Drivers must obtain a Temporary Permit, available from the rental company on presentation of a valid driving licence and payment of US$12. If you are driving out into the country, take a reasonable map because there are few roadsigns. The roads are not brilliant (the 40mph speed limit is quite appropriate), and driving is on the left. If you wish to go off the main roads it is advisable to get hold of a four-wheel-drive car, of which there are plenty for hire. The price of a day's hire starts at US$50 for a car and $55 for a jeep. Car rental companies, which work out of St John's and often from the airport include: **Carib Car Rentals** (© 462 2062), **National** on All Saints Road, St John's (© 462 2113), **Dollar Rent-a-Car** (© 462 0362), and **Matthew's Car Rental**, St John's (© 462 4600). You can rent a bicycle through **Sun Cycles** (© 461 0324), who deliver to your hotel.

The **Antigua and Barbuda Department of Tourist** has offices in:

UK: 15 Thayer Street, London W1M 5LD (✆ 071 486 7073/6, fax 071 486 9970).

USA: 610 Fifth Avenue, Suite 311, **New York**, NY 10020 (✆ 212 541 4117). Also at the Trade Missions: 121 SE 1st Street, Suite 1001, **Miami**, Florida (✆ 305 381 6762) and 3400 International Drive NW, Suite 4M, **Washington** DC 20008 (✆ 202 362 5122).

Canada: 60 St Clair Avenue East, Suite 305, Toronto, Ontario MT4 1N5 (✆ 416 961 3085, fax 416 961 7218).

Germany: Postfach 1331, Minnholzweg 2, 6242 Kronberg 1 (✆ 06173 7091, fax 06173 7299).

On Antigua itself, the main office is at the corner of Thames Street and the High Street in the centre of St John's, PO Box 363 (✆ 462 0480/462 0029, fax 462 2483). There is also a desk at the airport. The Tourist Board publishes *Antigua and Barbuda Adventure*, a twice-yearly glossy with articles and lists of restaurants and boutiques, and the smaller guide *The Antiguan*.

In a medical **emergency**, there is a 24-hour casualty room at the St John's hospital, on Hospital Road (✆ 462 0251). The **IDD code** for Antigua is 809 followed by a seven-figure local number. On island, dial the seven digits.

Antigua has a number of **galleries** in which you will see the works of Caribbean painters as well as arts and crafts. **Seahorse Studios** are located in Redcliffe Quay and there you will find originals and reproduction prints and jewellery. **Harmony Hall** is difficult to find on the east coast at Brown's Bay, but there too you will find arts and craft from all over the Caribbean (Harmony Hall has a sister property in Jamaica)—Haitian buses and colourful work with calabashes and baskets. It is good for a daytime visit; there is a restaurant and a bar in the old windmill.

Money

Antigua and Barbuda share their currency, the Eastern Caribbean dollar, with the other countries in the OECS (Organization of Eastern Caribbean States), from Anguilla in the north down to Grenada in the south. The EC$ is linked to the US$, at a rate of about US$1 = EC$2.65. US dollars are accepted everywhere on the island, though change will sometimes be given in EC$. Credit cards are also widely accepted by hotels, restaurants and shops and as security for car hire. Though confusion rarely arises, it is a good rule to establish which currency you are dealing in.

Life in Antigua can be quite expensive. Not only do most necessities have to be imported, but the government imposes no income tax, preferring instead to raise taxes through sales of food and goods. Even in the markets, where fruit and vegetables might be relatively cheap, prices are quite high.

Banking hours are 8am–2pm on weekdays with an extra two hours on Fridays, 3–5pm. Exchange can always be made at the larger hotels, but the rate will not be as good. **Shops** tend to be open daily except Sundays, between 8.30am and 4 or 5pm, with an hour off between noon and 1pm. They will often stay open later when a cruise ship is in dock.

Beaches

Between them, Antigua and Barbuda have some of the loveliest beaches in the Caribbean. Time was, not so long ago, that Antiguan families would simply move on if anyone was already on their favourite beach when they arrived for the Sunday picnic. Now they are relatively crowded—perhaps ten people scattered over a mile of isolated sand. If you want it, you can be alone on the beach in Antigua.

There is something for every taste, and for once the tourist brochures' claims are correct: you can walk alone on a mile-wide scalloped bay of silken sand, where coconut palms bend and brush the beach and the waves fizz around your toes; or you can cut a windsurfing dash on crowded strands where the body-beautiful roam. In some places, though, the sandflies do bite and mosquitoes dive-bomb you as you doze and so you might have to evacuate in late afternoon. Take some repellent if you go off the beaten track.

If you like an active beach, then your best bet is **Dickenson Bay** on the west coast north of St John's, where a clutch of hotels is situated. Superb sand and all the watersports and posing you will ever want; also plenty of watering holes to retire to. It extends into **Runaway Bay** to the south, which is also active and has lovely sand. **Fort James Bay** beach just to the south (closer to St John's) is popular with the Antiguans at the weekend, but tends to be uncrowded in the week.

There are a number of other beaches on the west coast and they become steadily more deserted as you go south. The **Hawksbill Bay** area has some small strips of

sand. The farthest from the hotel is a nudist beach. Past the ever popular **Jolly Beach** (also called Lignum vitae after the wood) you come to some of the deserted, mile-long strips with fantastic sand: **Ffrye's Bay**, the palm-backed **Dark Wood Beach** and **Johnson's Point**.

On the south coast in **Carlisle Bay**, where the Curtain Bluff hotel stands, the waves splay in fans on the steep sand and there are reefs to explore. The rest of the south coast is indented with bays and you will find half-moon coves of soft and mounded sand, for instance, at **Mamora Bay** where the St James's Club is situated. On English Harbour, a water-taxi-ride from Nelson's Dockyard, is **Galleon Bay**, and nearby on Falmouth Harbour are one or two good strips of sand.

On the east coast, where the weather is a bit rougher, there are one or two protected spots such as **Half Moon Bay** and **Long Bay**. For those who would prefer to tame the Atlantic weather, the east coast is the best place for **windsurfing** and a couple of recommended places are **Jabberwock Beach** on the northeastern shore (you can hire equipment at the Beach Hotel) and **Hodges Bay** around the corner to the north. In between these main beaches are any number of small coves where you can be alone. Ask an Antiguan.

Beach Bars

There are a string of bars to retreat to on Dickenson Bay. Among them **Shorty's Bar** or **Miller's** is popular, where there is often a band playing in the afternoon. A little quieter is **Spinnakers**, where you can get a pleasant meal after sizzling in the sun. For something a little more secluded, head down to Fort James Bay, where there are a couple of bars right on the sand, including **Russell's Beach Bar**, which operates on Sunday afternoon. On the endless strands of the southwest you will find the **Darkwood Beach Bar**, good for a beer and a view of the sunset. Finally there are all the nautical bars in Nelson's Dockyard, which collect an amusing crowd of yachtsmen, looking for a brawl, as they have done for a couple of centuries.

Sailing

If there is a single island in the Caribbean which offers the most complete sailing experience, it is Antigua. It has isolation and hectic activity, fantastic beaches and protected coves, all backed up by the services that sailors need.

The heart of Antigua sailing is English Harbour in the southeast of the island, which is very attractive and still has the historic buildings, now called Nelson's Dockyard, from its heyday as a naval headquarters two centuries ago. There is a good marina with water and fuel available and plenty of anchorage space. Onshore there are a number of hotels, and plenty of bars and restaurants, some right on the coast, others a short walk away. There are also supermarkets, a bakery, even a bookshop, and plenty of technical assistance in the chandleries and boatyards. Canny sailors will anchor in the huge Falmouth Harbour (a mile or so around the headland by sea, but within easy walking distance), where the rates are lower but the facilities just as good. Here you will find a couple of marinas, at the Catamaran Club and the Antigua Yacht Club, where all the requisites for a sailing holiday are on line.

Heading east from here, you will find excellent stopovers in the many recesses of the coastline: Indian Creek, which is isolated and away from the crowds, and Mamora Bay, home of the St James's Club, where things are more active. Nonsuch Bay is a popular anchorage and there are some good spots for a daytime stopover in the protection of Green Island just offshore. The northeastern corner of Antigua offers good cruising among the many smaller islands, where there are plenty of quiet anchorages, but it is also quite difficult sailing and should not be attempted except by experienced sailors. There is a marina near the town of Parham.

For those who are cruising down the west coast of the island there are plenty of stopovers on the magnificent beaches of bright white sand. Dickenson Bay is usually calm unless a northerly swell creeps around the northwestern point. There are more sheltered stops at the entrance of St John's Harbour and further south in Five Islands Harbour. There is a marina in Jolly Harbour with good facilities and some good daytime anchorages on the beaches towards the southern tip of the island.

Yachts of all sizes and styles can be hired, crewed or bareboats, for days, a week, or longer. Charter companies include **Nicholson's Yacht Charters** (℗ 460 1530, fax 460 1531) and **Seagull Yachts** (℗ 460 3049, fax 460 1767), both at English Harbour, and **Sun Yacht Charters** (℗ 463 2113, fax 463 2115) at Parham Harbour. For technical assistance and boatyard repairs, contact **Antigua Slipway** (℗ 460 1056) in English Harbour, **Seagull Yacht Services** (℗ 460 3040) at Falmouth and **Crabbs Marina** (℗ 463 2113) in Parham. There are **customs and immigration** facilities at English Harbour in the southeast, Parham in the northeast and in the capital St John's. Cruising fees are payable in Antiguan waters. You do not need to register if you move on to Barbuda.

Antigua stages one of the major regattas in the Caribbean sailing year. **Race Week**, or Antigua Sailing Week, is held at the end of the winter season, before all the yachts take off across the Atlantic to spend the summer in the Mediterranean. It attracts sailors from everywhere, and so for two weeks around the actual event the Antiguan waters are busy with craft of all sorts. There are five major races, each with a number of different classes, all followed by another fleet of yachts along for the ride. Many of the races skirt the island and so Antigua's hills offer a fantastic view of the proceedings if you would prefer a land-based vantage-point. But the races seem to be just an excuse for what the Caribbean does best, which is to mix a rum punch and get everyone to 'jump-up' afterwards. There are plenty of silly races and wet T-shirt competitions for non-sailors and the week winds up with the Lord Nelson's Ball, a formal affair (for the Caribbean anyway) and prize-giving. For information, contact PO Box 406, St John's (© 462 0036, fax 462 2627). In the following week is the **Classic Yacht Regatta** which brings together yachts of 'classic design', many of them fantastically beautiful with long-forgotten configurations of sails (three races). Contact the Classic Yacht Regatta (© 460 1093, fax 460 1542).

Watersports

Antigua caters well for sports-minded people. The best beach for general watersports is Dickenson Bay and here you can hire windsurfers and small sailing craft such as sunfish and hobie cats through **Halcyon Cove Watersports** (© 462 0256). Hotels on other beaches will usually have watersports equipment available to their guests. **Wet-bikes** and **waterskiing** are best arranged on Dickenson Bay beach, as is **parasailing**. **Windsurfing** can also be fixed up there, but intermediate and advanced windsurfers should go to **Patrick's Windsurfing School** (© 463 3094) at the Lord Nelson Beach Club on the east coast where the winds are stronger. **Deep-sea fishing** trips, casting for marlin and tuna, can be fixed up through some of the large hotels, try *Obsession* or *Legend* (© 462 0256).

Snorkelling is good in many places around the island and equipment can be borrowed from most hotels. There are reefs on all sides of Antigua, which offer excellent marine life, including sergeant-majors, parrot fish and larger fish like rays and the occasional dolphin, for **scuba diving**, down to 70ft. Some good dive sites are: **Cades Reef**, a 2-mile protected reef off the south coast, and nearby **Farley Bay** and **Rendezvous Bay**, and **Boon Point**, the northernmost tip of Antigua. The reefs have also claimed quite a few ships over the years and so there are plenty of wrecks to dive. **Dives** can be arranged through **Dive Antigua** (© 462 0256) at Halcyon Cove on Dickenson Bay and **Dive Runaway** (© 462 2626) on Runaway Bay. **Dockyard Divers** (© 464 8591) operate from the Copper and Lumber Store in Nelson's Dockyard and cover reefs and wrecks on the southern coast. *Instruction is available at the above places; a one-tank dive costs around US$45.* **Shorty's** glass-bottom boat (© 462 2393) works out of Dickenson Bay.

Other Sports

On land, you can play **golf** at the 18-hole **Cedar Valley Golf Club** (© 462 0161), northeast of St John's. There is a 9-hole course just near the Half Moon Bay Hotel in the east of Antigua (© 460 4300). **Riding** through Antigua's rolling dry hills or along the beaches can be arranged with the **Spring Hill Riding Club** near Falmouth (© 460 1333) and **Wadadli Stables** (© 461 2721).

Fortress Foraging

In the 18th century, Antigua's coastline bristled with forts and fortlets, many of which still exist, though they are mostly buried in 15ft of scrub. Aficionados and fort boffins will enjoy rootling around the ruins, and of course they still have the fantastic views for which they were built in the first place.

Fort James (early 18th century) and **Fort Barrington** guard the entrance to St John's harbour. Fort Barrington, on the south side, has a plaque commemorating William Burt, the Governor in whose tenure it was built. On it he signs himself *Imperator et Gubernator insularum Carib* (Emperor and Governor of the Leeward Islands). This Governor had some difficulties with the islanders, especially after drawing his sword at dinner and attacking some imaginary intruders supposedly lurking behind his chair.

Johnson Point Fort is at the southwestern corner of the island. Farther east, as you pass through Falmouth, **Monks Hill Fort** (as it is known to most Antiguans, though its name was officially Great George Fort) looms up on the hill. Built in the 17th century, it was a refuge for the women, children, slaves and cattle in case of attack by the French and their Carib allies. The track to the fort turns off the main road at the village of **Liberta**, and is only passable by four-wheel-drive vehicles. **Fort Berkeley**, a short walk beyond Nelson's Dockyard, was built in 1744 to guard the entrance to English Harbour. Its soldiers would haul up a chain boom if an invasion was threatened. Above Fort Berkeley the ground is crawling with earthworks and gun emplacements and of course the other side of the harbour are the major fortifications of Shirley Heights. *The Old Forts of Antigua* by T. R. St Johnston gives a run-down of the fortifications which made the island the most fortified place for its size in the world.

St John's

Antigua's capital, St John's, stands on gently sloping ground above a large bay. The central streets are laid out on a gridiron plan and although some are now being taken over by strips of concrete modernity, many of the older wood and stone buildings with overhanging balconies are still there, as they were a century ago.

Over one-third of Antiguans live in or around St John's, and the town is showing the fruits of the island's prosperity with shops full of computers and clothes from all over the world. But a more traditional West Indian life can be seen just a few minutes' walk out of the centre of the town, where you will see the chaos of the market or fishermen making lobster pots and mending their nets.

Many visitors arrive in Antigua by the harbour, passing beneath the two defensive outposts at Fort Barrington and Fort James at the mouth of the bay. First steps ashore will lead into the air-conditioned environment of a duty-free shopping arcade, **Heritage Quay**, but the life of St John's is not far beyond.

Just close by, a stroll along the boardwalk, is **Redcliffe Quay**, an area of old St John's that has been restored, with townhouses and warehouses with stone foundations and clapboard uppers. It is also a shopping complex, but worth a detour for its cafés and restaurants even if you're not on the hunt for a bargain.

Towering above the town's activity from its stately position at the top of the rising ground are the twin grey towers of the **Cathedral of St John the Divine**. The octagonal structure was erected in 1845 after one of Antigua's relatively frequent earthquakes, and to prevent similar damage the interior has been completely lined with pine. The two life-size statues that stand at the gates of the Cathedral, St John the Baptist and St John the Evangelist, were destined for French Dominica in the 18th century, but they were captured by a British warship and brought to Antigua.

The **Old Court House**, on the corner of Long Street and Market Street, dates from 1747, though it has been rebuilt a number of times, most recently after the earthquake in 1974. Now it is home to the **Museum of Antigua and Barbuda** (© 462 1469), *open weekdays 8.30–4, and Sat 10–2, adm free*, and houses an exhibition of Amerindian Antigua (known to them as 'Wadadli'), with *zemies* from the hundred archaeological sites on the island, as well as colonial and more modern Antiguan memorabilia, including the cricket bat of Viv Richards (an Antiguan), used when he broke the world record for the fastest Test century.

A walk through downtown St John's will take you to the **market**, an enclave of traditional West Indian mayhem, where the banter seems as much a part of the game as buying the local fruit and vegetables on display.

Since Antigua began to host West Indian cricket Test Matches in 1981, the venue has been the stadium up above the Cathedral. In 1736 this area was used as an execution ground following a slave rebellion. The ringleader Prince Klaas and four others were broken on the wheel (a punishment in which the victim was strapped to a cartwheel and his bones broken one by one), six were 'put out to dry' (hung in chains and starved) and 58 were burned at the stake. The Antiguans now enjoy watching the similar roastings meted out to visiting cricket teams. If there is a game on while you are in town, go to it.

The Northern Coastline

The area north of St John's is the most developed in the island, both by the tourist industry, which has built hotels on the beaches at Runaway Bay and Dickenson

Bay, and by prosperous Antiguans who have moved out of town to live in large villas set in hibiscus and bougainvillea gardens.

At the eastern side of the northern coast is **Long Island**, a low island lying a few hundred yards offshore, once used for grazing cattle and sugar cultivation. Now home to the Jumby Bay Hotel, it was traditionally famed for exporting far more sugar than it could possibly produce, all illegally shipped in from Guadeloupe. Having sworn in seven hogsheads for export before the magistrate, the owner would promptly add the letters 'ty' and ship out that amount to eager British markets.

The main road passes Vere Bird International Airport and beneath hills littered with windmill shells and modern communications aerials before returning to St John's.

East of St John's

Travelling due east from the capital on the Old Parham Road, you pass through lowlands that once were covered with canefields. A turn left leads to the old town of Parham, one of the first settlements and oldest harbours on the island. The few remaining old buildings are now surrounded by small clapboard houses set among the palm trees and recent tourist development around the marina.

One of the oldest sugar plantations on the island, **Betty's Hope**, *open Tues–Sat*, is off the main road to Indian Town Point on the east coast. The estate house has gone, but the twin cones of the sugar works and several outhouses, including the boiling house, have survived and they contain exhibits of the sugar age. One windmill has been restored with all its machinery.

The main road continues to the east coast, which has been buffeted and carved into limestone brittle over the millennia by the Atlantic's wave action. The coastline gives some cracking views. The much vaunted **Devil's Bridge** is a natural span cut out of the rock at Indian Town Point. On a rough day the area is spectacular as the full force of the ocean thrashes against the coral coastline and bursts up through blowholes. Antigua's coastline has many indentations here, creating deep and well-protected bays, and just around the corner from all the spray are beaches tucked in the coves, as at Long Bay.

Just farther south, the village of **Freetown** was settled soon after Emancipation in 1834. The liberated slaves formed their own villages away from the plantations, often in remote areas such as this where they could settle on unused land.

St John's to English Harbour

If St John's was the administrative centre of the Leeward Islands, the British Navy maintained its rule of the Caribbean waves (often successfully) from the southeast of the island, at what is now English Harbour. The All Saints road leads south out of St John's past the market through the centre of the island, rolling scrubland dotted occasionally with the cone of a windmill. **Liberta** is another small town created by the freed slaves.

The secluded cove of **English Harbour** is now considered one of the prettiest and most picturesque spots in the Caribbean, but two hundred years ago the West Indies was a hardship posting, and one visitor considered Antigua 'one of the most infernal places on the face of the globe'. On his first visit, the future Admiral Nelson thought of Antigua as a 'barbarous island' and the dockyard now bearing his name as a 'vile spot'.

Nelson's Dockyard

Set on a point deep in the tortuous recesses of **English Harbour**, Nelson's Dockyard is a conglomeration of restored stone warehouses, workshops and quarters that once made up an 18th-century naval station. Were it not for the flowery tropical shirts on the tourists and the gleaming white of the yacht hulls, you might hear the whistles and drum-rolls of an active barracks. The waters are still plied by sailing craft, and it is a sight to watch the yachts manoeuvring between the headlands and making for open water much as they did two hundred years ago.

You approach the dockyard on the road that skirts the eastern edge of Falmouth Harbour. At the entrance, once guarded to deter intruders, you will be waylaid by the inevitable T-shirt sentry at the small shopping arcade (*there is an admission charge*). Once inside, the charm of the place takes over. The quarters, with gently sloping roofs that reach out and shade balconies, have all been repaired, as have the old sail-loft and workshops. Cannon and the odd anchor stand proud in mock menace and the boathouse pillars and sprays of tropical flowers give an air of groomed antiquity.

The dockyard was abandoned by the Navy in 1889 and fell into disrepair, but was restored by the Society of the Friends of English Harbour and re-opened in 1961 as Nelson's Dockyard. Even if it has his name, Nelson himself certainly had no love for the place. He was based here for three years, as the young captain of HMS *Boreas*, between 1784 and 1787. He cruised the Leewards for much of the time, but

Nelson's Dockyard

during the hurricane season, when the French fleet was absent from the area, he spent time in the dockyard, jokingly threatening to hang himself.

He fell out with the islanders by enforcing the Navigation Act, which declared their profitable trade with American ships illegal (he had to stay on board his ship for eight weeks to avoid arrest when they took him to court). It was a pretty miserable time, though he found some solace in his marriage to Fanny Nesbit, a young widow from the nearby island of Nevis. He was happy to leave the Caribbean and did not return except briefly in 1805, hot on the tail of Villeneuve and the French fleet, in a chase of thousands of miles that culminated in the Battle of Trafalgar.

Nelson's Dockyard is a bit of tourist trap, with hotels, bars and restaurants, and you can expect to see a few blistering-red package-holiday conscripts press-ganged on to tour-bus lunches. However, with all the yachts, the place also retains a nautical air and there are always a few latterday sailors loitering on shore for a few days, looking for grog and a brawl like their predecessors in centuries past. There is a small **museum** in the Admiral's House, where you will see maquettes of naval ships, uniforms and buttons from the era of empire and today's racing cups.

On the opposite shore from the dockyard, **Clarence House** stands on the hill. This handsome Georgian Caribbean house, built of coral rock and with a large louvred veranda, was built in 1787 for Prince William Henry, later to be King William IV, who was in command of HMS *Pegasus* stationed at Antigua. He was a friend of Nelson and gave away Fanny Nesbit at their marriage. Today Clarence House is the official country residence of the Antiguan Governor General, though it is not often occupied. It is open to the public when he is not in residence (© 463 1026) and you can see some elegant antique colonial furniture including a fine commode.

Scattered all over the heights above English Harbour is the garrison of **Shirley Heights**, another extended family of barracks with arched walkways, batteries, cisterns and magazines. It was fortified in the 1780s by General Shirley, the Governor of the Leeward Islands from 1781 to 1791, in order to defend the harbour below. The fortifications had an uninterrupted view across to Guadeloupe, giving advanced warning of any impending French invasion, which means that the view is exhilarating. Once the fortress was constructed, the French never considered invading again, of course. The site was abandoned in 1856 and fell into ruin, but some buildings have been repaired. There is a small visitors' centre as you enter the area, with wall displays and maquettes of colonial soldiers, but at the top of the hill you will find the major exhibit, the **Dow's Hill Interpretation Centre**, *open daily, adm*. A multi-media show takes you through a fairly simple but quite lively display of Antigua's history, through American Indians, European explorers and settlers, planters and merchants and then naval years to modern Antigua. There is also a gift shop and a café with a view.

The Southwest

Many of Antigua's fine beaches are on the west coast south of St John's and these include Deep Bay, Hawksbill Beach and Darkwood Bay. Inland is Green Castle Hill, where there are some odd rock formations that have come to be known in tourist lore as the megaliths, imaginatively thought by some to have been used by the Caribs as a sort of shrine. The view is particularly good from the top of the hill.

The road emerges on the sea and skirts the coastline for several miles, in the lee of the Shekerley mountains, Antigua's biggest hills. The tallest among them is the 1319ft Boggy Peak, from which the view extends to Guadeloupe in the south and as far as St Kitts to the north on a clear day. It is also possible to see Barbuda, Antigua's sister island. To reach the peak you must take the steep road inland from Cades Bay on the south coast. The coastal road is a pleasant drive, through an undeveloped part of the island, where you can see fields of black pineapple, a small and succulent variety that Antigua exports.

At Carlisle Bay and the town of Old Road (from the old word 'roadstead' meaning harbour), the coastal road cuts inland into the island's lushest and most attractive area. At the village of Swetes, the road forks south towards English Harbour or north back towards St John's.

Festivals

For 10 days or so in late July the **carnival** competitions wind up to the finals: Calypso King and Carnival Queen (Antigua also stages the Caribbean Queen competition which brings contestants from all over the area), steel bands (if you hear them practising, then just wander in) and junior competitions. The traditional *j'ouvert* (pronounced jouvay) takes place on the morning of the first Monday in August, and then the streets will pulse to the carnival parades until Tuesday evening. On 1 January old-time Christmas characters parade on the streets. There is an annual **jazz festival** held over three days, usually in late May. Obviously the sailing regattas mentioned above (*see* p.59) are very lively occasions.

© (809)—

Where to Stay

Antigua has a host of fine resort hotels, tucked away in their own coves along the tortuous coastline. Many of them are extremely expensive retreats, ideal for the luxurious seclusion that the Caribbean does so well, and one or two sit in splendour in the historical setting of English Harbour.

Antigua has also gone for the all-inclusive plan in a big way recently, in which you live in a compound where everything is paid for in advance and you do not need to use any money. With echoes of a British heritage in Antigua, just a couple of places expect men to wear a jacket and even a tie at dinner, but where else could you be served afternoon tea in a hammock? Hotel rooms in Antigua are by no means cheap and the bill is then supplemented by a 7% government tax and usually by a 10% service charge (except in the all-inclusives).

luxury

Antigua's finest and most elegant hotel is **Curtain Bluff**, PO Box 288 (*©* 462 8400, fax 462 8409, US reservations *©* 212 289 9888). It stands on a bluff on the south coast, above a superb beach where the sand is carved into scallop patterns by the waves. This hotel is stately and quiet, with 66 suites and rooms scattered on the small promontory overlooking the two beaches, each from their own balcony. There is a beauty salon, a gym, tennis courts and a good restaurant with an extremely fine wine list; a jacket and tie are required for dinner. The hotel closes during the summer months, daily rate includes meals. Another stately and reclusive resort with the air of a country club is **Jumby Bay Island**, PO Box 243 (*©* 462 6000, fax 462 6020, UK reservations *©* 071 730 7144), which is set on its own island a couple of miles off the northeastern coast. Roofed with Spanish terracotta tiles, sumptuous villas and rooms are dotted around the island, most within a half-minute's walk of the excellent beach on Jumby Bay (from a West Indian word for 'ghost') as well as the restaurants and bars. Any farther and you may wish to use bikes, which are provided in plenty. The ferry crosses from the dock near the Beachcomber Hotel, north of the airport on Antigua, about once an hour. For now, Jumby Bay has 38 rooms in cotttages and 20 villas, but development plans are in the air, and these will inevitably affect the atmosphere of seclusion, all meals included.

very expensive

A hotel with a difference is **Galley Bay**, PO Box 305, St John's (*©* 462 0302, fax 462 4551, US *©* 800 223 6510, UK *©* 0435 835801), which stands on a spit of land between a magnificent cove and a lagoon on the west coast, where there are 31 rooms dotted around a park beneath a screen of palms, some in cottages overlooking the beach and others in palm-thatch cabins 'à la Gauguin' on the lagoon. Berbice planters' chairs (with extendable arms to support outstretched legs) for admiring the sunset, no telephones or televisions; fans chop the still evening air. A charming and very low-key retreat. Similar in style is the **Long Bay Hotel**,

PO Box 442 (℃ 463 2005, fax 463 2439, US ℃ 800 448 8355, UK ℃ 0345 835801), tucked into a typically secluded Antiguan cove on the eastern shore of the island, overlooking a lagoon one side and a pretty beach on the other. Family-run, it has just 20 rooms in a block and six cottages, no telephones or televisions. Little known, it is ideal as a quiet retreat for tired executives, as you can tell by all the magazines and books. Watersports—windsurfing, snorkelling and scuba—are available if you're feeling active. The **Hawksbill Beach Resort** (℃ 462 0301, fax 462 1515, US ℃ 800 223 6510) takes its name from the oddly shaped rock off one of its four beaches, looking like the bill of a hawksbill turtle rising from the water (alternatively a frog with a crown). From an old plantation house and windmill on a promontory, the 95 rooms are strung out along the waterfront, where the palm trees burst in an explosion of scratchy fronds. Most watersports, tennis, very comfortable rooms and some evening entertainment. For a small and well-run hotel right on the sands of Dickenson Bay, you can try the **Siboney Beach Club**, PO Box 222 (℃ 462 0806, fax 462 3356). The 12 very comfortable suites are set in a block festooned in tropical gardens, slightly removed from all the noise of the beach bars. It has a lively restaurant and bar looking over the beach.

expensive

If you would like to stay within the old English Harbour area, there are some good hotels, two of them in restored barrack buildings, the sail-lofts now converted into rooms. The **Copper and Lumber Store**, PO Box 184 (℃ 460 1058, fax 460 1529), has been historically re-appointed with a Georgian dining-room, rum puncheons in the courtyard, and suites named Hardy, Dreadnought and Victory. It is well restored and attractive, and does have an air of the 18th century in the brick arches, ship beams and stained wood staircases. An aloof view of all this activity can be had from **The Inn at English Harbour**, PO Box 187 (℃ 460 1014, fax 460 1603, US ℃ 800 223 6510), of which the main house commands the heights and has a fine view of the yachts manoeuvring into harbour from the dining terrace where you are sheltered with date palms. The six cottages are dotted over the forested hillside and 22 rooms stand in blocks on the beach, just a short trip by boat from the Dockyard. Expensive to very expensive. The **Yepton Beach Resort**, PO Box 1427 (℃ 462 2520, fax 462 3420) has 38 studios and apartments with full kitchens standing above a nice beach.

moderate

It is possible to stay in Antigua without making a visit to the IMF beforehand, though very cheap beachside accommodation is hard to find. The

Admiral's Inn, PO Box 713 (© 460 1027, fax 460 1534), stands next to the odd pillars that once supported the boat-house near the entrance to English Harbour. The Inn has beautiful worn bricks that were shipped out as ballast and dark wooden beams, but this is perhaps less the officers' accommodation and more the able seamen's—you could find yourself in the sail-loft. You won't have to share a bathroom with 50 others nowadays, though, and there is a friendly atmosphere, with a tar's tale or two told in the bar. An excellent spot on an isolated beach, particularly good for windsurfers, is the **Lord Nelson Beach Hotel**, PO Box 155 (© 462 3094, fax 462 0751) on the windswept northeastern coast. The hotel is family-run and there is an easy air around the restaurant and bar. The 20 rooms are comfortable and good value, best to have a car for some time at least. You can get to within a shout of Dickenson Bay at the **Island Inn**, PO Box 1218 (© 462 4065, fax 462 4066), which is has 10 self-contained rooms set in a modern block on Anchorage Road. Restaurant but no pool. Finally you will find good value at the **Catamaran Hotel**, PO Box 958 (© 460 1036, fax 460 1506, US © 800 223 6510), with eight rooms on Falmouth Harbour. It is set in a modern block with mock-classical pillars; comfortable rooms, kitchenettes, beach passable, watersports on offer, cheap to moderate.

cheap

Less expensive rooms can be found at **Roslyn's Guest House** (© 462 0762) on Fort Road leading out of town, with just four rooms and at **Murphy's Place** (© 461 1183) on the All Saints Road leading out of town, with four reasonably comfortable apartments with kitchens and a hearty Antiguan welcome. Very cheap rooms can only be found in the south of town, beyond the market. The **Montgomery Hotel** on Tindale Road (© 462 2793) and **Miami Hotel**, Market Street (© 462 0975), will offer a different side of Antiguan life. There are some guest houses that can be contacted through the Tourist Board.

© (809)– **Eating Out**

The food in Antigua is quite similar to that of other British West Indian islands: hotels tend to offer studiedly 'international' fare and local food has a good mix of fresh local fish and traditional Caribbean ground provisions. There are some exceptions, though, in a few hotel dining rooms and restaurants where you get good food in the best Caribbean settings. There is also good variety in the restaurants, with French, Italian and even Argentinian as well as West Indian. There are some lively local and tourist haunts, but Antigua has suffered recently because so many of the hotels have turned all-inclusive (their guests have paid for their meals in advance and venture out to restaurants less). Restaurants add a service charge of 10% and there is a 7% sales tax on top. Categories are arranged according to the price of a main course: *expensive*—EC$50 and above; *moderate*—EC$20 to 50; *cheap*—under EC$20.

Around St John's

expensive

Chez Pascal (© 462 3232) is on Cross Street in St John's and you dine in the calm and elegant interior of a classic wooden Caribbean town-house. The service and the cuisine are traditional French (even *escargots* are on offer), though Pascal, the chef, also uses the best of Caribbean ingredients: the *vichyssoise Franco-Antiguaise* is made with leek and local breadfruit. Follow with the *gougeonette de mérou au vin*, grouper cooked in a rich red wine sauce or *crevettes provençales*, shrimps in a tomato coulis and garlic butter. Dinner indoors and lunches in the garden, under bowers of tropical plants. At **Le Bistro** (© 462 3881), in the Hodges Bay area in the north of the island, you dine in a pretty dining room hung with plants and trelliswork. The menu is French and international, with good fish dishes including shrimp in dill. Dinner only, closed Mon. There are a number of lively places around town. On Long Street you will find the **Lemon Tree** (© 462 1969), with a large, cool and bright dining room upstairs with white louvres and high-backed wicker chairs. There is a lively atmosphere and a long menu, served both at lunch and dinner—from burgers and pastas to a chicken tarragon or a Caribbean gumbo. **Hemingway's** (© 462 2763) is open for lunch and dinner in one of St John's most charming wooden houses on Mary Street. Eat on the gingerbread veranda if you can. The fare is local and international—an excellent lobster soup followed by chicken tropical with fruit salsa and hot sauce. Both moderate to expensive.

moderate

O'Grady's is another lively haunt in an attractive wooden St Johnian house where louvred doors open onto the veranda. It is popular with expatriates and serves 'pub food' Antiguan-style, including an excellent fish and chips. You will find the ever-popular **Pari's Pizzas** up the hill in Dickenson Bay. You can take out or eat in, seated in deck chairs on a covered red and green veranda with trelliswork and hanging plants. Pizzas and pastas, ribs and chicken. Another popular haunt with the tourists and locals is the **Crazy Cactus Cantina** (© 462 1183) on the All Saints Road heading out of town. A Tex/Mex menu, lively atmosphere. There are a number of smaller, local restaurants in St John's, good places to stop for lunch and to gather for a drink at the end of the day. **Calypso** (© 462

1965) is on Upper Redcliffe Street and has tables scattered around a court-yard garden. Mostly local fare, curried chicken or flying fish in a beer batter, or a burger if you want it, closed Sun. **Brother B's** (℗ 462 0616) is similar in style and stays open for dinner as well. You will find it in a court-yard on Long Street and Soul Alley. If you want to eat more **cheaply** in town, there are a number of snack joints in the market area where you can grab a chicken or a pattie.

Around English Harbour

expensive

There is an excellent setting at **La Perruche** (℗ 460 3040), at the turning down to the yacht club in Falmouth Harbour. You dine by candlelight, inside at very pretty tables or in the evening air on a covered deck, looking onto a profuse tropical garden with palm-thatched parasols and benches. The cuisine is French creole: couliba of daurade, dorado with mushrooms and spinach wrapped in puff pastry or marinated breast of chicken in a Caribbean fruit sauce; good wine list, closed Sun. **Le Cap Horn** (℗ 460 1194) is also set on a pretty veranda, with greenery around the trellises. French and Argentinian fare, including huge churrasco steaks, or pizzas cooked on a wood fire if you want a take-away, moderate to expensive.

moderate

Nations is a much lower-key spot, a small shack with its own garden behind a pink and white fence, where some of the food is grown. Chicken or fish (the menu depends on what has been landed that afternoon) in a coconut sauce with rice and peas and fried plantain. An excellent rum punch and exotic fruit juices. Not far off, **Abracadabra** sometimes has live music under the palm trees in the garden. Inside, the fare is Italian and so you get home-made pastas and pizzas as well as fish dishes. A very popular spot for a pizza is at **G & T's** at the Antigua Yacht Club, where you look through the palms at the yachts in dock on Falmouth Harbour. Farther east you will find a lively Italian restaurant, **Albertos** (℗ 460 3007), which stands on the hillside in Willoughby Bay. You will get pastas and pizzas or an excellent grilled snapper with lemon. Sometimes dancing.

Bars and Nightlife

There are some fun and lively bars which offer happy hours where you can take Antigua's light and tasty home-brewed lager 'Wadadli' on a test run, particularly along Dickenson Bay, in town and around English Harbour. In Nelson's Dockyard itself there is a day-long view from the balcony at **Limey's Restaurant and Bar**. At 5pm the yachties congregate around the **Galley** on the waterfront for a happy hour and a half. You might try Twofers (two for one) at the **Main Brace**, the Copper and Lumber Store on a Tuesday or a Sunday. A popular place to move on to is **G & T's** at the Antigua Yacht Club in Falmouth (quite busy any night). **Dougie's Bar** overlooks Falmouth Harbour from upstairs and gathers a crowd of yachties doing a bit of liming by day. The Shirley Heights **Lookout** is something of an island institution on a Sunday afternoon when a band plays in the sunset (starting at 3pm) high above English Harbour. It attracts a riotous crowd by the early evening.

In Dickenson Bay you will find a lively haunt with loud music and wicked drinks behind Pari's Pizzas at **Shooters Club**, a tin-roofed hall peopled by latterday pirates (complete with handkerchiefs on their heads); shooters include Cerebral Haemorrhage, Brain Tumour, Deep Throat and Fuzzy Mother, closed Mon and Tues. **Millers** on Dickenson Bay beach itself is often lively (late on Sunday the residue of the Shirley Heights crowd roll in). On Sunday a crowd gathers at Russell's Beach Bar at Fort James Beach for a spot of afternoon jazz and drinking.

Discotheques include **Tropix**, an air-conditioned hang-out downtown at Redcliffe Quay, St John's and **The Zone** in the deepwater harbour. There is a circuit of shows that perform in the hotels: steel bands and the usual limbo dancers. There are three **casinos** on the island, with slot machines and betting tables open until 4am: **King's Casino** at Heritage Quay in St John's, the **Royal Antiguan** and the **St James' Club**.

Further Reading

Antigua was lucky in that the English wife of a planter, a Mrs Lanaghan, wrote *Antigua and the Antiguans* in 1844, describing the island and the customs of its people (recently reprinted in two volumes). You may also find a copy of *To Shoot Hard Labour*, in which an Antiguan, Samuel Smith (1877–1982) tells stories going back to emancipation (his grandmother was a slave) and his working life. A modern Antiguan writer who now lives in the States is Jamaica Kincaid, author of *Annie John*, a disturbing book about a childhood on the island, and *A Small Island*.

There are also one or two informative booklets that describe the historic sights of the island. *The Romance of English Harbour* deals with Nelson's Dockyard and *Shirley Heights* by Charles Jane tells the story of Shirley Heights and its defence of the island. **The Map Shop** in St Mary's Street in St John's has a good selection of Caribbean books and there is a good bookshop in English Harbour, **Lord Jim's Locker**.

Barbuda's great attractions are its marine life and its beaches, which are measured in miles and where it is difficult not to be alone. The reefs are forested with corals that move gently with the water and teem with fluorescent fish. And the sand on Barbuda is supreme. There is so much that they even export it. The island is 60 square miles of scrubland that barely clears the water, lying about 30 miles north of Antigua. It is made entirely of limestone coral deposits that have encrusted an out-crop on the same geological bank as Antigua. The Highlands, in the north of the island, struggle to top 130ft. The contours of Dulcina, as the island was known to the Spaniards, are even gentler than Antigua's and the pace of life much slower.

Caribs prevented early settlement of the island, but when they were wiped out, Christopher Codrington leased the whole island as a private estate, paying rent to the Crown of 'one fat sheep, if demanded'. It stayed within his family from 1674 until about 1870 and, because the soil was not fertile enough to support sugar-cane, it was used as a ranch for stock and work animals, a farm for provisions, a deer-park and eventually a cotton plantation. Many of the animals are still seen wandering about much as they always have, and the ubiquitous Caribbean goat gets everywhere. There are even rumours of its having been used as a slave-farm, where the tallest and strongest slaves were encouraged to breed. Amateur anthro-pologists maintain that this is the reason for Barbuda's abnormally tall population.

In 1976 the 11-person Barbuda council was set up and the island was granted elected government (with just two appointed members). But, as in so many island partnerships, the Barbudians do still complain that they are neglected by the gov-ernment in St John's. There are occasional words about the advantages of being independent of Antigua, but they are not very loud.

With just 1200 inhabitants, Barbuda is extremely quiet, and it is still surprisingly undeveloped as Caribbean islands go (petrol is hand-pumped here). The main activ-ities are fishing and traditional West Indian subsistence agriculture with some building. 'Wrecking' was another source of income, as the reefs around Barbuda have been known to claim many ships in their time. Tourism amounts to two extremely expensive hotels, a small resort and local guest houses.

The few hundred Barbudians left on island (many have emigrated but revisit their families often) have a tight-knit community, nearly all of them living in the only town (really a village), Codrington. The most common names (most people are called one of them) are Harris, Beazer, Thomas, Punter and Nedd and they have a welcoming interest in visitors. One person claimed that on arrival at the airport not so long ago, he was greeted with the words: 'But nobody said you were coming...'

Barbuda (airport code BBQ) is 20 minutes north of Antigua by plane and **Codrington** is served by a return flight morning and afternoon by LIAT. If you have booked with the Coco Point Lodge, you will arrive at their airstrip in the south. It might also be possible to catch a ride on one of the ships that make the run with tinned food and essentials; ask around at the main dock in St John's.

There are just one or two cars available for hire. Bargain for them. Alternatively try to hitch a ride. Most drivers that pass will offer you a ride, but with few cars headed anywhere you might want to go it can be a long wait. Because most of the food and other essentials of life are imported, Barbuda tends to be quite expensive. Bring things that you cannot live without. You are advised to change any EC$s that you will want in Antigua (it is good to have a few here, though US$s are widely accepted). If you would like a tour of the island, contact the knowledgeable Ivan Pereira a couple of days in advance (© 460 0258). The beaches are of course superb. The best is probably the main south coast beach which runs between Coco Point and River (the port area), but others include Low Bay by the Lagoon on the western shore and Two Foot Bay and North Beach on the northern coast.

Around the Island

The **Codrington** family influence is everywhere on the island: in the only settlement, just a few streets of concrete or clapboard houses and an airstrip, in the lagoon on which it sits, and in **Highland House**, their estate house that was built in 1750 but never really occupied. Its ruins, just walls, outhouses and a cistern steadily being reclaimed by the scrub, are visible a few miles north of the village. The island's other main sight is in marginally better condition. **River Fort** is a martello (round) tower that stands on the south coast, its gun turrets without cannon now, but still guarding the approach to the original docking area and harbour. For many years the island was a deer-park for the Codringtons and it is still possible to hunt them and to shoot duck.

For those with a more peaceable interest in wildlife, a visit to the **Codrington Lagoon** to see the thousands of frigate birds is very rewarding. You take a boat out into the mangroves, where the birds, with their distinctive dark arrow shape with scissor tails, circle overhead to thousands of feet. The best time to go is between October and February—the mating and later the hatching season. You will see the males display, with their impossibly large gullets puffed up like vast red footballs so that their heads are forced skyward and their throats resonate with a clacking noise. The females cruise around and make their choice. From December their

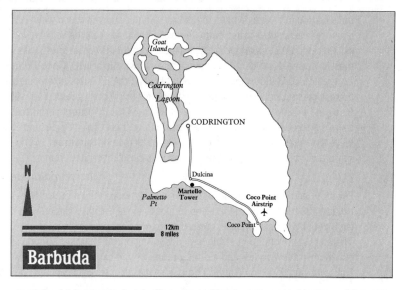

Barbuda

ungainly chicks start to hatch. To arrange the trip, ask around in town. There are **caves** in the northern part of the island, including **Dark Cave**, where a passage leads 100 yards underground.

Coral reefs grow off nearly all Barbuda's coasts, waving forests of staghorn and elkhorn where angelfish, trumpetfish and wrasses flit, and they make extremely good snorkelling. The corals are so close to the surface that it is hardly necessary to dive, so divers have to look after themselves.

The sandbars and coral reefs which make for such good beaches and snorkelling in Barbuda also make it difficult for **sailors**. The shoals appear at about the same time as the island comes into view as you head north from Antigua. The best anchorages are near the southeastern tip, either side of Coco Point, and off the western shore.

© (809)–

Where to Stay

luxury

The island's limited accommodation includes two incredibly expensive and luxurious enclaves, both located on the south coast. The **K Club** (© 460 0300, fax 460 0305, US © 800 648 4097), set on its own ½-mile of spectacular beach, is the inspiration of fashion designer Krizia. The 20 villas and cottages are stretched along the waterfront either side of the huge main house, taking the best of old Caribbean style, with modern comforts. The resort is decorated in jade and bright white. Each cottage has a huge bedroom, a veranda open to the breeze and a shower with a view. It is a luxury beach club—watersports, tennis and golf. After all the activity, you can enjoy gourmet meals in the main house with the few other guests. Stars most welcome. Next door (a couple of miles down the beach), **Coco Point Lodge** (✆ 462 3186) stands on the point beyond the K Club. The emphasis there is on seclusion from the outside world for its 50 or so guests. You will fly to the private airstrip near to the hotel (no K Club visitors permitted: there's a story in that one) and lodge in one of the exquisitely decorated villas that look over the superb beach from a screen of palm trees. Watersports available, all-inclusive rate (the resort is closed over the summer).

cheap–moderate

For those without spare millions there is a small resort, the **Palmetto Hotel** (✆/fax 460 0326). The rooms stand in blocks above a sloping garden with a large pool by the main house, dressed up in old Caribbean style; moderate. There are some **cheap** guest houses in Codrington. The **Sunset View** just outside has a few rooms and a dining room, or you can try **Nedd's** Guest House (✆ 460 0059) or **Walter Thomas's** Guest House, all cheap.

Redonda

The chain of Caribbean volcanoes passes by about 30 miles west of Antigua and among its peaks rises the tiny pimple of Redonda, so named because of its nearly round shape. It stands between Montserrat and Nevis, a circle of cliffs sparse on top, uninhabited except by birds. For nearly four hundred years after its discovery by Columbus it was ignored, but eventually in the 1860s somebody realized that centuries' worth of birdshit could be put to good use. Guano mining began, and at the height of production thirty years later the island produced 3–4000 tons of phosphate annually. That the island should be worth something to somebody was enough to bring claims of sovereignty from all the powers in the area, and so before long Redonda was annexed by the British and attached to Antigua.

However, a rival bid was made by an Irishman who happened to sail past in 1865. One Matthew Shiel, born in Montserrat, claimed it as a 'fiefdom' for his son, later King Felipe I. The sovereign's courtiers were literary folk and the line passed to the poet John Gawsworth, self-styled King Juan I, whose peers included J. B. Priestley and Rebecca West. This most illustrious of Caribbean lineages was thought to have gone into decline, but it was traced to the county of Surrey or Sussex in Britain, where it resides with the monarch, Jon Wynne-Tyson. The King made a visit in 1979 with his court historian and reaffirmed his suzerainty over the domain by planting his flag, blue, brown and green in colour and 'made from pairs of old royal pyjamas by Her Royal Highness, Jennifer Wynne-Tyson'.

Montserrat

humming bird & nest

Montserrat, the most southerly of the Leewards, has a jumbled interior of rainforested mountains worthy of one of the Windward Isles to the south, but its serried peaks are smaller, its slopes are gentler and island life is even slower. Even so, much of the island's 39 square miles are pretty inaccessible (it is 11 by 7 miles at its widest point), and only a few houses are cut into the central hills of the island. Most of the 12,000 islanders live on the sheltered Caribbean coast. The (relatively) flat lands around the shoreline, where the villas and estates of modern Montserrat are springing up, are littered with estate ruins that speak of rich plantation days.

The island does not attract a large beach-bound crowd (it has few beaches anyway) and seems generally undeveloped, though tourism is in fact the main foreign exchange earner. Montserrat tends to attract a more stately visitor. Without the airborne invasion suffered by so many islands, the island maintains some of the tranquillity now lost to the rest of the West Indies. Montserrat can be relied upon. Many people retire here.

Montserrat has a considerable, if distant, Irish heritage which, along with its luxuriant appearance, has led to it being called the 'Emerald Isle' of the Caribbean. Many of the place-names are clearly Irish, and although the islanders are obviously of African descent, at times it seems that you can hear an Irish lilt in their speech, momentary strains of brogue in the stream of West Indian. Whether this is imagined or not, Montserratian speech is one of the softest and most attractive of all variations in the English-speaking Caribbean. For all the Irish heritage (and there is a shamrock on one of the eaves of Government House), the island has been a British colony for most of its history. It is one of just five British Crown Colonies remaining in the Caribbean, administered by a Governor appointed from London in partnership with the island legislature.

Montserrat is stable and almost entirely crime-free. Life is extremely easy-going and the islanders are exceptionally welcoming and friendly—both to outsiders and amongst themselves. To judge by how often the locals say 'Hello', or 'yeah man!' walking along the street, they must all know each other anyway.

History

Alliouagana (thought to mean 'land of the prickly bush') was deserted when Columbus passed on his second voyage. The Caribs were off raiding elsewhere. He

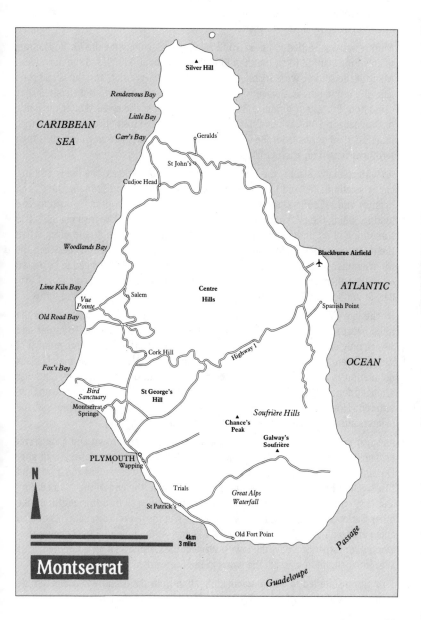

Silver Hill

Rendezvous Bay

Little Bay

CARIBBEAN
SEA

Carr's Bay

Geralds

St John's

Cudjoe Head

Woodlands Bay

Blackburne Airfield

Lime Kiln Bay

Salem

Centre
Hills

ATLANTIC

Vue
Pointe

Spanish Point

Old Road Bay

Cork Hill

Highway 1

OCEAN

Fox's Bay

Bird
Sanctuary

St George's
Hill

Montserrat
Springs

Soufrière Hills

Chance's
Peak

Galway's
Soufrière

PLYMOUTH
Wapping

N

Trials

Great Alps
Waterfall

St Patrick's

4km
3 miles

Old Fort Point

Montserrat

Passage

Guadeloupe

paused long enough to name the island Santa Maria de Montserrate after the abbey near Barcelona in Spain and sailed for Hispaniola. Only pirates braved the Caribs' attention over the next 140 years.

Montserrat was settled in about 1632 as a separate colony for the Catholics from mainly Protestant St Kitts, the then English island about 40 miles to the northwest. Many of the settlers were Irishmen, as was the first Governor, and the island soon gained a reputation as a place where Catholics and the Irish were welcome. They came from Protestant Virginia, and the population was also swelled after the Battle of Drogheda in 1649, when Cromwell sent many of the Irish prisoners of war. Irish indentured labourers from the other islands would make their way here once their term was served on another island.

As with so many islands, the first half-century of colonization was a litany of hurricanes, earthquakes and seaborne attacks. The raiders were French, Dutch and Spanish and, of course, the Caribs, who arrived in their thousands, burning and looting, killing the men and carrying off women and slaves. The Irish colonists had something of an understanding with their French co-religionists and often when the raids took place their property would be left alone. But relations between the Montserratian settlers themselves were hardly more peaceful. Laws had to be passed to prevent them from hurling insults at each other, 'English Dog, Scots Dog, Cavalier, Roundhead and many other opprobrious, scandalous and disgraceful terms'.

By the late 17th century the land was covered with sugar-cane well up into the hills. Because of the steep terrain, the cured sugar was loaded on to mules and casked only on the shore before shipping. Sugar meant slaves and a large number of Africans were brought in to work the canefields, giving Montserrat its mainly black population today. The occasional rebellions were put down ruthlessly. One was arranged for St Patrick's day in 1768 when the slaves intended to take over Government House, but the plans were overheard by a slave-woman who told the planters and the rebels were captured and executed.

As sugar failed and Emancipation came, other crops were grown and Montserrat became famous for limes. It was the second Caribbean exporter of the fruit after Dominica and much of the crop, 180,000 gallons one year, went to Crosse and Blackwell in Britain. Cotton became an export crop at the end of the 19th century and formed the basis of the Montserratian economy well into this century. Like other Caribbean islanders, the Montserratians had moved on to small plots of land and were leading a simple agricultural existence. At the time of Emancipation they worked for sixpence a day, the lowest wage in the Caribbean and, a hundred years later, their situation was still the worst in the Leewards.

This pitiful state led to considerable emigration from the island when a better life seemed possible elsewhere, and so most Montserratians have a relative who left for the canefields in the Dominican Republic or to work in oil in Curaçao. The exodus culminated in the 1950s, when 5000 left for Britain. Since then an influx of 'resident tourists', as they are known, many of them retired Americans and Canadians, has brought the population back to about 12,000. Most recently there has been a wave of Dominicans and Guyanese, who came to work in the construction industry in the aftermath of Hurricane Hugo.

Montserrat had a late start on the political scene. Robert Griffith and William Bramble led the Montserratians in their efforts to obtain a fair wage and in their political aspirations. The Montserrat Labour Party took all five seats in the first elections in 1951 and again in 1955. Today the island government, the Legislative Council, which has control over internal affairs, is led by Chief Minister Reuben T. Meade of the National Progressive Party. In elections in October 1991, they won four of the seven Parliamentary seats. Elections to the Council are held every five years. As a Crown Colony, ultimate executive power rests with the Governor, Queen Elizabeth II's appointed representative, but he would be very unlikely to use his overriding prerogative on internal matters. Independence is mentioned less now in island politics, but anyway it would not be considered before Montserrat is economically independent.

Hurricane Hugo, which struck in 1989, caused terrible destruction to both human and natural life and in places the damage is still visible. There were 10 deaths. Not a single electricity pole was left standing and an estimated 95 per cent of houses were damaged. Apart from this upset, the standard of living in Montserrat has risen steadily over the last twenty years and though there is a visible disparity between foreigners and the simple Montserratian farmers, the island is very stable.

Blarney

Of all the echoes you hear in West Indian English, the strongest in the speech of Montserrat is the Irish. Some visitors have claimed that the Montserratians have the gift of the gab and a truly Irish wit. The West Indians have a pretty mean sense of humour anyway (just nip down to the market and catch the banter), but particularly after a few rum punches, you might just think that you are in Galway.

In the 17th century, there were about 1000 Irish families on the island, but since then, most of the original white settlers have left. However, their names certainly live on in black Montserratian families, such as Farrel, Daly and Ryan, as a quick look at the Montserrat telephone directory will show. The Irish harp is a national symbol and appears on the Montserratian stamps.

There is a nice story from the 19th century about an Irishman who arrived from Connaught to find himself addressed by a black man in Connaught brogue. He asked how long the man had been in Montserrat. 'Shure, yer honour, and three years it is that I've been here.' Flabbergasted, the Irishman replied, 'Glory be to God. And do ye turrn black in thot toime?' and got on the first ship back home (*The Pocket Guide to the West Indies*, Sir Algernon Aspinall, 1938).

Flora and Fauna

Montserrat has the same botanic exuberance as the Windward Isles to the south—the thick dark earth cultivates a luxuriant flora: explosions of bamboo, mosses on the march, creepers grappling down below, and above orchids and airborne ferns. The national flower is the yellow *Heliconia caribaea*, known locally as lobster claw because of its odd shape, and the island tree is the hairy mango.

The national bird, the Montserrat oriole, is indigenous to the island. Its plumage is black and yellow and it can be found up in the mountains along with the purple-throated carib, one of Montserrat's three hummingbirds. Thrashers and bananaquits abound in the hibiscus and bougainvillea of the lower slopes and you might be lucky and see a chicken hawk hovering, spying out a meal. On the shoreline, particularly in the 15-acre mangrove-swamp coastal reserve at Fox's Bay Bird Sanctuary, you can see waders such as the common gallinule and some species of heron, alongside cattle egrets, kingfishers and the odd booby or a tropicbird with its long tail feathers.

Montserrat's landborne wildlife is limited to agouti (very shy, guinea-pig-like rodents), lizards, 'mountain chickens' (frogs) and tree frogs, which make their shrill night-time call all over the Caribbean. You have a good chance of seeing iguana, a prehis-toric-looking, tank-like lizard, at a daily feeding session; contact the Vue Pointe Hotel.

© *(809)–*   **Getting There**

Blackburne airport, 9 miles across the island from Plymouth, cannot take long-haul traffic, so you will have to make a connection. The best route is via **Antigua**, which has links to Europe and North America. Montserrat Airways (© 491 6494) has scheduled flights each day, as does LIAT (© 491 2533), who also put on an occasional service from Sint Maarten and St Kitts. Montserrat Airways offers charter flights (fax 491 6205, UK reservations © 0279 680144). There is a departure tax of EC$20 or US$8.

© *(809)–*   **Getting Around**

Buses, usually minivans, cruise the main routes around the island from Plymouth: **Highway 2** to St John's in the north and **Highway 1** over the hill. They leave from different places around the town according to the destination. In the country you can wave them down where you want. EC$3 gets you as far as you can go. The best way across to the leeward coast from the airport is by taxi. Generally, hitching works pretty well on Montserrat.

Taxis, many of which are also minivans, are readily available at the airport (© 491 4291) and in town (© 491 2261) and can be arranged through any of the hotel desks. Drivers are happy to take you on an island tour, which can be fixed through a hotel or the Tourist Board, at about EC$30 per hour. Some sample fares, fixed by the government: **airport** to Plymouth: EC$30 and to Vue Pointe: EC$42, and **Plymouth** to Vue Pointe: EC$13.

Hire-cars cost about US$35 per day. Driving is on the left and visitors must obtain a temporary licence (EC$30) from the airport or the Treasury upstairs in the post office in Plymouth. Companies include **Pauline's Car Rental** (© 491 2345) and **Edith's Car Rental** (© 491 6696). **Reliable Car Rental** (© 491 6990) will hire you a mini-moke for about US$30.

Tourist Information

In **Britain** (and in Ireland), write to 3 Epirus Road, London SW6 7UJ (© 071 730 7144, fax 071 938 4793). **USA**: PACE Advertising Agency, 485 Fifth Avenue, New York, NY 10017 (© 212 818 0100, fax 212 818 0120). **Canada**: Travmark Group Inc, 33 Niagara Street, Toronto, Ontario M5V 1C2 (© 416 362 3900, fax 416 362 9841). The **Montserrat Tourist Office** can be contacted at PO Box 7, Plymouth (© 809 491 2230, fax 809 491 7430), and when you are on island, tourist information can be obtained from the Tourism Department on Marine Drive. The Tourist Board publishes a small magazine, *Holiday Montserrat*, with some current information on activities and restaurants.

In a medical **emergency**, there is a 24-hour accident and emergency room at the Plymouth hospital (© 491 2552) on Princess St on the hill above town.

If dialling Montserrat, the **IDD code** is 809 followed by a seven-digit island number which begins 491. When on-island dial the full seven figures.

Money

The currency of Montserrat is the Eastern Caribbean dollar (fixed to the US dollar at EC$2.65 = US$1) which is used on islands from Anguilla to Grenada. The US greenback is also widely accepted, but expect change in EC dollars. **Banking hours** are Mon–Thur 8–1 or 3, and Fri 8–1 and 3–5.

Beaches

Most of Montserrat's beaches are mostly thin strips of dark volcanic sand, some in coves lined with palms; but on the northwestern coast coral reefs have thrown up some light brown sand. There is not much in the way of beach facilities, so if you go far afield, take a picnic, but some beaches are close to the hotels and you can get a drink or lunch there. Getting to the only white-sand beach, **Rendezvous Bay**, involves a difficult walk over the hills from Little Bay, or a boat trip. This can be arranged with a fisherman, or through one of the day sail and snorkelling trips. The very secluded **Little Bay** is the next best beach and **Carr's Bay**, where fishermen keep their boats, is worth a look too. Heading south there are good strips of sand at **Woodlands Bay**, which has some changing facilities, **Lime Kiln Bay, Old Road Bay** and **Fox's Bay**.

Beach Bars

There is a nice beach bar, the **Nest**, beneath the Vue Pointe on Old Road Bay, where you can get a snack or a drink, and on Barton Bay beneath the Montserrat Springs, where you can linger at **Las' Call** until 8pm at the weekends.

Sailing

If you are passing down the inner chain of islands it is possible to **anchor** on the leeward coast of Montserrat. The best places to stay overnight are at Old Road Bay, where you will find the Nest beach bar and the View Pointe Hotel, and off the main town of Plymouth, where there is a bight off the Yacht Club and the string of restaurants in Wapping within walking distance. In the north there is a good anchorage and a day stopover at Little Bay, from where you can take the dinghy round to the white sand of Rendezvous Bay.

There is not much in the way of **yachting facilities** in Montserrat, but in Plymouth you can take on water and there are a few small shops and of course the market where you can stock up on provisions. Plymouth is the only **port of entry** on the island.

Watersports

Danny Watersports (✆ 491 5645) at Old Road Bay will fix windsurfing, sunfish, sailing trips and snorkelling, which is very good in Little Bay and Rendezvous Bay. **Scuba diving** can be arranged with **Sea Wolf** Diving School (✆ 491 7807), who offer resort courses for novices. *Dives from US$40.*

Land-based sports include **golf**; there is an 11-green course at Belham Valley (✆ 491 5220), where different tees make up 18 holes; green fees about EC$60. The Montserrat Open is held in March. There are **tennis courts** at the Vue Pointe Hotel (✆ 491 5210) and the Montserrat Springs Hotel (✆ 491 2481). If you would like to explore the island by mountain bike, **Island Bikes**, PO Box 266 (✆ 491

4696 evening, fax 491 5552) will hire you an 18-speed mountain bike. They also offer maps with trails and **guided bicycle tours** including a 90% downhill tour from Windy Hill through Paradise Estate. If you are happier on foot there are **hiking trails** from Galway's Soufrière to the Bamboo Forest, where you have a chance of seeing the national bird, the Montserrat oriole, and from Vue Pointe to Fox's Bay. Guides can be booked through the tourist board and the hotels.

Plymouth

The small capital of Montserrat, **Plymouth,** lies on an open bay on the southwest coast of the island and has a population of around 3500. It was supposedly named after the Pilgrim Fathers' Plymouth in Virginia, and it became the capital town in 1640 when Kinsale to the south was abandoned. Set on the waterfront on the slopes of the gentle Montserratian mountains, it is a classical British West Indian town where the arched stonework of the old Georgian warehouses is topped with wooden upper storeys, shaded balconies and red tin roofs. The streets hardly bustle, but customary West Indian 'limers' hang around chatting at key points, and the odd policeman in a starched shirt and trousers will wander by. A short walk from the town centre, the back streets soon become lined with simple wooden shingle houses shaded by breadfruit trees in small yards of beaten earth. Clambering up into the hills above the town and along the coast, the new Montserrat of concrete villas is establishing itself behind hedges and gardens.

On Fridays and Saturdays mornings, the **Plymouth Public Market**, guarded by its cannon, becomes traditional West Indian mayhem. Country ladies sit, their skirts rolled above their knees, presiding over stacks of ground produce, yam, tannia and eddoe, and exotic Montserratian fruits, soursop, christophine and banana.

Parliament Street leads through the business centre of the town and past the government buildings to the Anglican **St Anthony's Church**, where there are two silver chalices which were presented to the church by the freed slaves: 'as a thank-offering to God for the blessing of freedom vouchsafed them on 1st August, 1838'. The church has been rebuilt several times, following military raids and hurricanes, since the first was erected on this site in 1636 by Anthony Briskett, Montserrat's first Governor. **St Patrick's Roman Catholic Church** stands on George Street.

Across Fort Ghaut, heading south, the road descends into the area of Wapping, where the old stone warehouses have been restored. On the hill above is **Government House**, the official residence of the Montserrat Governor, an attractive creole house built in the 19th century and decorated on one gable with a shamrock. The landscaped gardens are worth a visit (*open on weekdays 10–noon*) and the house itself has paintings and period furniture.

Highway 2 leaves town in the shadow of the principal fort in the extensive ring of defences that guarded Plymouth in the 18th century. **Fort St George** stands 1200ft above the town. Built in 1782 by the French, its scattered battlements cover acres and are overgrown. Some cannon are in place in the two open-plan gun batteries and some cannon have been mounted, commanding a magnificent view and once again covering the town and its approaches from north and south.

Down below, the road leaves the town via St Anthony's Church and **Sturge Park** where inter-island sports matches and carnival competitions take place. The **Montserrat Museum** (© 491 5443), *open Sun 3–5 year-round, Wed 1–5 in Dec–Apr winter season and when a cruise ship docks, adm free*, is situated in a restored 18th-century sugarmill and its exhibits cover Montserratian life from the time of the the Arawaks, through early colonization and the sugar years to the island's success as a producer of limes in the 19th century. The museum is run on donations and contributions from the Montserrat National Trust, which you can join for EC$5.

On the coast beneath the museum is the **Fox's Bay Bird Sanctuary** (*see* p.82). Marked walks lead through the swamp. *There is no admission fee.* The remains of a fort can be seen on Bransby Point itself. You can see herons, mangrove cuckoo and kingfisher stalking and flitting in the mangrove and manchineel.

Back inland, a side road (Highway 4) cuts up into the mountainside to St George's Hill, but the main road continues through a series of small villages, Salem and Weekes among them, and the open slopes of the Centre Hills. At Waterworks stand the old **Montserrat Air Studios**, the world-renowned recording studios that were opened in 1979 by George Martin, one-time producer of the Beatles. They are defunct now, but a whole string of famous artists has worked there, including the Rolling Stones, the Police, Stevie Wonder, Paul McCartney and Duran Duran.

North of Woodlands the expensive villas evaporate and the land becomes drier as the Centre Hills tail off and the Highway wiggles through the West Indian villages of Cudjoe Head, St John's and Geralds, where you will see farmers walking barefoot or riding a donkey to their small plot of land in the hills. Carr's Bay, an idyllic fishing cove, is on the Caribbean coast at the foot of Silver Hill.

From here the road crosses over to the uninhabited Atlantic coast, where the views are spectacular and the mountains more rugged, eventually coming to the airport at Blackburne. This area is completely undeveloped. On the flatlands around the airport the restored remains of the sugar estates and their mills and chimneys stand out against the mountains. From here, it is a 6-mile ride back up into the high fertile hills on Highway 1, where there are a couple of simple villages on the heights, before the road descends into Plymouth.

Past Government House on the coast road, a turn leads inland to the dropping-off point for the fairly steep climb to **Chance's Peak** (3002ft), the highest on the island. It takes a couple of hours but the stunning views from the summit (on a clear day) make it worthwhile. There are 2360 steps and the occasional rest-house for a breather. There is a legend, also heard elsewhere in the Caribbean, that you might meet a mermaid combing her hair on a rock at the summit, with a diamond snake next to her. If you can seize the comb, get it down to the sea and wet it before the snake catches you, her treasure will be yours. Island lore does not relate what happens if you fail. A guide for this walk can be arranged at the Tourist Board.

Another side-road leads to Galways Estate, *adm free*, where a sugar plantation was first established in the 1600s and was worked for 200 years. The sturdy dark stone remnants of the estate buildings have been partially restored; in the overgrowth you can see the boiling house, the great house, a windmill and an animal-driven mill.

There is a smell of sulphur on approach to **Galway's Soufrière**. It is a short walk from the end of the road. Cut into the fertile hills is a brown scar, Montserrat's vent to the volcanic underworld, which periodically belches and continually lets off stinking gases through discoloured sulphur pools and fumaroles (in 1902, when volcanic activity was seen all along the island chain, the ashes were so bad that Plymouth had to switch on the lights at midday). Water runs milky white, smelly and at near boiling point, discolouring the rocks all around, often the yellow of sulphur. The clay ground can be too hot to stand on, but as long as you are careful it is a good walk. The tourist board publishes a page of advice about how to avoid scalding yourself on the visit. 'Persons who wear spectacles should make provision to clean them regularly on the trail.' You can walk from here to the Bamboo Forest.

The **Great Alps Waterfall** is 45 minutes' walk upriver into the hills from just out-side St Patrick's. The water, only really impressive in the wet season, cascades from 70ft into a dank ravine strung with lianas and elephant ears and crawling with mosses. You can cool off with a 70ft shower when you arrive—take your swimsuit.

Festivals

St Patrick's Day (17 March) has recently been resurrected in Montserrat and is now celebrated with fêtes and beach parties, particularly in the southern village of St Patrick's. The Queen's Birthday on the second Saturday in June is more formal, but August Monday (from Emancipa-tion Day, 1 August 1834) is remembered with blow-outs, Caribbean style. On Labour day, 6 May, there are more beach picnics and also a fishing competition. The major festival is **Carnival** at Christmas. The activities start at the beginning of December, with the elimination rounds of the calypso and Festival Queen competitions, and culminate in a week-long series of masquerade parades, jump-ups and feasting. The main celebrations start on Christmas Eve and finish with Festival Day on 31 December, when the island dances from dawn and masquerades all day and night.

Fans of soca music will recognize the name of (the Mighty) Arrow, from Montserrat, whose calypso 'Hot Hot Hot!' made it to the top worldwide.

© (809)–

Where to Stay

hotels

There are just a few hotels in Montserrat, with a couple at the top of the comfort range and several smaller guest houses. There is a 7% government tax on hotel rooms and villas and usually a 10% service charge will be added to your hotel bill. The **Vue Pointe Hotel**, PO Box 65 (© 491 5210, fax 491 4813), has ultimate easy old-time Caribbean elegance and an attentive and welcoming air. The rooms are ranged regularly around the sloping, lawned garden in three small blocks and 30 very comfortable octagonal rondavels, with balconies, huge beds, and louvres and fans to coax the island breezes. Vue Pointe is family run, and a friendly crowd of regulars often gathers at the bar and restaurant. There are watersports on the bay. The **Montserrat Springs Hotel**, PO Box 259 (© 491 2481, fax 491 4070, US © 800 223 9815), has gone for a more typical Caribbean air of clean, cool comfort, with large, air-conditioned suites and rooms in blocks on the hillside ouside Plymouth. There are 34 rooms in bright white and pastel colours, pool, tennis, watersports and beach bar. There is a smaller hotel in town, the **Flora Fountain**, PO Box 373 (© 809 491 6092, fax 491 2568) on Parliament Street, with 18 comfortable rooms set around a tropical garden courtyard in an odd circular building; moderate to cheap.

guest houses

You are guaranteed a fine welcome at **Providence Estate House** bed and breakfast, St Peter's (© 491 6476, fax 491 8476), which is set in fantastic gardens in the northwest of the island, where it looks towards Redonda and Nevis from a hillside setting of 600ft. The two rooms, furnished with antiques, but with televisions, are downstairs in a recently restored stone and timber-frame plantation house. Breakfast on the balcony, a kitchenette for your use and dinner on request, an excellent Caribbean retreat, cheap to moderate. **Marie's Guest House**, PO Box 28 (© 491 2745, fax 491 3599), has just four simple rooms in a modern Montserratian house a short walk outside Plymouth to the north. Private baths, living room with television and kitchenette, very cheap. In Kinsale there is **Niggy's Guest House** (© 491 7489), just five very simple rooms around a popular bar and restaurant, very cheap. Also in Kinsale, **Moose's Guest House** (© 491 3146).

villa hire

There are several villa companies and real estate agents with villas. **Isles Bay Plantation**, PO Box 64 (© 491 4842, fax 491 4843) is one of the most comfortable places to stay: a small cluster of four-room villas on the hillside in Belham Valley above the golf course, offering modern Caribbean luxury with pools; maid service includes cordon bleu cooking. Contact **Caribbee Agencies**, PO Box 223 (© 491 7444, fax 491 7426), **Montserrat Enterprises Ltd**, PO Box 58 (© 491 2431, fax 491 4660) or **Neville Bradshaw Agencies**, PO Box 270, Plymouth (© 491 5270, fax 491 5069).

© (809)–   # *Eating Out*

Montserrat's cuisine is mainly West Indian, based on the tropical vegetables and fruits on sale at the market, and the fish and animals that can be caught. Recently the supermarkets have catered for the influx of Americans and Europeans by bringing in food from outside, which is comparatively expensive. The island's Irish heritage reaches as far as the food in **goat water**, a stew of goat meat with herbs, often served at ceremonies. Another local delicacy, only served on Dominica and Montserrat, is **mountain chicken**, which hops wild in the hills before it reaches your plate. In fact, it is not a chicken at all, but an outsize frog. The hotels have popular dining rooms—the Vue Pointe has a barbecue on Wednesdays and a Sunday brunch, and the Montserrat Springs a barbecue with music on Fridays and a buffet lunch on Sunday afternoons. There is a nice clutch of restaurants in the restored stone warehouses of Wapping south of town. It is best to book in season and you might request a dish while on the phone. A service charge of 10% is usually added. Categories are arranged according to the price of a main course: *expensive*—EC$40 and above; *moderate*—EC$20–40; *cheap*—less than EC$20.

expensive

At the **Belham Valley** restaurant (© 491 6623), you look out from an ornate veranda onto the golf course. The menu is international with some local fare: conch fritters served with a dill mayonnaise or with West Indian hot sauce, followed by chicken sautéd with shallots and cream brandy sauce. Finish off with a mango mousse. In Wapping you will find the **Emerald Café** (© 491 3821), a popular stopping point for visitors—seafood crêpe, sautéd lobster or mountain chicken diable. The **Blue Dolphin** (© 491 3263) has a strong West Indian feel, set in a modern Montserratian house in Amersham above Plymouth. The building has dolphins painted on a blue wall, but ask if you're having trouble finding it. White lace netting over bright-coloured tablecloths, local music, fish, steaks and seafood with local vegetables.

moderate

The **Golden Apple** (© 491 2187) also has excellent local food in a typical West Indian setting. Red tablecloths and flowers accompany a fish, conch or chicken dinner, or a goat water. Ring to reserve. **Ziggy's** (© 491 8282) is set in a newly built, Caribbean-style house above Belham Valley, wooden with window shutters standing at angles on stilts. Sandwiches, salads, steaks and plenty of local fish and conch. **Niggy's Bistro** (© 491 7489) is set in a modern house behind a white picket fence in Kinsale. The dining room has a boat bar. The food is continental, with chicken, fish and steaks. Friendly and fun. **Andy's Village Place** (© 491 5202) is a cavernous, tin-roofed bar and restaurant in Salem. Old cable drums as tables, where you get marinaded barbecue chicken and ribs or a fresh fish. Classic rum-shop attached. In town you will find a pleasant stopover on the veranda at the **Ocean Terrace**. Simple meals overlooking the centre of town from a pretty yellow and green balcony. At **Oasis** (© 491 2328), you can catch a calypso chicken or a burger in a Wapping old stone house or in the garden.

cheap

There are several local Montserratian haunts and rum shops, which double as bars and simple restaurants. In Weekes, **Nep Co Den** serves the best rotis (boneless) on the island and in the far north, in the village of St John's, is **Mrs Morgan's**, where you will get the best goat water, or local fish if you prefer. It has a concrete hut, plastic tablecloths and a crowd of limers. In town you can take away a fry chicken at the **Evergreen Pastry Shop**.

Bars and Nightlife

Montserrat is pretty quiet after dark, though hotels occasionally have bands. You might stop for a game of pool in the **Golden Apple** in Cork Hill, while in Weekes, **Nep Co Den** is popular— fluorescent posters, cotton wool on the ceiling and loud music. In town, **Casuarina** is upstairs in an old warehouse and the **Yacht Club** is busy at weekends. The **Green Flash** in Kinsale has a rumbustious bar and **The Inn** on Sugar Bay has occasional lively evenings. Discos include **La Cave** opposite the Evergreen take-away in town, **Images**, upstairs at Angelo's Supermarket, and the **Uprising Club**, south of town.

St Kitts and Nevis

Rum Shop

St Kitts and Nevis stand side by side in the arc of diminishing volcanic peaks in the Leeward Islands. Their concave slopes rise gracefully through shoreside flatlands to rainforested and often cloud-capped summits, fertile greens offset against the blues of the tropical sea and sky. They have strikingly beautiful views of one another, across the Narrows, a channel just 2 miles wide.

The two islands live fairly amicably together (they are bound politically), but each has a distinct character and maintains its own identity. Internal rivalry is of course very strong—every Kittitian has a relative on Nevis and vice versa—and the annual inter-island cricket match is a fiercely contested event.

Unless you hide out in the tourist ghetto or lock yourself away in plantation splendour (St Kitts and Nevis have a stunning collection of plantation house hotels), you cannot help but notice life around you in St Kitts and Nevis. There is a strong and vibrant West Indian culture, unlike on some of the other islands nearby, where life has been swamped by the international tourist industry. Expect to be accosted in the street. You may be asked for money or given a slug of rum. Either way, the Kittitians (pronounced as in 'petition') and Nevisians (as in 'revision') will let you know their thoughts on life. The country has a population of 44,000, of which about 9000 live on Nevis (many more Nevisians live in St Kitts).

Since their Independence together in 1983 St Kitts and Nevis have faced difficult economic times, recently compounded by the recession up north, and despite the slowly developing tourist industry the islands are pretty poor. Visit, though, and you will find two quite different Caribbean islands, both welcoming and laid-back in classic old-Caribbean style.

History

St Kitts was once known as the 'Mother Colony of the West Indies', because it was the first island in the Lesser Antilles to be settled permanently. Liamuiga, the Carib name for St Kitts, supposedly means 'fertile land' and it was the verdant growth that attracted European colonists in the early 17th century. Despite the hostility of the Carib Indians and risks from a local infestation of pirates, they came to plant tobacco. The first settler was the Englishman Thomas Warner, who arrived in 1623. Next year he was joined by a French privateer, Pierre Belain d'Esnambuc, who called in to repair his ship after a fight with the Spaniards near the Cayman Islands. Welcomed by Warner, the Frenchman stayed for a while and then went to

France to persuade settlers to return with him to St Kitts. The two men arranged to share the island and in 1627 divided it into three, with the French in the north and around Basseterre, and the English in the middle.

One of the main reasons that the French and English were happy to team up was that they needed to protect themselves against the Caribs, who were none too pleased about this intrusion into their islands. The battles began even in 1626, with the Caribs rallying in their canoes from other islands including Dominica and Guadeloupe, but the Europeans held their own. Steadily the Caribs were forced out and Liamuiga became St Kitts. The Spaniards were no more pleased at this intrusion into their backyard in the New World and in 1629 their fleet attacked the settlement. During the skirmish the colony was destroyed, but as was to be the routine all over the islands, as soon as the invaders were gone the settlers filtered back and got on with their planting.

The new settlers also started to look farther afield. Competition for empire was hotting up and English expeditions were sent to settle nearby islands. Nevis was one of the many 'Charibby Islands' made over arbitrarily to the Earl of Carlisle by Charles I in 1627 and the next year Oualie was promptly taken from the Caribs by the British. Montserrat and Antigua were settled in 1632. The French boldly took on the larger and more hostile Windwards to the south, heading for Martinique and Guadeloupe.

On St Kitts itself, the scene was set for the next two hundred years—the French and British would be constantly at each other's throats. At one stage they managed to fall out on the basis that a tree had grown. A banyan marking the border in the north of the island had enlarged by putting out a few years' worth of aerial roots and the land enclosed by it just happened to include 250 French houses. War was just averted on that occasion, but St Kitts passed from one power to the other like a shuttlecock. Brimstone Hill was built and besieged. As the navies whittled through the islands Nevis took a fair beating too. In 1706 the French swooped in, destroyed what they could (about £1 million's worth), and left with around 3000 slaves.

At the beginning of the 19th century, the British finally gained the upper hand in the endless series of wars and eventually both islands found themselves in the hands of the British, with whom they remained until Independence. Only a few hints of French influence remain in St Kitts today: a fleur de lys on the national coat of arms and, most notably, the name of the capital—Basseterre.

When the islanders were not being besieged, they were planting sugar-cane furiously. Nevis stuttered on its route to prosperity, but prosperous it became. At one stage a fleet of twenty ocean-going ships was devoted entirely to serving that island, sailing out with luxuries and manufactured goods such as tools and returning loaded with sugar-loaves. She was dubbed the 'Queen of the Caribbees'. The sugar industry also needed slaves and in the late 17th century Nevis had a slave market. Vast numbers of Africans were brought over and when the ships arrived in port these frightened men and women would be oiled up before being made to parade through the streets singing, prior to being taken to auction.

With the 19th century, the West Indian sugar industry went into decline and the mansions into decay, though the planters kept up their balls and finery as long as they could. And after Emancipation in 1834, the 'apprenticeship' system soon broke down in 1838 and the slaves were finally freed. On such small islands, many were forced to remain on the plantations, but eventually independent villages like Challengers on the leeward coast of St Kitts grew up.

The late 19th century was a lean period for all the Caribbean islands and St Kitts and Nevis slipped into obscurity. The sugar industry had more and more difficulty competing in the world market as Cuba and Santo Domingo gained the ascendancy. Today, apart from a small income from sugar, St Kitts–Nevis is dependent on a slowly expanding tourist industry.

Politics

St Kitts and Nevis are united in a constitutional Federation, in place since Independence from Britain in 1983. The two islands were originally shunted together in 1882, as the colonial authorities in London made one of their many political rationalizations, and they formed a part of the Presidency of the Leeward Islands. The island of Anguilla was appended to the Basseterre administration in 1871.

The three islands followed much the same course as the other British colonies in the 20th century, led by the clamour for political change in Jamaica, Trinidad and Barbados in the 1930s. In 1951, the islanders were given the vote and the St Kitts and Nevis Labour Party, rallying the voices of people who had had no political say before, swept the board. 'Associated Statehood' in 1967 brought more internal self-government, but at this point Anguilla, which had felt neglected by the government in St Kitts, staged one of the world's lesser-known revolutions and made its claims for secession heard (see p.124). After a 15-year row, Anguilla eventually left the State of St Kitts–Nevis in 1982.

At Independence in September 1983, the Nevisians wanted to make sure they would not end up in the same position as Anguilla and so they renegotiated the settlement, inserting an 'escape clause' that allows them to secede from Federation with St Kitts if two-thirds of the Nevisians choose to do so. Nevis has its own five-member elected assembly to govern its own affairs. For the moment, political unity between the islands is reasonably secure.

In the 11-member House of Assembly of St Kitts–Nevis, three of the seats are allotted to constituencies on Nevis and these can easily hold the balance of power. St Kitts–Nevis remains within the British Commonwealth. At the moment it is headed by Prime Minister Kennedy Simmonds, whose party, the People's Action Movement, is in coalition with the Nevis Reformation Party.

Flora and Fauna

The lower slopes of St Kitts are bright green with sugar-cane, but both islands have thick and fertile growth, starting as scrub and grassland at the shoreside and rising to rainforest, where you will find swathes of elephant ears, and gommier and Spanish oak trees whose upper branches dangle with lianas and explode with orchids and cycads. Close to the summits of the mountains the rainforest gives way to stunted elfin woodland. The wildlife in St Kitts and Nevis is relatively unspoilt.

Around the bright red flamboyant tree, poinciana (named after St Kitts' first French Captain General, de Poincy), and bougainvillea, you will see typical island birds such as the purple-throated carib and other hummingbirds, daring bananaquits and bullfinches. Offshore, you can see pelicans and the occasional frigate bird, and in the lowland thickets you may spot a warbler or a pearly-eyed thrasher.

St Kitts' few deer have moved to the northern part of the island now that the road on the southeast peninsula has disturbed their peace, but they are shy and difficult to see. You are more likely to come across the green vervet monkey, which was introduced in the 17th century. It stands about 1ft high, lives in the hills and travels in packs of about forty. You can tell when they are angry by the white line above their eyebrow which they wiggle at you furiously.

© (809)–
Getting There

Golden Rock airport, 2 miles from Basseterre on St Kitts, has no direct scheduled services from Europe or from the USA, so you will have to make a connection. Newcastle airport on Nevis can only take short hopper flights, but there are easy links both from Antigua and from St Kitts itself (by plane or by ferry, see below for connections between the two). There is a departure tax of EC$20 (US$8).

By Air from the UK: The easiest connections from the UK and other European countries are via Antigua, from where hopper flights link up with British Airways and BWIA services from London and Lufthansa from

Germany. It is also possible to make same-day connections to the islands from Paris (Air France) or from Amsterdam (KLM) via Sint Maarten.

By Air from the US: The easiest connections from the USA are made in Antigua and Sint Maarten, but another alternative is to fly via the American Airlines hub in San Juan, Puerto Rico, from where there are regular flights on American Eagle. Some charter airllines do fly in from the USA.

By Air from other Caribbean Islands: St Kitts is easily accessible by the hopper flights that pass up and down the island chain touching most of the islands between Antigua and San Juan, Puerto Rico. Most of them also stop in Nevis too. Airlines with scheduled flights include LIAT (© 465 2286 St Kitts, © 469 5302 Nevis). Winair (© 465 8010 St Kitts, © 469 7583 Nevis) flies in from Sint Maarten. If you need to charter an airplane, you can contact **Carib Aviation** (© 465 3055, fax 465 3168) which has nine-seater and five-seater planes, **Air St Kitts–Nevis** (© 465 8571, fax 469 9018, © 469 9241 Nevis) or **Nevis Express** (© 469 9755).

Travel between the Islands: LIAT flights operate half-a-dozen times a day, but are often fully booked. The local inter-island 'bus' service is really the ferry (usually twice daily both ways; no services Thurs and Sun; about 45 minutes; EC$20 return). Out of the winter season, you can take the Four Seasons ferryboat which leaves from their terminal on the waterfront in Basseterre, timings according to the flights. The views are magnificent as the mountains shift slowly above you. Kenneth's Dive Centre run a water-taxi service for a minimum of four passengers (© 465 2670).

Tourist Information

The St Kitts and Nevis Tourism Offices are:

UK: 10 Kensington Court, London W8 5DL (© 071 376 0881, fax 071 937 3611).

USA: 414 East 75th Street, **New York**, NY 10021 (© 212 535 1234, fax 212 879 4789, toll free © 800 562 6208); Presidents' Plaza II, 8700 West Bryn Mawr, Suite 800 S, **Chicago**, IL 60631 (© 312 714 5015, fax 312 714 4910).

Canada: 11 Yorkville Avenue, Suite 508, Toronto, Ontario M4W 1L3 (© 416 921 7717, fax 416 921 7997).

The **IDD code** for St Kitts and Nevis is 809 followed by a seven-digit local number, beginning with 465 in St Kitts and with 469 in Nevis.

Money

The currency of St Kitts and Nevis is the Eastern Caribbean dollar, which is shared with the other former British colonies in the area. It is fixed to the

US$ at a rate of US$1 = EC$2.65. US dollars are accepted all over the island, though. Major credit cards are accepted in the tourist areas and it is a good idea to make sure which dollar currency you are dealing in.

Banks are open daily 8–3 and many remain open on Fridays until 5pm. The St Kitts and Nevis National Bank also opens on Saturday mornings, 8.30–11.30. Shopping hours are 8.30–midday and 1–4pm.

St Kitts

The familiar name St Kitts (from St Christopher) has been used by the Kittitians since the 18th century. It is not known how the island took the name of the travellers' saint (Christopher Columbus, who passed the island on his second voyage, did not call it this), but perhaps later explorers named it in his honour.

St Kitts is the larger of the two islands (68 square miles) and is shaped a bit like a paddle, set in the water so that the handle points southeast. The blade is covered in a ridge of volcanic mountains, tumbling steeply from the summits and then flattening out towards the sea. The slopes are traced with *ghauts*, or ravines, which look a bit like huge volcanic stretch-marks and give an idea of the upheaval that the mountains once underwent.

Like many islands in the Caribbean, St Kitts became very wealthy as a sugar factory in the 17th and 18th centuries (it was worth building the massive Brimstone Hill to defend it), but unlike most other islands, the slopes of St Kitts are still covered with canefields. The industry hardly pays its way—it was bought out by the government in 1975 and kept going because it employs a large number of islanders. Recently, however, cane-cutters have been brought in from Guyana and St Vincent.

In contrast to Nevis's quiet and almost comatose mature, there is a slightly raw air about St Kitts, typical of the larger Caribbean islands. You might expect it in a poor and undeveloped country. The majority of the Kittitians are charming, though, and will happily engage you in conversation. It is worth getting out to explore the northern areas of the island.

Getting Around

The ride from the airport into town is little more than a mile, but if you do not want to go by cab (EC$13), then it is a short walk over the sugar railway to the main road where a minibus will pick you up in a matter of minutes and take you to Basseterre for EC$1.

Buses, now Japanese minivans, run the roads of St Kitts intermittently from 6.30am until about 8pm. Headed to the main part of the island (there are no buses to the southeast peninsula), they leave from the waterfront in

Basseterre when they are full or when the urge takes the driver. They do not generally circle the island, but run along either one coast or the other, which means that you can be stranded in the northern canefields if you are on a round-island tour. If this happens, **hitch**, which is quite a good alternative anyway. Getting on to a bus is as easy as flagging it down on the roadside; to get off you must shout 'Driver, Stop!'. The buses are inexpensive and EC$4 will get you to the north of the island.

Taxis are readily available. In Basseterre you will find them at the Circus and they can also be arranged through any of the hotels. Fares are fixed by the government. Some prices are **Golden Rock Airport** to: Basseterre—EC$13, Frigate Bay area—EC$25, Rawlins Plantation or Golden Lemon at the northern end of the island—EC$55; and from **Basseterre** to: Frigate Bay—EC$18, Brimstone Hill—EC$30, Rawlins Plantation or Golden Lemon—EC$50. Most taxi-drivers will also be willing to take you on an island tour, which costs around EC$130 for three hours. Taxis can be ordered through the St Kitts Taxi Association (℗ 465 4253).

Car hire gives the most mobility, particularly if you are staying in the north of the island, and a car can be hired from about US$35 per day or a mini-moke for slightly less. Before driving on St Kitts, you must purchase a local driving licence, obtainable on production of your own licence and EC$30 at the police station in Cayon Street, Basseterre. Driving is mostly on the left, though there are recognized chicanes to avoid the numerous potholes in the road. Some hire firms are: **Caines** on Prince's Street, Basseterre (℗ 465 2366), **Delisle Walwyn and Co.** just off the Circus in Basseterre (℗ 465 8449), **TDC Rentals** (℗ 465 2991) and **Sunshine Car Rentals** (℗ 465 2193). You can hire a scooter through **Easy Ride Moped Rentals** (℗ 465 3429).

Organized island tours, to sights including Brimstone Hill and hikes up into the crater of Mount Liamuiga, can be arranged through **Kriss Tours** (℗ 465 4042) and through **Greg's Safaris** (℗ 465 4121).

Tourist Information

On St Kitts, the Department of Tourism can be found in Pelican Mall on Bay Road, PO Box 132, Basseterre (℗ 465 4040, fax 465 8794). There is also a helpful office at Golden Rock Airport. The Tourist Board put out a glossy magazine *The Traveller*, with essential information on restaurants and where to go shopping. There are a couple of **art galleries** worth visiting in St Kitts. The **Spencer Cameron Gallery** (℗/fax 465 1617) is set in a pretty colonial building on Independence Square. It exhibits some

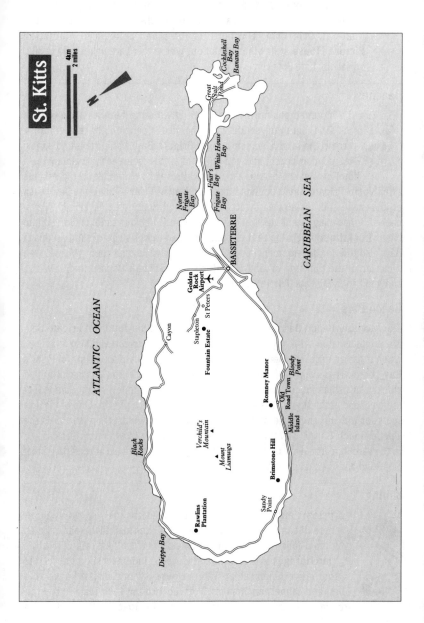

St. Kitts

4km
2 miles

N

ATLANTIC OCEAN

Dieppe Bay

Black Rocks

Rawlins Plantation

Sandy Point

Verchild's Mountain

Mount Liamuiga

Brimstone Hill

Cayon

Stapleton

St Peters

Fountain Estate

Romney Manor

Middle Island

Old Road Town

Bloody Point

Golden Rock Airport

BASSETERRE

North Frigate Bay

Frigate Bay

Friar's Bay

White House Bay

Great Salt Pond

Cockleshell Bay

Banana Bay

CARIBBEAN SEA

African but mostly Caribbean paintings, some painted by Kittitians and residents on the island, but also artists from elsewhere in the Caribbean, open Mon–Sat, 9am–4pm. The north of the island is home to **Plantation Picture House** at Rawlins Plantation, where there are paintings and silks on sale by Kate Spencer.

Beaches

In the mountainous northern areas of St Kitts the beaches are mostly of black sand, but in the south, which has been opened up by the peninsular road, the sand is golden brown. **Frigate Bay** is still the island's most popular beach, and you will find all the facilities for watersports, a hotel nearby and bars to get a drink. Its opposite number on the Atlantic side, **North Frigate Bay** is pounded by ocean waves. **Friar's Bay** is the best beach on the island and it is now easily accessible (though soon to be developed). Palm-backed, it has magnificent views and superb mounded golden sand. Looking out to Nevis from the southern tip of the island there are other strips of sand—Banana Bay (also due for development) and Cockleshell Bay. Beyond them you will find seclusion at the thin strip of sand at **Major's Bay**. There is windsurfing, kayaking and good snorkelling at **Turtle Beach**.

Beach Bars

The **Monkey Beach Bar**, an octagonal wooden hut at the bottom of **Frigate Bay**, is a popular haunt with daytime bathers and watersportsmen and also at sunset, when it has an excellent view across the waves. And beneath the palms on **Friar's Bay** there are a couple of lean-tos from paradise where you can get a grilled chicken or fish and a cool beer to stave off the heat. Definitely recommended, at the weekend and festivity days, or whenever a cruise ships puts in. One of the best spots for a drink and a view of Nevis (perhaps after windsurfing across) is the **Turtle Beach Bar** (© 469 9086), which collects a lively crowd on its terraces and in the garden, particularly on Sundays. Follow the south peninsular road past Great Salt Pond and then take a left.

Sailing

Customs and immigration are in Basseterre and you can stop over here in comfort and take in the life of the small town (also take on provisions from the supermarkets), but the best sailing and the **anchorages** are really off the steep, indented shoreline of the southeastern peninsular. White House Bay and Ballast Bay are the best and calmest anchorages. You can also put in to Major's Bay just around the southern tip of the island. **Brooks Boat Co** (© 465 8411) in the deepwater harbour just south of Basseterre can make limited repairs. Basseterre is the only port of entry into St Kitts, but you do not have to clear again when moving on to Nevis.

Watersports

The best place for watersports is **Frigate Bay**, in the hotel area south of Basse-terre, where you can find waterskiing, parasailing, jetskis and snorkelling equipment. **Windsurfing** and small boat sailing is also popular here (try **R & G Watersports**). There are often sunfish races here and there is an annual windsurfing race in July between Frigate Bay in St Kitts and Oualie Beach on Nevis. Another good spot for windsurfing, snorkelling and kayaking is at Turtle Beach on the southeast peninsula. **Deep-sea fishing** trips for steely-eyed shark-fishermen or women can be arranged by **Tropical Water Sports** (© 465 4167) and **Leeward Islands Charters** (© 465 7474) or on *Panda* (© 465 1617).

Scuba diving, to see black coral, sting rays and underwater volcanic vents, can be arranged through **Kenneth's Dive Centre** (© 465 2670, fax 465 6472) in Basse-terre or **Pro Divers** (© 465 3223, fax 465 1057), based at Fisherman's Wharf in town and at Turtle Beach (© 465 9086). *A single-tank dive costs around US$40* and operators have underwater photographic equipment. **Snorkelling** is good off Old Road Town on the island's leeward side and Dieppe Bay on the northern coast. A glass-bottom boat, *Jazzie II* (© 465 3529), offers tours to the southeast peninsula.

Other Sports

On land there are well-organized **walking tours** around St Kitts, that make a close and informative inspection of plantation ruins (the conical windmills and square steam chimneys that you see from the road), and follow rivers up through the ever-encroaching undergrowth to hidden rockpools to seek out crayfish. The most rewarding walk takes you up 3792ft to the top of St Kitts's highest peak, Mount Liamuiga (from Belmont Estate in the north), and down into its crater (400ft down), a trip that lasts all day. Another trip takes you past Verchild's Mountain and across the island on the route of the old English military road from the 17th cen-tury, which linked the two coasts. It also passes close to the **Dos d'Ane** pond. You are advised to take a guide if you go high into the hills. If you wish to join a guided tour contact **Greg's Safaris** (© 465 4121) or **Kriss Tours** (© 465 4042).

A more leisurely look at St Kitts's plantation history may be had on horseback, **riding** around the island or simply cantering along the beach. This can be arranged through **Trinity Stables** (© 465 9603). Off-season, between July and January, you can sometimes ride on the sugar-cane train (© 465 8157).

For **golfers** there are two courses on the island: an 18-hole championship course in the Frigate Bay area (*green fee around US$35*) and a 9-hole course at Golden Rock.

Basseterre

Basseterre, the small capital of St Kitts, has plenty of charm. It stands on the mile-wide sweep of a south-facing bay; a grid of streets lined with stone and wooden West Indian houses and sheltered by the magnificent green slopes of Monkey Hill and the South Range. It is home to about 15,000 Kittitians (just under half the island's population).

The name Basseterre and its protected site have come down from the French, who first settled the area. The town was adopted by the British in 1727, in preference to their capital at Old Road, but apart from this and the (not quite) gridiron layout of the town, nothing else French survives. Today, the church towers, stone Georgian buildings and even the pointed iron railings speak of the island's 350-year assocation with Britain. Life itself is changing as the colonial memory recedes, but echoes remain in the pith helmets of the police, Bedford trucks and the clock-chimes.

Visitors in the 19th century entered Basseterre through the arch of the **Treasury Building**, the domed colonial structure on the waterfront that housed the customs. From here they emerged in the heart of the town at the **Circus**, where an elaborate green Victorian clock-tower stands beneath a ring of royal palms. Fading 19th-century Basseterre, warehouses with dark stone foundations and bright white upper storeys, spreads out along Bay Road, parallel to the sea. St Kitts's notorious *ghauts* (pronounced gut), or river-ravines, are channelled down the middle of the streets (when in flood they are fearsome and have been known to wash parked cars out to sea).

the Circus
St Kitts

To the west of the Circus, the Government Buildings can be found on Church Street and **St George's Anglican Church** on Cayon Street, built and rebuilt on the site of a French church of 1670. Travelling further west you come to the large villas in the gentrified district of Fortlands, locally referred to as the old aristocratic area. The Governor General's residence can be seen from the road in Greenlands, but it is not open to the public.

Walking east from the Circus you come to **Independence Square**, known until 1983 as Pall Mall Square, where the goats mowing the lawn spike the imposing grandeur of the imperious Georgian homes and the **Roman Catholic Cathedral** with its impressive rose window. Further east on the waterfront, you come quickly to the boats and drying nets in the fishermen's district. In the yards of beaten earth, small clapboard houses are shaded beneath a breadfruit tree or a palm.

Visitors do not arrive at the Treasury Pier any more and so it has fallen into disrepair, used only by kids casting a line for fish or as a perch for pelicans between dive-bombing sorties. Instead, the new **customs pier** 50 yards away to the east is a hive of activity twice a day with the arrival of the ferry from Nevis. Traditional island sloops also dock here to collect anything from crates of drink to building materials before sailing off to Nevis. With a boom as wide as the mast is tall, they offer a graceful sight plying between the islands.

Clockwise around the Island

A coastal road runs around St Kitts, circling the island beneath the central mountain ranges, winding in and out of the ghauts, surrounded by canefields. Today the cane is crushed in one central factory, fed by a circular railway line around the island, but the ruins of the old windmills and steam chimneys still stand proud behind curtains of bright green cane. Now that most of them are dilapidated, it is hard to imagine the atmosphere of a functioning plantation, but the rusting copper vats and the crushing gear still give a hint of the ceaseless human activity.

A couple of miles west of Basseterre, **Bloody Point** was the scene of an early massacre of the Caribs in 1626 when, in spite of their differences, the English and French teamed up. They were tipped off by a Carib woman that the Indians were preparing to attack and so the Europeans ambushed them, supposedly killing 2000. Strangely, the infant son of the Indian chief, Tegreman, was allowed to live and was brought up in the family of Ralph Merrifield in England. At **Old Road Town**, capital of the English part of the island in the 17th century, you can see one of the Indians' artistic memorials, their rock carvings: lozenge-bodied and antennaed cartoon characters waving at you from the face of black volcanic rock.

Just above the town is **Romney Manor**, *open Mon–Fri, 8.30–4*, an old plantation house that is the home of **Caribelle Batik**. The Indonesian process has been borrowed and has been turned to creating scenes with West Indian colour—anything from the fluorescent fish-life to the pastel nightlife. A mile farther on is the town of **Middle Island**, where you will find the tomb of Sir Thomas Warner, the pioneer British settler, who was knighted at Hampton Court by Charles I for his efforts. He first arrived in 1623 and died here in 1648, a 'noble and much lamented gent'. From St Kitts, he had settled the islands of Nevis, Antigua and Montserrat.

Brimstone Hill

Beyond Middle Island, an 800ft peak rises next to the coast, on the flank of Mount Liamuiga itself. Its contours appear square because a massive fortress sits on the summit—a 38-acre stronghold with a citadel presiding over bastions, miles of ramparts, barracks, powder magazines and an amphitheatrical cistern. Brimstone Hill, *open daily 9.30–5.30, Thurs and Sun 2.30–5.30, adm*, named because of the sulphur which you can still smell nearby, is a fitting name for this monster—the whole edifice is built of burnt black stone.

The hill was first fortified in the 1690s, and with walls 7ft thick added almost a hundred years later it was considered impregnable, but it was stormed successfully by the French in 1782. They shelled it for weeks until there were breaches in the ramparts 40ft wide and not a building was left standing. Once the fighting was over, the fortifications were rebuilt and this lumbering giant became known as the Gibraltar of the West Indies. It was never attacked again. Today much of Brimstone Hill has been restored and it bristles with cannon once more. But despite the odd whiff of sulphur the hellish aspect of Brimstone Hill has gone: the ramparts are overgrown with bougainvillea, and cannon lie around useless. The view from the summit is magnificent and ranges from Montserrat and Nevis in the south to Statia, Saba, St Martin and St Barthélémy in the north. The citadel now contains a museum, displaying uniforms and weapons alongside the history of St Kitts.

Sandy Point, a typical West Indian town, with clapboard rum shops and the odd old stone building jostling new concrete, is the second-largest town on the island. **Charles Fort** was the island's leper asylum. From here, the road runs through the canefields around the northern point of St Kitts, in the shadow of Mount Liamuiga. In the 17th century the Dutch were the great traders in the Caribbean and they kept warehouses at Sandy Point. A fire in 1663 cost them 65 warehouses full of tobacco. The island which lies 5 miles off the coast is Dutch St Eustatius.

Mount Liamuiga (pronounced 'Liar-mweagre') is the highest point on the island at 3792ft, and there is a crater lake just below the lip. The volcano, which was known for most of its history as Mt Misery, is (almost) inactive; it has been known to rumble very slightly once in a while. **Dieppe Bay** takes its name from its French heritage, which lasted until the early 18th century. The dilapidated stone and wooden buildings give an idea of the town's former prosperity as a sugar port. Returning down the Atlantic coast to Basseterre, the road passes the **Black Rocks**, volcanic extrusions that have blackened into weird black shapes since their eruption millions of years ago.

At Cayon a road cuts inland to Basseterre, running through the villages of Stapleton and St Peter's. Just beyond Stapleton is the Fountain Estate House, built on the site of **La Fontaine**, the residence of illustrious French Governor de Poincy in the

1640s. Not only was he Captain General, but he was also Knight of Malta. He arrived with due pomp and circumstance and promptly erected himself a four-storey château in keeping with his station. The magnificent building was destroyed by an earthquake in 1689 and only the chapel and the steps remain.

The inland road rejoins the coast road as it approaches Basseterre, just by the central **Sugar Factory**. This monster is a proper factory, with conveyor belts feeding vast metal maws, banks of crushers that squeeze the very last drop of juice from the cane, and disgorge just a white pulp known as *bagasse*. All St Kitts' cane is brought in on the narrow-gauge railway track that runs around the northern part of the island. Among the modern equipment, vast brightly coloured baskets full of cane, you can see the discarded coal-fired engines of seasons past. There are no regular tours of the factory, but it is usually possible to visit it during the cane-crushing season, between February and June, by asking at the gate.

South of Basseterre

Passing through the last of the canefields, the road south from Basseterre descends into the tourist enclave of Frigate Bay, cut off from the heart of St Kitts. In times past, Frigate Bay itself was the scene of early morning duels between slighted members of the St Kitts nobility, but now it tends to be clubs at dawn on the golf-course and a bit of jousting on jetskis.

In 1989 a road was built that opened up the south of the island beyond Frigate Bay, and large international hotel companies have begun to muscle in on the beaches. From Frigate Bay, the road leads past the old salt ponds, common property in the days when the island was shred by the French and English, and comes to Cockleshell Bay and Banana Bay, where there are magnificent views of Nevis.

Festivals

The main event in the Kittitian calendar is **Carnival**, which takes place just before Christmas and lasts into New Year. It is a week of jump-ups, calypso and beauty queen shows and masquerades. Not many tourists attend, though plenty of Kittitians return to the island for the festivities and it is fun to watch the events in the stadium at Warner Park and around the streets of Basseterre. Grab a chicken leg and a *Carib* lager from one of the ladies fanning braziers at the edge of the park and join the crowd. There are other smaller events in the year, more dancing in the streets of Basseterre: the Westbourne Ghaut **Block-out** (they block off the streets and have a party there with live bands) on the Queen's Birthday, **Easterama** at Sandy Point at Easter and **Village-arama** in St Johnston's, which sees fashion parades and the calypsonians sparring with one another in song. Independence Day, 19 September, is celebrated with traditional Caribbean feasting and festivities.

Where to Stay

St Kitts (and Nevis) has far and away the finest collection of plantation house hotels in the Caribbean. Many are still surrounded by sugar cane as they were two hundred years ago and they still retain the grace and hospitality of the era—they are small and are run in the style of a private house. As former estate houses, most are not on the beach, but the hotels run beach shuttles a couple of times a day. Children are sometimes not encouraged at these hotels. There are no really good beach hotels on St Kitts as yet, but the Frigate Bay area has some purpose-built shoreside condominium complexes. Hotels are being constructed on the southeast peninsula. St Kitts also has a number of villas for hire all over the island: details can be obtained from the Tourist Board. A government tax of 7% is added to all hotel bills.

Plantation Houses

very expensive

Rawlins Plantation, PO Box 340, St Kitts (© 465 6221, fax 465 4954), has one of the Caribbean's supreme settings in an old estate house on the slopes of Mt Liamuiga, looking north to Statia and Sint Maarten. There are just 10 rooms, scattered in stone outbuildings and cottages among the tropical trees and hedges of the lawned estate gardens. But the house itself, with library and dining room, is the nerve centre, where you take cocktails and then dinner overlooking the grounds. A bewildering variety of tropical fruits for breakfast, followed by a buffet lunch (worth attending if you are not staying there, for the saltfish and funchi and the candied sweet potato) and then dinner of chicken and mango or lamb in guava sauce. If this sounds over-indulgent then you can walk in the forests above the estate or knock a ball about on the grass tennis court. It is very expensive, but there are few places like it anywhere in the Caribbean. Close by is the **Golden Lemon Inn** (© 465 7260, fax 465 4019, US reservations © 800 633 7411), which is set in a 17th-century trading warehouse on the waterfront in Dieppe Bay. It is now meticulously restored and the old stone walls are more likely to echo with piano and singing accompaniment after dinner than the rumbling of rum barrels. There are 16 rooms, with wooden floorboards and louvred windows, gracefully furnished with antiques and with huge beds. But most charming are the 10 suites, which have been exquisitely decorated, each in a different style; tropical, oriental, Egyptian, and so on. The **White House**, PO Box 436 (© 465 8162, fax 465 8275), used to be the military mess and the officers made sure to choose a superb site high above Basseterre for their retreat. The drawing room and dining rooms are furnished to suit the period (perhaps a little more luxuriously than the original), with rugs, chaises-longues and rosewood chairs. The bedrooms are also far more comfortable than you might find in an old coach house. Just 10 doubles, painted white with four-poster beds. Tennis, croquet, golf nearby and other officer-like pursuits.

moderate–expensive

Ottley's Plantation Inn, PO Box 345 (© 465 7234, fax 465 4760, US © 800 772 3039), is set in magnificent grounds. From the colonial grandeur of the enormous rooms and balconies you look over restored stone outhouses and a superb lawn backed with royal palms to the Atlantic Ocean beyond. Again a private house atmosphere, centred on the stonework terrace of the old boiling house, where you will find the dining room and the pool. Expensive. The **Ocean Terrace Inn**, PO Box 65 (© 465 2754, fax 465 1057, US © 800 524 0512), is close to town, but isolated from the relative hurly-burly in a walled garden that rambles across the hillside. The 54 rooms (air-conditioned with satellite television) make it sound large, but they are scattered around the main house and garden pool, where you can swim or take a jacuzzi and drink at the pool bar before dinner with a view of Nevis. Expensive. The **Fairview Inn**, PO Box 212 (© 465 2472, fax 465 1056), is set in a pretty Kittitian great house over-looking the Caribbean coast, with wooden floors and ceilings. It hasn't quite the style of the other inns of St Kitts, but prices itself accordingly. There are 23 rooms in stone cottages behind the great house, which has a busy and friendly bar, moderate.

Hotels, Self-catering and Guest Houses

expensive

The best of the hotels in Frigate Bay is **Colony's Timothy Beach Resort**, PO Box 81 (© 465 8597, fax 465 7723, US © 800 777 1700) at the southern end of Frigate Bay. There are 60 plush and very comfortable rooms and suites in blocks and a walkway of crotons and bougainvillea down to the pool and restaurant just above the beach. There are kitch-enettes in some rooms. **Sun 'n' Sand Beach Resort**, PO Box 341 (© 465 8037, fax 465 6745, US reservations © 800 223 6510, Canada reserva-tions © 800 424 5500) have a collection of cottages and studio apartments in a tropical garden around a pool and tennis courts, on the windy Atlantic coast. Pretty bedrooms with air-conditioning and ceiling fans, kitchenettes and cable television, housekeepers.

moderate

Less expensive self-catering accommodation in Frigate Bay is available at the **Gateway Inn**, PO Box 64 (© 465 7155, fax 465 9322). Walking distance from the beach, simple air-conditioned rooms with cable television. Also try **Conaree Beach Cottages**, PO Box 259 (© 465 8110), moderate to cheap. There is a pleasant stopover in very centre of town, with all the comforts for a businessman or a passing traveller, **Palm's Hotel** (© 465 0800, fax 465 5889). It's air-conditioned and carpeted, with cable television and video recorders, situated right above the Circus.

cheap

There are two typically West Indian guest houses in Basseterre where you can find a simple room. Try the **Park View Guest House** (© 465 2100), next to the bakery on Victoria Road, private or share baths, or very cheap, the **Windsor Guest House** (© 465 2894) on Cayon Street, share baths.

© (809)–   **Eating Out**

The food in St Kitts is fairly typical of the British Caribbean: chicken, fish or goat, often in a stew, served with a tonnage of Caribbean vegetables. The more adventurous dining rooms will also serve more exotic ingredients in tropical fruit sauces and some traditional European recipes. There is of course the rather less traditional burger to be found in the resort hotels, but it is well worth getting out to find a more Caribbean meal, either in the plantation houses, which serve excellent buffet lunches and set dinners, or in the side streets of Basseterre. Not many places accept credit cards. There is a government tax of 6% added to all bills and usually a 10% service charge as well. Categories are arranged according to the price of a main course: *expensive*—EC$40 and above; *moderate*—EC$20–40; *cheap*—under EC$20.

expensive

At the **Patio** (© 465 8666) in Frigate Bay, you dine on the veranda of a private house with tables lit by candle-lamps and served by waitresses in French creole madras costume. The menu is continental, with Caribbean adaptations—seafood pasta or lobster with crab, followed by tropical fruit parfait or chocolate mousse pie with a brownie crust, by reservation only. **Fisherman's Wharf** (© 465 2754) has a waterside setting looking back at Basseterre, on a wooden deck with bench seats. Seafood and grilled fare including barbecue shrimp, seafood kebabs and shark steak. Quite a lively atmosphere, particularly at weekends. The **Lighthouse** (© 465 8914) sits on the cliff just above the deep-water harbour to the south of town, on the site of the old Fort Smith (from which it has taken its mock crenellations). It is air-conditioned and plush, with grill foods and West Indian and continental dishes—dover sole St Christopher—followed by fruit sorbets. Open Tues–Sat. There is a bar on the point itself for a cocktail with a view. **The Anchorage** (© 465 8235) has a pleasant setting in a villa just off Frigate Bay beach. Mixed international food, but a seafood speciality of lobster or shrimp, entertainment in season.

moderate

A popular spot in Basseterre, for a daytime drink or a cocktail at dusk, and light or fuller meals day long, is the **Ballahoo** (© 465 4197), where you sit on a veranda right above the Circus in the centre of town. Quite a few tourists, but some locals too—shrimps parmesan or blue parrotfish fillet and always a vegetarian dish, closed Sun. **Arlecchino** (© 465 9927) serves Italian food in a simple West Indian courtyard; pastas, pizzas and full platters—*pollo alla Cacciatora*, hunter-style chicken.

cheap

Pisces is an excellent local restaurant, where whelks, saltfish and less exotic stew fish and curry chicken are served with a volley of local ground provisions. Plastic tablecloths and HBO on the television, tropical fruit juices in season and a good local crowd. **Chef's Place** (© 465 6167) on Church Street serves West Indian food to a local crowd. Delicious pumpkin or carrot soup, followed by turtle, saltfish and local fish. Open lunch and dinner. There are plenty of local hide-outs in Basseterre where you can get traditional chicken or fish. Try **Victor's** (© 465 2518) in New Town, where you dine on mock-leather benches and plastic table-cloths in a modern pink town-house. Local juices to accompany Kittitian fare—plates of curry goat heaped with green fig and sweet potato. You can get an excellent take-away pizza or a roti at the **Pizza Place** on Central Street in town. And if you would like a fry chicken to go, try **Gilly's** on Sandown Road or **Wendy's** on Cayon Street. On Fridays and Saturdays the Kittitians cook up chicken and fish on braziers at the streetside.

Bars and Nightlife

Much of the entertainment in St Kitts is centred around the hotels, whether it be singing along to Broadway tunes at the Golden Lemon or joining in the Jack Tar toga party. However, if you fancy a drink with some Kittitians after work, there are plenty of rum shops around the island. Try **Five-Ways**, on the junction of five roads at the western end of Central Street, which collects a crowd of ministers and limers, and **Tiffin**, off Pond Road—turn at Uncle Jerry's corner. There are regular Sunday afternoon events, making a good day out, at the **Turtle Beach Bar** in the south and the **Monkey Beach Bar** on Frigate Bay. The Kittitians also make picnic trips to Brimstone Hill on Sundays and holidays.

There are a few clubs you can move on to. You can hear live music at the **Fisherman's Wharf** at the weekend. The **Cotton Club**, at Conaree past the airport, pulls in a lively crowd on Fridays and Saturdays and **Reflections** upstairs at the Flex Fitness Centre on Frigate Bay Road, opens Thurs–Sat with a varied crowd. The **Lighthouse**, just out of town, has a clifftop bar with a view and an occasional discotheque at the weekends.

Nevis

At times it is the only cloud in the sky, but there is always a cloud on the summit of Nevis. Like all the tall volcanic Caribbean islands, Nevis blocks the path of the racing Atlantic winds which, as they rise and condense, stack in huge immobile cumulus clouds. This permanent white wreath supposedly reminded the Spanish travellers of the snow-capped peaks of home and so the island came to be called Nuestra Señora de las Nieves, Our Lady of the Snows. Gradually, the name has been shortened to Nevis (pronounced Nee-viss).

Nevis is almost circular (6 by 8 miles) and from the sea can look like a regular cone; deep green slopes rise in sweeping curves to the central Nevis Peak at 3232ft. About 9000 Nevisians live in settlements dotted all over the island.

The stateliness of the old-time West Indies is vanishing all over the Caribbean, but it is still just visible here. Once, the island was known as the 'Queen of the Caribbees' because the society was so august and the estate houses were so grand that ladies could walk down the stairs three abreast, panniered skirts and all. 'Old-time' Nevis is mostly gone now as the finely crafted bridges and dark stone walls are being swallowed up in the ever-encroaching jungle, but the plantation house hotels retain the old grace and finery of centuries past and they are some of the most exquisite hotels in the Caribbean.

A hundred years of association across the Narrows may have forged close relations, but it has not diminished Nevis's own traditions. When the Deputy Governor-General of St Kitts and Nevis is in residence you will always see two flags flying: one is for the Federation of St Kitts with Nevis and the other Nevis's own flag.

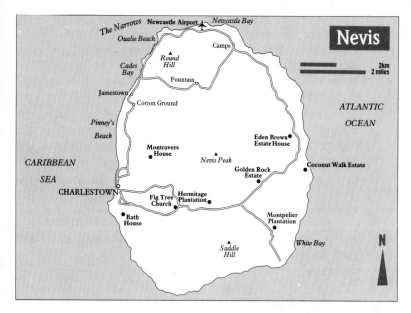

Nevis is the smaller and quieter partner in the Federation with St Kitts and the Nevisians go more placidly than their fellow-countrymen. In school, the children learn that there were no slave rebellions in the island's history which, if it were true, would probably make Nevis stand alone throughout the whole Caribbean. Certainly the Nevisians are extremely polite and they all have time to stop and talk to a stranger. It is a good time to visit the island. Nevis is developing, building steadily but only slowly and it has not yet joined the headlong rush for the tourism dollar. The quiet, small island charm still remains.

Getting Around

There is a scant **bus** service that sets off from Charlestown in both clock-wise and anti-clockwise directions. Buses leave from the town centre and run until 6.30pm (8pm on Saturdays), maximum fare possible is about EC$3. Hitching works quite well in Nevis.

Taxis are available near the pier in Charlestown, at Newcastle airport, through the hotels or through the Nevis Taxi Drivers Association (© 469 1483). Some sample prices are **Charlestown** to: Pinney's Beach—EC$13, Oualie Beach—EC$25, Newcastle airport—EC$30, the Golden Rock Hotel—EC$30. Taxis can also be hired for a three-hour island tour for around EC$120.

You need a local licence if you wish to drive in Nevis, and it can be obtained on presentation of your own licence and EC$30 to the police in Charlestown. Mini-mokes are popular and easily available. There is basically one road, about 20 miles long, that runs around the island, with one or two branches leading off it. Watch out for the goats who seem to find the tastiest grass at the roadside.

Car rental costs around US$45 per day and a mini-moke slightly less. Hire firms are: **Nisbett Rentals** (© 469 9211) next to Newcastle airport, **Gajor's Car Rental**, in Bath (© 469 5367) and **Skeete's Car Rental** at the airport (© 469 9458), who also hire out mopeds.

Details of getting to Nevis are given under 'Getting There' and 'Travel between the Islands' on pp.95–6.

Tourist Information

The helpful **Bureau of Tourism** is on Main Street in Charlestown (© 469 1042, fax 469 1066).

Beaches

Nevis has a stunning 3½-mile strand in **Pinney's Beach**, which starts just north of Charlestown and is backed along almost its entire length by a confusion of palm trees, trunks growing at all angles. The golden brown sand shelves steeply into the sea and the scene is perfected by some cracking views of St Kitts. It is a good long walk and there is the occasional beach bar where you can stop to fortify yourself or linger over a sunset view. The Four Seasons Hotel sits smack in the middle and has brought large-scale watersports to the beach; windsurfing and small boat sailing can be arranged there.

Following the coast around to the north you come to **Oualie Beach**, with more golden sand and a superb view across to St Kitts. Beyond here there are a couple of indentations with sand overlooking the Narrows: one long strip between Hurricane Hill and the airport (there are no facilities and not much shade, but you are quite likely to be alone) and **Newcastle Bay**, which has more steep-sloping sand and quite big waves. The Nisbet Plantation Hotel is set on its own small beach.

Beach Bars

Pinney's Beach has a number of very pleasant shoreside stopovers, ideal for lunchtime and a lazy afternoon on the beach. Just north of the Four Seasons is the **Beachcomber**, which is set in a converted villa: daytime snacks and endless drinks with a rum crowd of latterday pirates. At the deserted top end of the beach is the **Fort Ashby Bar**, a few old battlements just back from the sand, where you can get well-priced salads and sandwiches under the banyan and palm trees; it has a watersports shed and Monday night football on the television. The **Mariner's Pub** has some watersports, a changing room and a great view of St Kitts, but the building is a bit ghostly and empty. Elsewhere on the beach there are impromptu shacks where you can get a beer and a barbecue chicken or fish: the **Shack** offers local fare and **Shazzy's** is a lime-green lean-to with ribs, chicken and fish to go with an easy sunset view. Further north, **Prinderella's** is a pretty gingerbread bar set on a brown-sand beach in a small cove, serving good food. And further round you will find a good place to linger at the **Oualie Beach Bar**, with some watersports. Finally, a popular haunt on the north coast is the **Newcastle Bay Marina**, with a restaurant and shops above a small strip of sand.

Sailing

Sailing down to Nevis across the Narrows from St Kitts gives one of the most glorious views in the eastern Caribbean. And then there is the magnificent and calm stretch of Pinneys Beach. The best **anchorage** is off the town of Charlestown in the southwest and you can explore the island from here or stop over along Pinney's Beach during the day. There is a calm spot tucked into the shoreline in the lee of Cade's Point. There are limited services for yachts in the town, but there are supermarkets where you can get provisions and ice. The only **port of entry** to Nevis is in Charlestown. You do not need to clear again if you move on to St Kitts.

Watersports

For waterskiing and small boat sailing the calm waters of Pinney's Beach are ideal. Watersports equipment can be hired through the **Four Seasons Hotel** and at the bars at the top end of the beach. As you head around the coast the winds pick up, so windsurfing and sailing are popular here too. You can hire a board or a sunfish at Oualie Beach through **Nevis Water Sports** (© 469 9518). Near the airport the **Newcastle Bay Watersports Centre** (© 469 9394) offers mainly windsurfing, but also arranges sailing and kayaking, and snorkelling on the nearby reefs. A day's sail, with snorkelling and a barbecue picnic, is available through the catamaran *Caona* (© 469 9494). **Scuba-diving** rental and instruction is available through the **Scuba Safaris** (© 469 9518, fax 469 9619) at **Oualie Beach** and at the **Four Seasons Resort**. The are good caves for diving on the south side of the island.

Other Sports

For **walkers**, there are some worthwhile hikes into the Nevisian jungle, taking a look at the island's more exotic flora. From the slopes of Mount Nevis there are some spectacular views to the surrounding islands, when it is not shrouded in cloud. A good route to the peak leaves from the Golden Rock Hotel to the Source, for which you are advised to take a guide. Guided walks can be arranged through **Eco-Rambles** (© 469 2091) and **Top to Bottom** (© 469 5371), who take walks to Gallow's Bay, Montravers and the Tower Hill Estate.

The old sugar estates provide excellent foraging ground for the walker/historian. There are endless ruins on the island, where the skeletons of mansions gape in their decay and the long-overgrown gardens are littered with cane-crushing rollers and boiling coppers. The Nevis Historical and Conservation Society, which is based at Alexander Hamilton House (the museum), organizes a monthly hike and other events. (For a calendar of events, call them on © 469 5786.)

There was once an Upper Round Road which ringed Nevis above the plantation estates, linking Zion, Rowlands and Hamilton. Much of it is still walkable, if a little overgrown. Down below you will find **Montravers House** inland from Pinneys Beach. It was the finest on the island when Nevis was the Queen of the Caribbees (it even had a moat). **Bath House** is just south of Charlestown, and on the windward coast there are fine ruins at **Coconut Walk Estate**. Not far north on the Atlantic coast is the **Eden Brown Estate House**, famous for its ghost, the tortured bride who lost her husband in a duel with his best man on the very night of her wedding.

Riding: a ride in the foothills of Nevis Peak or a canter through the surf can be arranged through **Cane Gardens** (© 469 5464, call evenings) or the **Hermitage Inn**, where carriage rides are available. **Golfers** can play on the 18-hole, Robert Trent Jones II course attached to the Four Seasons Hotel. There is still an active **Jockey Club** in Nevis, with race meets on certain holidays.

Charlestown

The island's capital and only town is Charlestown, a few streets of charming old stone buildings with balconies and gingerbread woodwork ranged along the Caribbean coast. It is home to 1500 Nevisians, whom you will see hanging out in the Court House square at the town centre—hucksters selling sweets and drinks, and a small crowd of 'limers' passing the time of day. The odd countryman still rides into town on his donkey.

The town also has a strong spirit of 'when the boat comes in'. The atmosphere of sedation switches to one of hectic activity twice a day with the arrival of the ferry from Basseterre. All supplies have to be brought in by boat and as the inter-island sloops or the ferry chug into harbour, loaded to the gunwhales with crates of bottles and boxes of tins, so the Nevisians race to the pier. Business complete, the activity is eclipsed and Charlestown snaps back into its customary slumber.

Just along the waterfront from the pier is the **market**, at its busiest on a Saturday morning, when the fruits and spices are heaped on the tables and lightning banter fills the air from soon after dawn.

Main Street, where the few shops and offices are situated, leads to the small Independence Square where you find the War Memorial and the Court House. Close by you will find a gallery, the **Plantation Picture House**, with paintings and hand-painted silks on sale. On the southern outskirts of the town is **Government House**, built in 1909, the official Residence of the Deputy Governor-General of St Kitts and Nevis.

Close by is the **Bath Hotel**, *open Mon–Fri 8–5, Sat 8–12, adm*, a huge block of a building constructed in 1778 in grand Nevisian style, complete with ballroom, balconies and accommodation for 50 guests.In Nevis's heyday people would come and stay here in order to take the waters, which come out of the ground at temperatures as high as 108°F and supposedly resemble those of Baden-Württemburg. The waters were first mentioned by some visitors before Nevis was even settled. Captain John Smith, leader of the Jamestown settlers of Virginia, called here first in 1607. Some of his fellow travellers had supposedly been scalded by manchineel sap when they sheltered under the tree in the rain, but here they found 'a great poole, wherein bathing themselves they found much ease...they were well cured in two or three days.' The hotel is a ruin now, although it has survived the earthquakes and hurricanes well. (At the time of writing it was temporarily occupied by the police.) The bath-house is still functioning, however, so if you are scalded by a manchineel tree, you can rush around here and take the waters.

Close by is the **Horatio Nelson Museum** where the exhibit 'Nevis in the Time of Nelson' details Nelson's life and time in the West Indies alongside a description of Nevis's sugar prosperity. There is an impressive collection of Nelson memorabilia; letters, maquettes of ships and pottery from toby jugs made in his image to the porcelain used at his marriage feast.

Alexander Hamilton

At the northern end of town, on a lane called Low Street, is **Alexander Hamilton House**, the birthplace and home for five years of the architect of the American Constitution, Alexander Hamilton, whose face you will see on the US$10 bill. The house was built in the 1700s and Hamilton was born there in 1757 of a Nevisian mother and a Scots father. When he was five, they moved to St Croix, from where Alexander eventually left to complete his education in the States. A patriot during the American Revolution, he was George Washington's aide-de-camp. He was known as the 'Little Lion' because he was 5ft 7in tall and his blue eyes were said to turn black when he was angry. It was he who, having trained as a lawyer, first suggested the Federation of the American States in the form that was eventually adopted, and with its founding he became First Secretary to the American Treasury. He died in a duel with a political opponent, Aaron Burr, in 1804. The attractive building houses the **Museum of Nevis History**, *open weekdays and Saturdays in season, 8–4, adm free*, where there is an excellent chronological display of Nevis from Amerindian times to the present, with ghostly Arawak faces in pottery, pictures of 'old-time' Nevis and documents from the life of Alexander Hamilton himself. The Nevis House of Assembly holds its parliamentary sessions upstairs in the building.

Anticlockwise on the Island Road

Once past Government House, the town quickly thins into countryside with scattered houses sitting on small plots of beaten earth. Here you will come across age-old stand-pipes, delivering water as they have for the last hundred years, and impromptu roadside markets which switch sides at midday to avoid the sun.

Fig Tree Church, a small stone sanctuary in a tropical garden, is famous for the register of Horatio Nelson's marriage to the Nevisian girl Fanny Nisbet. He was based at English Harbour in Antigua on the HMS *Boreas* in the 1780s, but was unpopular with the West Indians because his job was to enforce the Navigation Laws which banned their very profitable trade with countries other than Britain (they even sued him once and he had to stay on board his ship for eight weeks to avoid being locked up). However, eventually he found solace with the young widow Fanny, whom he first met at Montpelier House. Prince William Henry, the friend of Nelson who later became King William IV, gave the bride away, and his signature can also be seen in the register. The couple soon returned to England, but the marriage did not last as Nelson became involved with Lady Hamilton.

In Clay Ghaut just off the main road you will find the **Eva Wilkin Gallery**, *open Jan–April, Mon–Fri 10–3*, which is set in a restored windmill. Eva Wilkin, who died recently, lived and painted for many years in Nevis and her work is on view alongside exhibitions of other painters. There is a shop downstairs, or call in advance (© 469 2242). Behind the gallery, **Saddle Hill** is the site of a huge hilltop fort, started in 1740, which now lies in ruins. During his stays on Nevis, Nelson would reputedly be seen each day on the hill with his spyglass pointed out

Fig Tree Church, Nevis

to sea. Now it is a good place to rootle around and of course, as a former lookout, the views are still magnificent.

At Camps near the northern side of the island, you can take a road that leads into the forest and through the hills, emerging on the Caribbean coast at Cades Bay at the **Soufrière**. This is an active volcanic vent that first appeared with a hiss and a sulphurous stench when an earthquake struck in 1950. It is a bit lukewarm now, with just the odd trace of stink-bomb and some heated and barren patches of earth, but is a reminder that the underworld is not so far away in the Caribbean.

The road returns to Charlestown along the Caribbean coast, behind Pinneys Beach. **Jamestown**, first capital of Nevis, which slid into the sea in 1680 during an earth-quake, is visible only to scuba divers just off the coast. It is said that one man escaped the quake when the jail collapsed around him. 'Redlegs Greaves', a Scots gentleman pirate who retired to an estate on Nevis after a lifetime of freebooting, had been recognized by a former comrade in revelry and had been thrown in jail. Having been spared by the earthquake, he was eventually pardoned.

Festivals

In Nevis, the island festival goes by the rather unwieldy name of **Culturama**. There are regular Caribbean Carnival activities, so you can expect to see calypso and string band competitions and costumed mas-queraders strutting through the streets of Charlestown. Culturama takes place in late July, coming to its climax on the first Monday in August. **Tourism Week** has displays of arts and crafts alongside horse-racing, a treasure hunt and music. If you are on island at Easter, look out for the kite-flying competitions and in May or June there is a sailing regatta, with some races for local fishing craft, which makes a colourful sight.

© (809)–

Where to Stay

Like St Kitts, Nevis has some extremely fine plantation hotels, where you can bask in 18th-century splendour just as the planters did two hundred years ago. They are low-key and quiet. Most are not on the beach, but there are usu-ally shuttles. If being right on the sand is important then there are also some nice beach hotels. Nevis is building steadily, some stylish hotels and some in simple modern concrete. A 7% government charge is added to all bills and most hotels also add 10% for service.

There are also a number of villas and cottages dotted around the island for those who would prefer to be independent and perhaps do the round of the restaurants in the evening. Contact the Tourist Board or **Sea Shell**, Main Street, Charlestown (✆ 809 469 1675, fax 469 1288, US toll free ✆ 800 457 0444), which has several houses and villas, mostly with pools, for rent.

expensive–very expensive

The **Hermitage Inn**, St John's Parish (✆ 469 3477, fax 469 2481, US ✆ 800 742 4276), has a supreme setting on the southern-facing slopes of Nevis. Around the great house, a classic West Indian timber-frame building from the 1740s, the rooms are set in neat cottages with traditional shingle walls and tin roofs, wrapped in gingerbread woodwork and bougainvillea. The rooms have wooden interiors and four-poster beds and many cottages have hammocks on the balconies from where you can savour the view. There is the easy-going air of a private house as guests gather for a rum punch and tannia fritters before dinner on the veranda. MAP. At **Montpelier Plantation Inn**, PO Box 474 (✆ 469 3462, fax 469 2932, US ✆ 800 243 9420) is another tropical island idyll of centuries past, where you will find a similar gracious old West Indian ambience, a little more English in style. There are 16 recently redecorated rooms, with grey-flecked marble floors, in cottages scattered around the grounds of a magnificent estate house, all linked with brick paths among flamboyant trees and frangipani. The plantation is lost in the southern hills of Nevis, but there are shuttles to the beach. The dining room, on a huge veranda above the lit gardens, serves excellent West Indian fare and after dinner guests linger and chat over coffee and liqueurs. Montpelier is quiet, luxurious and sedate and it will not let you down, expensive. **Nisbet Plantation Beach Club**, St James Parish (✆ 469 9325, fax 469 9864, US ✆ 800 344 2049), has the advantage among the plantation hotels of being on the beach, though as a larger hotel it lacks the intimacy of the others. The view from the great house to the seafront is superb—down an alley of tall palms beneath which the 38 rooms and suites are situated in cottages. They are luxurious, with cane furniture and sea-facing balconies behind tropical screens. The great house is a fine setting for dinner. Nisbet is a little up-beat, with some light entertainment over coffee in the drawing room and bar. MAP, very expensive. The **Golden Rock Estate**, PO Box 493 (✆ 469 3346, fax 469 2113, US ✆ 800 223 9815), is a smaller and simpler plantation hotel set 1000ft up the mountain side and threatened with being swallowed up by its 25 acres of garden. Old estate buildings have been converted into drawing-room and bar, the cistern into the swimming-pool and the shell of the windmill into the honeymooners' suite. Just 15 rooms, decorated with antiques, which stand in a modern block above the main house. Very comfortable and friendly, expensive. The **Four Seasons Resort**, PO Box 565,

Charlestown (© 469 1111, fax 469 1112, US © 800 332 3442, Canada © 800 268 6282), is a departure for Nevis. It is large, sumptuous, swish, brisk and without much character, but good for a body-holiday—massage parlour, health centre, watersports and day cruises, tennis and golf, low-calorie meals and king-sized beds. Room service, very expensive.

moderate

The **Oualie Beach** Hotel (© 469 9735, fax 469 9176) has much more casual Caribbean style: a small, much more laid-back beach hotel situated on the golden sand of Oualie beach. The 22 bright and breezy rooms have gingerbread fittings and superb views of St Kitts, which you can gaze at from the screened verandas. Some rooms have mahogany four-poster beds with canopies. There is a busy bar and restaurant serving West Indian meals and plenty of watersports are available right outside on the beach, moderate to expensive. Perched on the hillside above Oualie Beach are the 10 **Hurricane Cove Bungalows** (©/fax 469 9462). They are built of carefully finished wood, with muslin nets over the wooden beds, window shutters on stilts and magnificent views. One- and two-bedroom units with full kitchens, central pool but no restaurant. Secluded and comfortable.

cheap

There are simple self-catering apartments in town at **Meadville Cottages**, PO Box 66 (© 469 5235, UK © 081 771 5836) on Craddock Road. Neat, clean and quite comfortable, with balconies to sit and relax on. There are a couple of guest houses in town. The **Seaspawn Guest House**, PO Box 233 (© 469 5239, fax 469 5706), is on the edge of Charlestown and has clean and simple rooms each with a private bath. It is a good place from which to explore Nevis if your hotel is not the main point of the holiday. Close to the town-centre is **Daniel's Deck**, where there are no-nonsense rooms with private bathrooms at very cheap prices.

© (809)–   ***Eating Out***

The finest food and the best settings are found on the verandas of the plantation house hotels, but there is an increasing number of good restaurants outside the hotels in Nevis, both for international food and for a local meal with the Nevisians. Most restaurants add a 10% service charge to your bill. Categories are arranged according to the price of a main course: *expensive*—EC$50 and above; *moderate*—EC$20–50; *cheap*—under EC$20.

expensive

For an excellent and thoroughly original night out you can go to **Miss June's** (© 469 5330), who serves a compendium of Caribbean and other dishes in a restored stone estate house high in the hills of Stoney Grove. You start with cocktails on a verdant gallery and move inside for a set menu of five courses: soup, fish, a multiplicity of main dishes and vegetables on a buffet and then puddings, which Miss June talks you through (it can be as many as 20 dishes in all). Coming from Trinidad, she cooks plenty of spicy, Indian-inspired food, but also expect Asian and gourmet Caribbean. The menu varies nightly. By reservation only, but well worth making the effort to get there, set price moderate to expensive. In town you will find that the best restaurant goes by the unlikely name of **Eddy's Restaurant** (© 469 5958). It is set on Independence Square in a very attractive old town house, so you dine in the wooden interior on creaking floorboards or on the veranda looking out on to the square. Lively atmosphere, a popular gathering place with the ex-pats, local and international fare; daytime fritters and salads, burritos, night-time specials of catch of the day, Italian and stir-fry dishes. Some entertainment, bar attached.

moderate

Not far off is a quieter haunt, **Unella's** (© 469 5574), set on a stone-walled balcony and wooden deck upstairs overlooking the yachts on the waterfront and the lights of St Kitts. Lunchtime salads, evening local fare, grilled fish served with capers and lemon or shrimp scampi sautéd in garlic. **Prinderella's** (© 469 8291) serves food most nights, as does the **Newcastle Bay Marina** (© 469 9395) beyond the airport, where you can get pizzas and simple local dishes.

cheap

Also in Newcastle and well worth a stop for its local food is **Cla Cha Del** (© 469 9640). For the best in local food go to **Muriel's Cuisine** (© 469 5920) on Happy Hill in the back of town. Classic West Indian restaurant in a modern house, with flowery tablecloths and a daily varying menu of curries and stews and rotis, served with excellent johnny cakes. **Callaloo** in Charlestown has simple West Indian fare in an air-conditioned setting.

For a sunset drink you can wander along to any of the bars along Pinney's Beach, but in town **Eddy's** often has a lively crowd. Two more local bars are the brightly painted **Jelly Water** near Alexander Hamilton House and **Mariner's Wharf** on the waterfront. Some of the hotels lay on entertainment, perhaps a piano player or a steel band, but if you want to join in with Nevisians on their evening out you can try the local discotheques, **Dick's Bar** in Brick Kiln Village and **Club Trenim** on Government Road in Charlestown.

herding zebus

Anguilla

Anguilla is a flat and barren island, 16 miles by 3 and mostly 15ft deep in scrub. Inland, the 'eel' is hardly attractive, but along its writhing coastline Anguilla has some of the Caribbean's most spectacular beaches—mounds of sumptuously soft and blinding white sand, set in an electric blue sea. On a coast 45 miles long, there are about thirty of them.

Anguilla is the most northerly of the British Leewards and it lies about 5 miles from the French part of St Martin, looking north and east into the Atlantic. Sombrero Rock, its dependency, is the northernmost point in the chain of the Lesser Antilles. The 9000 Anguillians are pretty cool—for a small island there is a remarkable air of independence and self-assurance. The island is quiet to the point of sedation and it seems that nothing could ruffle Anguilla's calm. But it is worth remembering that twenty years ago, when they wanted to secede from St Kitts and Nevis, they took to the scrub and staged a revolution.

As with so many Caribbean islands, the Anguillians you meet here are only half the story, as there are probably more abroad than there are on the island. Anguilla has never been able to offer its people a living and so traditionally they have travelled. The money they send home and money from tourism has made the island quite rich.

As you travel around Anguilla you will see the grey skeletons of partially built houses protruding from the scrub. You might think they were the failed dreams of ex-patriots, paradise homes that have foundered on classic West Indian business inertia. But this is not the case at all, as most of them are owned by Anguillians abroad. In time-honoured tradition, the traveller returns when he has earned enough to buy a plot, then leaves again to earn more in order to build on it. Steel reinforcements are left sticking into the sky ready for the time that the family outgrows the house and they need a second storey (it's also a tax dodge). Among all the development, however, there are still people who lead simple West Indian lives, in shingle and clapboard houses set in a small plot of beaten earth.

The Anguillians have been building fairly steadily for the tourism industry as well as for themselves. In the past the island has specialized in a brand of reliable low-key high luxury, but there are now some less expensive places to stay too. There are some good places to eat out and a string of lively beach bars and for the moment the island has an easy air because it is not too crowded.

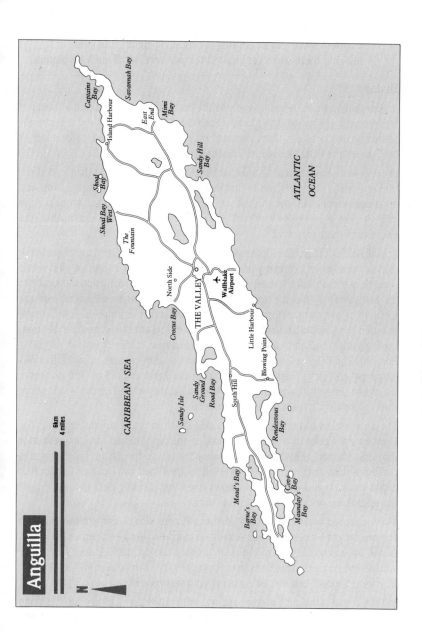

Anguilla

CARIBBEAN SEA

ATLANTIC OCEAN

Captains Bay
Savannah Bay
Island Harbour
East End
Mimi Bay
Shoal Bay
Shoal Bay West
Sandy Hill Bay
The Fountain
North Side
Crocus Bay
THE VALLEY
Wallblake Airport
Little Harbour
Blowing Point
Sandy Isle
Sandy Ground
Road Bay
South Hill
Rendezvous Bay
Mead's Bay
Barne's Bay
Maunday's Bay
Cove Bay

6km
4 miles

N

Apart from the impeccable beaches, it is the Anguillan people that make this barren islet a special place. As they greet you with the slightest wave and a soothing 'all right, all right', it is hard to imagine there was ever a raised temper here, let alone a revolution.

History

In Amerindian times, Anguilla went by the name of Malliouhana and although it was probably christened Anguilla by a Spaniard, Spain herself ignored it because it offered no quick returns. The Spaniards' only fleeting interest in the island was in 1633 when the Dutch moved in. They promptly attacked it.

In 1650 some Englishmen, an assorted bunch of rovers and misfits, had a go at settling the island. They arrived to find that Anguilla was 'filled with alligators and other noxious animals, but the soil was good for raising tobacco and corn, and the cattle imported multiplied very fast'. Salt could also be harvested and this has continued until quite recently.

Anguilla did not really turn out that well as a plantation island, perhaps because the settlers were more interested in other things; soon it was a 'nest of pirates and smugglers and outlaws, dangerous to every neighbouring island and a disgrace to the British name'. But the Anguillian settlers were themselves vulnerable to the usual raids and ransackings of the Caribs and other Europeans. The French defeated them and occupied the island and the Irish attacked a number of times, leaving settlers behind in their turn (you can just hear echoes of Irish in Anguillan English). The defenders had more success in the 18th century, though. In 1744 they repelled a large French force that landed at Rendezvous Bay. The story goes that when the Anguillians ran out of ammunition, they loaded up the weights from their fishing nets in order to keep up their fire.

The early settlers had made what they could of the barren land, renting it from the Crown for the price of 'a fat capon, a kid, or one ear of Indian corn on every feast day of St Michael the Angel'. Slaves were brought to the island, but the estates could not support them, so they were left to grow their own food or fish for four days a week. They were also encouraged to go abroad, using their skills as coopers (barrel-makers) or carpenters to earn a living.

They ventured as far afield as Trinidad and Puerto Rico, dealing in merchandise and practising a bit of smuggling. A tradition of boat-building grew up on the island. At one stage even the Governor was an 'honest old sloop man'. As they sailed, they would send home contributions from the money they earned abroad, 'remittances' that were the back-bone of the economy until very recently.

Initially Anguilla had no Governor and was administered by a notable on the island such as the doctor, who also acted as magistrate, but in 1825 the island was attached to St Kitts for administrative convenience. The Anguillians had very little in common with the people of this successful sugar colony founded on slave-labour, which in any case was about 60 miles away to the south. Occasionally they protested to the British Government, but without success. With little representation in the St Kitts House of Assembly, the Anguillians were treated as poor relations and they had to fight hard even to get their name added to the title of the country St Kitts and Nevis in 1951.

The Revolution

In 1967, when all the British Caribbean colonies were given internal self-rule as 'Associated States' with Great Britain, with the option of Independence not far off, Anguilla suddenly found itself faced with the possibility of Independence in union with St Kitts and Nevis. The islanders promptly staged a revolution. On 30 May 1967, they rounded up the Kittitian policemen and shipped them out, refusing to recognize the authority of the Basseterre Government.

From the beginning the situation bemused outsiders, who wrote it up as 'the mouse that roared' and 'the eel that squealed', but they did not reckon with the determination of the Anguillians, who went as far as staging a tiny invasion (unsuccessful) of St Kitts to pre-empt attempts to take Anguilla by force. They held referenda and wrote their own constitution.

Disbelieving colonial officials were dispatched to persuade the Anguillians to rejoin St Kitts–Nevis, but the islanders were adamant. With political tension mounting in 1969, British troops were sent to occupy the island in an operation which was later dubbed Britain's 'Bay of Piglets' after the invasion of Cuba a few years before. Not a shot was fired, and the soldiers arrived to find themselves welcomed by people singing 'God Save the Queen'. When the troops were withdrawn, the London Metropolitan Police took over. All around them Caribbean countries were shaking off the colonial yoke, but Anguilla decided that it did not want Independence at all. It preferred to remain a Crown Colony of Britain. The whole episode is hilariously retold in Donald Westlake's *Under an English Heaven*, recently republished, available in Anguilla and complete with priceless photographs.

The political solution was long in coming, but eventually in 1982 Anguilla was granted its own constitution, with Ministerial Government headed by a Governor and ministers chosen from a seven-member House of Assembly. The Government is led by Chief Minister Hubert Hughes, leader of an AUP/ADP coalition formed after elections in March 1994.

Today some Anguillians depend on fishing for their livelihood, sailing to catch lobsters, which sell for a very good price and are flown out to hotels as far off as Puerto Rico each evening. But most work in the construction industry or in tourism, which has taken off since the early eighties. On an island where life has been precarious for so long, Anguilla is probably more prosperous now than it ever has been.

Getting There

The modest Wallblake airport in the centre of the island cannot take long-haul flights and so you must make a connection in the Caribbean, but it is usually possible to reach the island in the same day. Transit points are Antigua, Sint Maarten and San Juan. The journey by sea from Marigot, St Martin is perhaps a more charming way to arrive. There is a departure tax of US$6 (EC$16) if you are leaving by air, US$2 (EC$5) by sea.

By Air from the UK: The easiest connections are made in Antigua, where LIAT (✆ 497 2238) links up with the regular British Airways flights to ensure a relatively trouble-free onward journey. An alternative is to take the BA flight to San Juan on Puerto Rico, and connect there on American Eagle. From elsewhere in **Europe**: Air France, KLM and Lufthansa fly to Sint Maarten, from where it is an easy hop by plane or boat.

By Air from the USA: The main gateway for Anguilla is San Juan. American Eagle (✆ 497 3500) has two flights daily from San Juan, where there are easy connections on American Airlines and other carriers with all the large US cities. It is also easy to make connections in Sint Maarten.

By Air from other Caribbean Islands: Winair (Windward Island Airways, ✆ 497 2748) provides an air link from St Thomas and Sint Maarten. LIAT (✆ 497 5000) serves Anguilla from Antigua, San Juan and the Virgin Islands. Finally, the island's carrier, Air Anguilla (✆ 497 2643, fax 497 2982) has daily services from St Thomas and they will charter from San Juan or Antigua.

By Boat: Ferries link the port of Marigot in the French territory of St Martin with Blowing Point on the south of Anguilla. Services leave roughly every 30 minutes during the day and the crossing is 20 minutes. If you can, take the gull-wing powerboat built by Rebel Marine on Anguilla, with an engine that makes a sonorous rumble. You will have to pay a departure tax from St Martin of US$2.

Getting Around

There is an almost mythical **bus** service in Anguilla, a couple of minivans that run from Blowing Point to The Valley, and occasionally on other roads, to an entirely unpredictable schedule. Track it down if you can. Hitch-hiking is workable and may introduce you to some amusing islanders.

Taxis can be arranged at the airport or at Blowing Point and at any of the hotels. Drivers are happy to drop you for the day on a remote beach and then return to collect you. Most will give impromptu tours of the island, but organized tours cost US$40 for a couple of hours. Prices for journeys are fixed (quite expensively) by the Government. Some examples are: the **airport** to Shoal Bay—US$10 (and from **Blowing Point**—US$15), The Valley—US$5 (US$10), Sandy Ground—US$8 (US$10), Cove Castles and the southwestern end of the island—US$20 (US$17).

Car hire gives the most mobility and cars are readily available, from about US$35 plus taxes. A local licence must be obtained, but this is easily done on presentation of a valid licence to the company when you hire, or to the police in The Valley, price US$6. Driving is on the left and the speed limit is 30 mph(!). Traffic usually proceeds at a stately pace, but watch out for the couple of roundabouts and the odd hanging traffic light. Some of the many companies are: **Apex Car Rental** (© 497 2462), **Island Car Rentals** on Airport Road (© 497 2723), and **Tripple K** (© 497 2934), both of which also hire out jeeps (at about US$45 plus taxes). **Scooters** can be hired through **Boo's** Cycle (© 497 2323), just above Sandy Ground and **Sandy Island Enterprises** (© 497 6395) in Road Bay who also have bicycles.

Tourist Information

UK and Europe: The Anguilla Tourist Office, 3 Epirus Road, London SW6 7UJ (© 071 937 7725, fax 071 938 4739).

USA and Canada: Medhurst and Associates Inc, 271 Main St, Northport, NY 11768 (© 516 261 1234, fax 516 261 9606, toll free © 800 553 4939).

On island, information and assistance can be obtained from the helpful office at the **Anguilla Department of Tourism** in the government buildings in the Valley, Anguilla, British West Indies (© 497 2759, fax 497 3091), which is open 8–midday and 1–4pm. There are information booths at the airport and at Blowing Point.

If telephoning from outside the Caribbean, the **IDD code** for Anguilla is 809 497, followed by a four-figure island number. If calling within the island, dial only the last four digits.

In an **emergency**, there is a 24-hour surgery at the Cottage Hospital in The Valley (© 497 2551).

Money

The currency of Anguilla is the Eastern Caribbean dollar (fixed to the US dollar at a rate of about US$1 = EC$2.65). The US dollar, best carried in the smaller denominations, is perfectly acceptable, though you will occasionally receive your change in EC$. If you are on a tight budget, it is better to use EC$. Credit cards are accepted at large and expensive hotels and in some shops, but do not expect to use them in smaller restaurants. **Banking hours**: Mon–Fri 8–3, with an extra couple of hours on Fri afternoons 3–5. **Shops** keep variable hours, though usually with a respectable lunch-break.

Beaches

Anguilla's superb sand makes her beaches some of the best in the Caribbean. There are miles and miles of it, glaringly white and so thick and soft that you stumble through it. Breakers clap and hiss as they race in a flurry of surf towards the palms and the seagrape.

You will not find any crowded beaches on the island, though you can find watersports equipment at the hotels if you want action. There are miles of strand to walk in the cool of the early morning, and you can sizzle to your heart's content in the heat of the day. So much of the coastline is sand that even the harbours are usually on a good beach. Get a little off the beaten track and you will find a whole cove to yourself, glorious, calm and scorching. Two words of warning: beware of manchineel trees, which bear a poisonous apple and will blister you if you sit under them in the rain, and skinny-dipping. Like many West Indians, the Anguillians are modest about nudity and so it is officially not allowed. If beaches are your thing, Anguilla is close to paradise.

Shoal Bay is the island's most popular beach and also one of its finest. Here the mounds of sand are carved into scallop shapes by the meandering waves and you can walk for miles. There are one or two hotels and beach bars to retire to if the heat of the sun gets too much and there are reefs offshore for snorkelling. All essential beach requisites are for hire at Skyline Beach Rentals—'beautiful lounge chairs, elegant floating rafts, long fluffy towels and reliable snorkelling gear'. Headed west there is a tiny cove just before town, **Little Bay**, which is cut out of the cliffs, so secluded that you must go by boat, unless you are prepared to clamber down the rockface (where there are ropes to assist you).

Sandy Ground is a busy half-moon bay with a line of bars and restaurants right on the sand. It is a working bay, with ships unloading at the jetty and yachts at anchor. It is possible to hire watersports equipment here.

Further west there long strips of blinding white sand at **Mead's Bay** and **Barnes Bay**, with hotels standing on the clifftops above them and fantastic sunset views. Both have bars to retreat to in the hotels, and watersports equipment for hire. At the far western end of the island you will find a couple of tiny inlets with golden sand, enclosed by cliffs, which are perfect suntraps.

On the south side of the island the most westerly bay is **Shoal Bay West**, a superb curve of sand where space-age villas cut the skyline and the swimming is impeccable. Headed east you come to the protected cove of **Maunday's Bay**, another magnificent strip of sand that is home to Cap Juluca, whose Moorish domes stick out of the tropical greenery.

Cove Bay has a fine curve of sumptuous sand and after this you come to the 2-mile stretch of **Rendezvous Bay**. It has seen some development lately, but it is good for walking morning or evening and it is easy to find an isolated spot with the hills of St Martin in view. Past Blowing Point, itself a respectable strand, there are fewer beaches until you come to the far east of the island, where you can take an outing to **Mimi Bay** and the wilder **Savannah Bay**. These two are quite windy and they are isolated, so take drinks and a picnic if you will want them. On the north coast is Island Harbour, a gathering point mainly for its beach bars, *see* below. In the far northeast you will find a perfect isolated cove in **Captain's Bay**, the ultimate secluded retreat. Anguilla's uninhabited **offshore cays**—Deadman's Cay, Sombrero, Scrub, Dog, Gorgeous Scilly Cay and Prickly Pear Cay—may sound like a surreal shopping list, but there are some excellent stretches of sand on them and you can arrange to visit on a day trip. Ask at the watersports companies below.

Beach Bars

There are some cool and easy beach bars around the island where you can find a fruit punch or a beer and a salad to fill a gap during the day's beach activity. Between the (relatively) more formal restaurants of Sandy Ground you will find a couple of bars—**Johnno's** and **Tropical Penguin**—two lively bars with meals in the daytime which stay open on into the night. At Shoal Bay on the north coast there are some popular haunts to retreat to: **Uncle Ernie's**, a wooden lean-to which is festooned with photos of satisfied customers and has a grill permanently on the go, and **Madeariman Reef**, an open-sided bar looking over the sand from the trees. A short walk down the sand is the quieter retreat, **Round Rock** Bar, a gazebo built around a tamarind tree.

Yet further east you come to Island Harbour, where **Smitty** has a shack under the palm trees covered with nautical buoys and nets, with chairs scattered in the sandy ground and television relayed to the garden. Offshore you can have a fun day 'liming' and snorkelling on **Gorgeous Scilly Cay**, which Eudoxie Wallace, Gorgeous to his friends, has landscaped with palms, conchshell walls and thatch shelters. Wave from the pier and they will come and pick you up. Both these two have music a couple of times a week in season.

Visible from Road Bay is **Sandy Island**, the archetypal paradise island, just a bar of sand and ten or so palm trees and excellent snorkelling. Perhaps this is where the

Lamb's Navy Rum girl lives. Day trips are arranged easily through **Sandy Island Enterprises** (℃ 497 6395).

Sailing

Anguilla and its offshore islands are popular cruising grounds (particularly with tourists from St Martin next door), and there are some excellent beaches where you anchor and head ashore for a picnic and an afternoon swim. There are, however, many reefs, particularly along the southern shore. The principal bay, and site of the customs office, is Road Bay on the northern shore, a wide harbour protected by a cliff. You will find a supermarket here and a number of good restaurants. West of Road Bay there are good daytime stopovers at Barnes Bay and Mead's Bay and to the east there is a protected anchorage at Crocus Bay, just below the Valley. Some of the best sailing is around the offshore islands: Sandy Island is the archetypal deserted island with just a couple of palm trees, and Prickly Pear is a traditional tourist idyll (there is nothing but a beach bar). Both have anchorages and make a satisfying day's sail and snorkelling from Road Bay. **Customs and immigration** are best completed in Road Bay on the north coast, but it is possible at Blowing Point. Cruising fees are charged in Anguilla. Anchoring is prohibited in Little Bay and Rendezvous Bay and restricted around the offshore cays to certain areas.

Watersports

In Anguilla's electric-blue water are some excellent coral reefs with good **diving** and **snorkelling**. The top spots for snorkelling are Little Bay (*see* 'Beaches' above) and Shoal (another name for reef) Bay. Dive sites are to be found all around the island, particularly towards the western end, where reefs flash with butterflyfish and angelfish or a shimmering cloud of fry, and also on the offshore cays. There are wrecks (some deliberately sunk), where you might see a jackfish or an octopus. Complete instruction and equipment hire are available through **Tamariain Watersports** (℃ 497 2020, fax 497 5125) in Sandy Ground. *A single tank dive costs US$40.* **Mike's Glass-Bottom Boat** (℃ 497 4155) organizes reef tours and snorkelling trips. If you wish to go **windsurfing** in small sunfish and hobie cats, try one of the hotels, perhaps Pineapple Beach. **Sandy Island Enterprises** (℃ 497 6395) go to Sandy Island of course, but also arrange watersports, snorkelling trips and day visits to other islands on *Shauna I* or *II*. If you would like a sunset cruise or day picnic on a catamaran, try *Wildcat* (℃ 497 3111). **Deep-sea fishing**, for wahoo and tuna and sailfish, can be arranged through Sandy Island Enterprises. *A half-day's sail with full tackle costs around US$350.*

There are **tennis courts** at a number of the bigger hotels.

The Valley (population about 800) is Anguilla's capital, though you should not think that this makes it a town; the density of houses is just slightly greater than elsewhere. Some official buildings and a few shops are bunched around a couple of hanging traffic lights. Blink and you will miss it.

Headed west from The Valley, the road moves into more open country very quickly, passing the airport and making towards the developed southwestern tip of the island. Anguilla's plantations were never very successful, but the **Wallblake House** is an attractive great house. Built in the late 18th century, it is set behind a white picket fence and has a cistern similar to those on the islands of Saba and Statia (Sint Eustatius) farther south. The house is private. Driving west there is a side road down to **Sandy Ground**, a small village with some traditional Anguillan houses set on a thin spit of land between the sea and the last of the working salt pans. The pans are disused now, but the water still becomes curiously discoloured, lavender and grey, as the sun and wind continue to do their work. The road snakes further west, throwing off side-roads to **Blowing Point**, the departure point for boats to St Martin and to the hotels and isolated settlements.

Heading north and east from The Valley, you pass quickly into open country once again, which is dotted periodically with Anguilla's attractive old wooden houses and the half-built newer ones. There are a couple of local settlements in this less developed area; one at **Island Harbour** on the north coast, from which many of Anguilla's fishermen set off. On the beach you will see the fishing boats, brightly painted so that they are more visible at sea, and built to a unique Anguillan design. In the main house of the Arawak Beach Resort there is a small display of Amerindian artefacts (plus some reproductions and some exhibits from modern-day Arawaks in Guyana)—*metape* strainers to get the poison juice out of cassava, pottery, cotton spindles and jewellery made of shells.

Anguilla's only historical sites are in this area. Just off the road close to Lower Shoal Bay, the **Fountain** (presently closed for renovation) is contained within a National Park and has a number of Amerindian rock carvings around the island's only reliable source of water, cartoon faces which are each struck by the sun's rays in the course of the year. At **Sandy Hill Bay** are the remains of a 17th-century fort.

Festivals

The main event in the Anguillan calendar is **Carnival**, which takes place in early August. It borrows a lot from other Caribbean carnivals, with floats and dancers 'jumping-up' as they cruise around town in masqueraders' costumes, and calypso competitions, where the Anguillians sing of island life and love. Held at the same time is **Race-week**, unique to Anguilla, the nation of seafarers and boat-builders. Traditional fishing boats are pitted against one another in races from bay to bay around the island.

© (809)–   ***Where to Stay***

There is a good range of accommodation in Anguilla, from a couple of the Caribbean's most exquisite hotels to the simplest guest houses. In between you will find some mid-range hotel accommodation; through the Inns of Anguilla you can get a room at around US$100 a night in season. There are also many condominium complexes. Most of the hotels are set on one or other of Anguilla's pristine beaches. Hotel rooms can be booked in the UK through the **Anguilla Reservation Service** (© 071 937 7725, fax 071 938 4793), but you may prefer to buy a package.

A good alternative is to stay in a villa of which there are many scattered around the island. Rental companies, who will often arrange a car for you, include **Anguilla Connection** (© 809 497 4402, fax 809 497 4402), **Select Villas of Anguilla** and **PREMS** (Property Real Estate Management Services), PO Box 256, The Valley (© 809 497 2596, fax 809 497 3309). Perhaps check them out while you are there before a return visit. The Government levies a room tax of 8% and most hotels charge service at 10%.

Hotels

luxury

The **Malliouhana Hotel**, PO Box 173 (© 497 6111, fax 497 6011) is one of the Caribbean's finest, and it stands on the cliffs above the mile-long stretch of Mead's Beach on Anguilla's northwestern coastline. Tall and slender arches and terracotta tiles on floor and roof give a Mediterranean impression, but the name Malliouhana is distinctly Caribbean, taken from the Indian word for the island. The 55 rooms and suites are luxuriously decorated and many have balconies overlooking the bay and the sunset, which you can linger over in time-honoured tradition. Watersports include windsurfers, skiing and sunfish; there are tennis courts, two pools, a children's centre and a gym with a view. Also a superb restaurant on the cliff-tops, with some of the best food on the island, French cuisine and a wine cellar of around 20,000 bottles. Extremely personable and dependably well run. **Cove Castles**, PO Box 248 (© 809 497 6801, fax 809 497 6051, US © 800 348 4716), is another haven of understated super-luxury, set on the magnificent curve of Shoal Bay West. The 12 rooms stand in striking white villas with windswept geometrical faces, staring at a superb vista of St Martin. Inside they are spacious and elegant, with curved white walls, rattan furniture and each one with a hammock with a view. Villas come with housekeepers and villa (room) service (according to a personalized pre-arranged menu) and plenty of watersports. **Cap Juluca** (© 497 6666, fax 497 6617, US © 800 323 0139) has its own inimitable style— white Moorish domes that rise out of Anguilla's superb southwestern sands, a surreal impression after a day in the Anguillan sun. The 98 rooms, suites and villas are palatial, and the bathrooms are no less than luxurious, jacuzzis in the sunlight. Plenty of watersports, a fitness centre and even croquet.

expensive–very expensive

The **Cinnamon Reef Beach Club**, PO Box 141 (© 497 2727, fax 497 3727), is set in the horseshoe cove of the isolated Little Harbour on Anguilla's southern coast. Villas and suites are set widely spaced in a tropical garden, in modern cottages splashed with bougainvillea and hibiscus, each with a hammock on the terraces. With just 22 rooms, it has a friendly and lazy feel and a pleasant terrace and sitting area with a library overlooking the calm beach and bay. Watersports and tennis, but generally a quiet resort. The **Arawak Beach Resort**, PO Box 98 (© 497 4888, fax 487 4898), takes the theme of the Arawak island idyll to 20th-century levels of comfort. Standing on a breezy cliff there are 14 rooms and suites recalling Arawak names—*coyaba* (heaven), *zemie* (an image of God), *toa toa* (mother) and *bohio* (thatched hut). The rooms are far more than thatched huts now, with huge beds, batique wall prints, Haitian carvings and Guyanese woodwork, sea grass matting and ghostly Amerindian faces on the lampshades. The best of the lazy Arawak life is there. There is a restaurant, **Arietos**, which offers light, Arawak-inspired and vegetarian food. In more typical 20th-century sybaritic style you can try the **Fountain Beach Hotel** (© 497 3491, fax 497 3493, US toll free © 800 342 3491), which is situated on the superb sand of Shoal Bay. There are 10 very comfortable rooms and suites, decorated with bright white tiles and antiques, some with kitchens and balconies looking to the sea. Very private and quiet, with pool, palm garden and a charming Italian restaurant, expensive. **La Sirena**, PO Box 200 (© 497 6827, fax 497 6829, US toll free © 800 331 9358) has a fine setting with buildings clustered around a pool at the western end of Mead's Bay. Very comfortable rooms and a busy atmosphere around the dining room and bar, some entertainment, expensive.

cheap–moderate

The **Rendezvous Bay Hotel**, PO Box 31 (© 497 6549, fax 497 6026, US toll free © 800 274 4893), is a quiet resort in an older Caribbean beach club mould. The rooms stand in blocks and there are some cottages in a sandy garden, each decorated with white tiles and wicker furniture. There is a tennis court and the magnificent Rendezvous Beach just a short walk away, moderate. If you want to be close to the action of Sandy Ground you can try **Sydans Apartments** (© 497 3180, fax 497 5381), cheap to moderate, and for cheaper rooms you can go to The Valley. Try **Florencia's** (© 497 2319) which serves meals, and for simple rooms, try **Norman B's** (© 497 2242) near Crocus Bay and **Lloyd's** (© 497 2351), both cheap.

Self-catering Villas

There is a good range of self-catering accommodation in Anguilla. Rooms and apartments tend to be set in a central building or clustered around a central garden; some will have a restaurant but all have kitchens. Some of the best are: the **Frangipani Beach Club**, PO Box 328 (© 497 6442, fax 497 6440, US toll free © 800 892 4564) which stands on the beachfront in Mead's Bay. The extremely comfortable and spacious rooms are set in a mock Spanish palace with curved roof-tiles and balconies with classical balustrades, very expensive. The **Carimar Beach Club**, PO Box 327 (© 497 6881, fax 497 6071, US toll free © 800 235 8667), has villas and apartments in modern blocks either side of a pretty tropical garden, everywhere exploding with bougainvilllea, leading onto the sand of Mead's Bay. Bright white and modern decor with wicker furniture in large living rooms and patio; one- to three-bedroom apartments, expensive to very expensive. **Shoal Bay Villas**, PO Box 81 (© 497 2051, fax 497 3631, US toll free © 800 722 7045), has an excellent setting lost in the palms of Shoal Bay. There are just 13 individually decorated units standing around a pool, with all the activity of Shoal Bay nearby. There is a dining room, the palm-thatched Reefside Restaurant, which stands beneath the palms on the sand, rooms expensive. There are two less expensive villa hotels in Island Harbour in the northeast: **Harbour Villas** (© 497 4393, fax 497 4196, US reservations © 206 822 0589) are set back from the sea. Simple fan-ventilated bedrooms in five units, full kitchens and living area with wicker furniture and a balcony, moderate. **Harbour Lights**, PO Box 181 (© 497 4435) has four rooms above the waves of Island Harbour. Quiet and simple.

© (809)–   *Eating Out*

Some of the best food in Anguilla is to be found in the hotel dining rooms (try Malliouhana, Cove Castles and Cinnamon Reef, all expensive), but it is worth looking around. There are places where you can have a quiet and intimate evening for two and of course livelier restaurants too. Obviously there is plenty of fish and seafood and it is worth tasting spiny lobster, caught in Anguillan waters (what remains after the rest has been shipped off to St Martin and San Juan). You will find local West Indian haunts where you can pick up a pattie or a chicken leg for lunch and trusted local fare for dinner. Eating out is not cheap in Anguilla, but credit cards are accepted in the major restaurants if you don't want to think about it at the time. Categories are arranged according to the price of a main course: *expensive*—US$18 and above; *moderate*—US$10–18; *cheap*—under US$10.

expensive

Hibernia (© 497 4290) is a small and charming restaurant in Island Harbour in the northeast, well worth making the journey to get there. You dine on a quiet, calm veranda with a view on to a lit garden, with meticulously prepared dishes presented by the owners themselves. The menu is French with Caribbean ingredients and a taste of Thai food—start with a combination of house-smoked fish (wahoo, marlin, tuna and dolphin) or *Tom Yam Taley*, a spicy Thai seafood broth, and follow with *magret de canard poêlé au miel et à la citronelle*, duck in honey and lemon grass. Finish with armagnac prunes in chocolate with chestnut ice-cream. Closed Mon. **Mango's** (© 497 6479) has a charming setting just behind the seagrape trees on Barnes Bay. The veranda is open to the evening breeze and its 'new American' cuisine gives exotic variations on Caribbean food— sesame snapper cooked in a soy sauce marinade and a house speciality of swordfish Caribbean in a gingered mango sauce. Dinner only, closed Tues. In town, **Koalkeel** (© 497 2930) offers a 'Caribbean dégustation' menu, Caribbean and Mediterranean fare in gourmet style, some of it cooked over a coal-kiln or outdoor oven. Ginger barbecued lamb with fungi (cornmeal) and island provisions, or shrimp sautéd in olive oil with couscous. There is a slightly rarified setting on the veranda of an old-island house. Set on the beach in Sandy Ground, **Riviera** (© 497 2833) has a charming, meandering dining room set under palm trees. The menu is French, with Provençal specialities, and you will start with a *ti punch* and the oyster bar, and then follow with a crayfish bisque and *daurade grillé*, fillet of dorado served in a lime butter sauce. The style is light sauces and *nouvelle* presentation, with set menus and salads at lunchtime for a good break from the beach.

moderate

As the name might suggest, **Smugglers Grill** (© 497 3728) has a secluded nautical air, tucked away in a quiet waterfront setting in Forest Bay on the south coast. You dine on a wooden deck, surrounded by oars, barrels and rigging, seemingly afloat as the waves break beneath you. Much of the food is grilled, and served with French style. Lobster specialities, served as a soup or in sauces from around the world—*moscovite, à l'indienne* and *exotique* (from Southeast Asia)—and some Caribbean dishes, grilled filet of mahi-mahi in a lemon-herb cream sauce, all topped off with flavoured Caribbean rums. Good value and a fun night out. There are a number of restaurants down in Sandy Ground: just behind the beach itself is **Ripples** (© 497 3380), a brightly decorated dining room with window-shutters on stilts. Check out the award-winning chef's red pepper snapper or pasta ripples, with seafood and vegetables in a light creamy sauce. The **Ship's Galley** (© 497 2040) has a pretty waterfront setting with white trelliswork hung with tropical flora. Lunchtime burgers and salads, dinner seafood speciality (fresh whelks) or a fillet of local catch. Not far off is **Chillis**, set in a red and yellow dining room painted with cactus, which serves Mexican fare. For a local meal you can go to **Lucy's Harbour View** (© 497 6253) where you overlook Sandy Ground from a veranda in a modern Anguillian house. Red snapper speciality, but other classic dishes like conch fritters and curry goat with a tonnage of ground provisions or seasoned rice.

cheap

A cheaper local meal can be found at the **Aquarium** in South Hill: stews, curries and local whelks on an upstairs veranda. There are other simple and local restaurants around town. You can get a roti or a fry chicken at the **Pepperpot** or in the **Roti Hut** opposite the airport (with its accompanying drive-in ice-cream stop).

Bars and Nightlife

The best bars are really the beach bars—there is a regular Sunday afternoon crowd at Shoal Bay—and the hotel bars. If you are feeling homesick for an English draught beer, then you will find Double Diamond, John Smith's and Guinness at **Roy's Place** just above the beach in Crocus Bay.

Anguillan nightlife is quiet (the locals sometimes take the ferry over to St Martin for the nightclubs there, and there are also casinos in Dutch Sint Maarten if that's your thing). There is sometimes a barbecue or a band at one of the hotels: **La Sirena** has a weekly show by a troupe of dancers, with the Anguillians often in attendance. It is definitely worth joining in the jump-ups at **Johnno's** in Sandy Ground, which gets wild and crowded at the weekends and at holidays.

Sint Maarten

Sint Maarten/Saint Martin is the smallest island in the world to be shared by two nations. The southern half is one of the Netherlands Antilles, a part of the Kingdom of Holland, and the northern part is a *commune* of France (*see* p.173). The distinct personalities of the two sides of the island are still just recognizable, though with the building mania of the last twenty years it has taken on a universal wash of concrete, and the feel of the island has changed irreparably.

Of Sint Maarten's 17 square miles, between 4 and 5 of them are under water in lagoons and salt ponds. Above the waterline, Sint Maarten is covered in yellow-green scrub, with startlingly steep hills that rise to around 1200ft. From the heights there are excellent views—Sint Maarten is surrounded by islands.

It is rather like a modern-day Babel—overdeveloped and confused. It has excellent beaches, dependable Caribbean sunshine and loose development laws. Together these are enough to have brought development corporations swooping in. They have built with abandon, throwing up resorts on any strip of sand they can find. Sint Maarten bulges with glittering casinos, shopping malls and fast-food joints. Hotels come in complexes, and tourists by the jumbo-load.

And the languages of Babel are there too. You will hear the drawl of a Texan vacationer alongside the clipped vowels of an Englishman on holiday; Dutch, French and Spanish fill the air. English-speaking West Indians have flooded in from down-island, Dominican girls sit and chat in upbeat Spanish, you will hear Haitian kreyol and the babble of Papiamento, the extraordinary language from the Dutch Windward Islands.

Sint Maarten has also adopted Sint Eustatius's traditional role as the Dutch entrepôt in the Windwards. The streets of the capital, Philipsburg, are lined with air-conditioned boutiques, brimfull with duty-free bargains. And cruise-liners disgorge still more tourists on one-day shopping extravaganzas. It is mercantile mayhem. The confusion is complete. But after centuries in the doldrums, the island is more prosperous now than it has ever been. The material benefits are obvious, but since tourism is a difficult industry, it could all be gone tomorrow, so who can blame them for taking advantage of it while the going is good?

But a million tourists arriving each year cannot but have an effect on island life—just imagine a national consciousness that is made up of

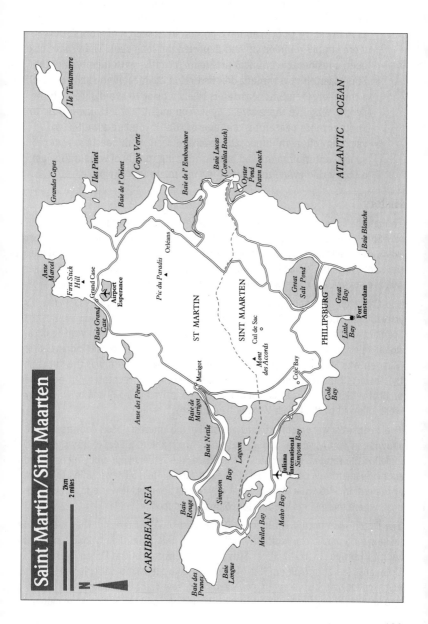

Saint Martin/Sint Maarten

N

CARIBBEAN SEA

2km
2 miles

ATLANTIC OCEAN

Ile Tintamarre

Grandes Cayes

Ilet Pinel

Caye Verte

Baie de l'Orient

Baie de l'Embouchure

Anse Marcel

First Stick Hill

Grand Case

Baie Grand Case

Airport Esperance

Baie Lucas (Coralita Beach)

Oyster Pond

Dawn Beach

Pic du Paradis

Orleans

ST MARTIN

SINT MAARTEN

Cul de Sac

Great Salt Pond

Baie Blanche

Anse des Pères

Marigot

Mont des Accords

PHILIPSBURG

Great Bay

Fort Amsterdam

Little Bay

Baie de Marigot

Baie Nettle

Cole Bay

Cole Bay

Lagoon

Simpson Bay

Baie Rouge

Juliana International

Simpson Bay

Mullet Bay

Maho Bay

Baie des Prunes

Baie Longue

waiters and maids. Dutch Sint Maarten officially has a population of around 30,000, and there is also a large number of illegals, perhaps as many as 10,000, who have poured in in search of work (5000 were simply rounded up and deported not long ago). There have also been considerable political problems recently, with members of the Sint Maarten government on corruption charges. If you style yourself a traveller, then Sint Maarten is really a place to avoid, although the people who live there swear by it. You might take a look *en route* to another more peaceful island nearby. But if you like a well-oiled vacation (often an impeccable package deal), with beaches, watersports, entertainment and a truly amazing variety of restaurants just a buggy-ride away, then Sint Maarten might be your place.

History

Though the PR moguls may swear otherwise, it is unclear whether Columbus ever saw Sint Maarten. He might have seen it on his second voyage, on 12 November 1493, as he sailed past Statia (Sint Eustatius) and Saba. He did name an island after the saint (St Martin's Day is 11 November), but this was probably Nevis. As other sailors came by, the name was fixed as Sint Maarten.

The Caribs and Arawaks continued to live here on and off for 140 years after his arrival. Settlement was difficult as there was no permanent water-supply. But the Spaniards were not initially interested in the island anyway, and only made occasional raids to take people to work in their gold-mines. To the Indians, Sint Maarten was Sualouiga, supposed to mean 'land of salt'. And it was the salt pans that attracted the first Europeans to Sint Maarten, as they ventured out from the original settlement in St Kitts. Some Frenchmen arrived in 1629 and in 1631 they were followed by the Dutch West India Company.

The Spaniards were spurred into action by the interest these countries were showing in Sint Maarten, and in 1633 they arrived with a fleet of fifty ships and expelled the settlers. But whatever they tried, the settlers kept creeping back and so the Spaniards eventually decided to put a garrison here. They fortified the point at the entrance to what is now Great Bay. By all accounts it was a miserable outpost, where the soldiers had rats for company and food.

The Dutch soon occupied Curaçao off the coast of Venezuela, but they were still looking for a port in the northern Caribbean, *en route* from their colonies in Brazil back to Europe. In 1644, Peter Stuyvesant, a director of the Dutch West India Company, led an attack on Sint Maarten to take the island back. It was in this engagement that Stuyvesant (later Governor of New York, then called Nieuw Amsterdam) was hit by a cannon-ball and lost his leg. In 1648 the Spaniards abandoned the garrison in Sint Maarten and the Dutch and French soon made their way back on to the island.

The agreement on sharing the island dates from 1648, and the traditional story tells of a Dutchman and a Frenchman setting off in opposite directions, with a bottle of liquor apiece to keep them going, walking around the coast until they met, whereupon a line was to be drawn between the two points. How the French got the bigger share is explained variously: the Dutchman's gin made him sluggish/he took time out under a tree/the wily, wine-drinking Frenchman sent a girl to waylay him (delete as applicable). The sad drab truth of the matter is that the two sides decided that they would do well to stop skirmishing and so they signed a treaty on a hill that came to be called Mount Concordia. The salt pans remained common property and the two sides arranged that they would not fight each other even if their mother-countries went to war. This happened many times and the treaty was broken with the same regularity. The island changed hands 16 times, often with British involvement. The communities had little to do with each other except to march over and skirmish on the other side, and so it was not until the 20th century that a road was built to link the two halves of the island.

Sint Maarten saw some small prosperity as a plantation island, cultivating tobacco and growing provisions for nearby Sint Eustatius in the boom years of the 18th century. Sugar and cotton were grown, and another industry that continued into the 20th century was the harvesting of salt from the inland ponds. At its height, Sint Maarten produced 4 million kg.

In 1848 the French emancipated their slaves in Saint Martin. Many of the Dutch slaves fled across the border, staying there until the Dutch declared emancipation in 1863. Gradually Sint Maarten's fortunes waned and it became poor and forgotten. Many of the islanders left in search of work elsewhere. And so it remained until about thirty years ago, when the tourist industry started to grow. In the 1950s, the population of the Dutch side dropped as low as 1500 but has increased out of all proportion since then.

© (599 5)– ## Getting There

Most flights arrive at Princess Juliana airport which is something of an air crossroads for this area of the Caribbean. It is particularly busy on Sunday afternoons, when many organized tours change over. A departure tax of US$10 is payable except for destinations within the Dutch Caribbean.

By Air from Europe: The French connections are the best. Air France (© 54212) operates three times a week from Paris and there are charter airlines to other French cities. There is a weekly flight from Amsterdam on KLM (© 54240), and one from Frankfurt on Lufthansa (© 52040).

By Air from the USA: American Airlines (© 53304) flies in direct from Miami and New York, and there are plenty of connections from other American cities through their hub San Juan. Continental (© 53444) and ALM (the Dutch Caribbean carrier, © 54240) also fly from New York.

By Air from other Caribbean Islands: Sint Maarten is well served from around the Caribbean. Winair (© 54210) is based in Sint Maarten and flies to all the nearby islands. LIAT (© 54203) flies hopper schedules along the island chain and touches most of the islands from San Juan, Puerto Rico down to Antigua and on further south. ALM flies daily to Curaçao, Aruba and Caracas, with occasional flights to San Juan, Santo Domingo and Port of Spain. There is a **ferry boat** from Marigot on the French side to Anguilla.

Getting Around

A stream of **buses** link Philipsburg to Marigot and Grand Case. Only the occasional bus strays onto the airport road. The fares are US$1–2 depending on your destination and buses are quite frequent until 10 or 11pm between Marigot and Philipsburg. Buses leave from Back Street in Philipsburg and in the country it is best to wait at recognized bus stops. **Hitch-hikers** will find that a large proportion of the thousands of cars on Sint Maarten pass without stopping. If you are patient, it works fine.

Taxis are the government-approved, quite expensive, tourist-recommended method of travel and they wait in superabundance at Juliana airport and in town. They are not metered, but rates are fixed by the Tourist Board. Some sample prices are: Juliana **airport** to Philipsburg—US$8, Marigot—US$8, Grand Case—US$16–18. From **Philipsburg** to Marigot—US$8, Grand Case—US$16. In the unlikely case that you cannot flag one down, there is a taxi-stand just behind the court house in Philipsburg, and you can also arrange them through any hotel.

Tours of Sint Maarten are available, though there is not much to see apart from the views of the island and other islands. You will ride from shop to hilltop to restaurant in a little safari buggy. Tours can be arranged through any hotel desk (they will pick you up) or through **Sint Maarten Sightseeing Tours** (© 52753) or **Island Reps Tours** (© 52392), US$15 for about 3½ hours. If you would like to tour by **helicopter**, Sint Maarten offers that too: **St Martin Helicopters** fly out of Juliana airport (© 44287).

If you want to test out the different beaches in the day and French restaurants at night, it is worth hiring a **rental car**, of which plenty are available from around US$35–40 per day or $45–50 for a jeep, plus insurance. Foreign driving licences are valid in Sint Maarten and driving is on the right-hand side of the road. Many hire companies are based just outside the airport, but companies will also deliver to the hotels. There are far too many cars on the island, so expect traffic jams in the three small towns. Some local as well as big international rental companies are: **Opel Car Rental** (℗ 54324), with offices just east of Juliana airport, **Caribbean Auto Rentals** (℗ 45211) on Union Road in Cole Bay, **Avis** (℗ 42316) in Cole Bay, **Budget** (℗ 54274) within walking distance of the airport building and **Hertz** (℗ 54314).

Sint Maarten is an ideal dropping-off point for four other islands, all of which are served by air and also by boat. **Anguilla**, the enigmatic British Crown Colony, is just a 20-minute ferry ride out of Marigot (in a gullwing speed-boat) and **St Barts**, perhaps the most chic piece of France anywhere, is 12 miles southeast of St Martin, reached aboard *White Octopus* or *Eagle* from Bobby's Marina, Great Bay (both ℗ 24096). **Island Reps Tours** (℗ 52392) arranges tours by plane to nearby islands with Winair.

The two other Dutch Windward Islands are easily reached: **Saba**, where pretty gingerbread villages are clustered on sheer volcanic slopes, is an hour's sail away in the motorboat *The Edge* and **Statia**, once the region's richest trading port (then known as the Golden Rock), is best reached by plane. **Winair** (℗ 42230) flies to these islands a couple of times a day from Juliana airport, return about US$60.

Tourist Information

There is no Tourist Office dealing specifically with the Dutch Caribbean in **Britain**. It is best to write to New York or to the islands themselves. In **Holland**, contact the Cabinet of the Minister Plenipotentiary of the Netherlands Antilles at Badhuisweg 175, NL 2597 JP, 'S Gravenhage, The Hague (℗ 070 512811).

In the **US**, you can get information from the Sint Maarten Tourist Bureau, 275 7th Avenue, New York, NY 10001 (℗ 212 989 0000, fax 212 242 0001} and in **Canada** from 243 Ellerslie Avenue, Willowdale, Ontario, M2N 1Y5 (℗ 416 223 3501, fax 416 223 6887).

On **Sint Maarten** itself the main Tourist Information Office is in the Imperial Building, 23 Walter Nisbett's Road, overlooking the lagoon, but there is also an information desk on the waterfront (just where the launches drop the cruise-ship passengers) and a booth at Juliana airport. Open weekdays 8–noon and 1–5. On the French side, there is a small Tourist Information office on the harbour in Marigot, open 9–12.30 and 2–5. There are also quite a few strategically placed information offices which encourage you to visit the time-share complexes as well as giving tourist information. The Sint Maarten tourist industry is well organized, and you will be bombarded with brochures and magazines telling you what to do and where to score your duty-free bargains from the moment of your arrival. The magazine most worth reading goes by the unlikely name of *Discover*, and is produced in tandem by the Tourist Offices from both sides of the island.

To telephone Sint Maarten from abroad, dial **IDD code** 599 5 followed by the 5-digit local number. Within Sint Maarten dial just the five digits, and from Saba or Sint Eustatius, dial 5 and then the 5-figure number. Phoning from the Dutch to the French side, dial 06 and then the six-digit number; from the French to the Dutch side dial 3 followed by the five digits. There are no coin-boxes on the French side and so you will need to buy a *télé-carte* from the post office or the few newsagents that stock them.

In the case of a medical **emergency**, the Sint Maarten Medical Centre is on Front Street in Philipsburg (℅ 31111).

Money

All transactions in tourist hotels and restaurants on both sides of the island can be carried out in US dollars. The official currency on the Dutch side is the Netherlands Antilles florin/guilder, which is fixed to the US dollar (rate US$1 = NAFl 1.78), but you will only see it if you are in a local super-market or on a bus. Where there might be confusion, make sure which currency you are dealing in. NA florins are not accepted on the French side.

Credit cards are widely accepted on the Dutch side, as are traveller's cheques. Personal cheques are not accepted. You can change money at any of the hotel front-desks, but the rate will not be as good as at a bank. **Banks**, of which there are five or six in Philipsburg, keep hours of 8.30–3 on weekdays with an extra hour on Friday afternoons, 4–5.

General **shopping** hours are 8–noon and 2–6, Mon–Sat, with hours extended to Sunday morning if there is a cruise ship in town. Sint Maarten is a free port and so there is no duty.

Beaches

The beaches all over the island are excellent (*see also* Saint Martin, p.178). In the irregular, indented coastline, wave action has ground down the coral and pushed up the grains in blinding-white mounds of sand on the shore. And with so many resorts and complexes, every conceivable activity is available on Sint Maarten. Modern-day knights joust on their jet-skis, dipping and darting on the waves, inspected from above by para-sailors and by scuba divers from below. Screaming children can be frightened into rapt silence by being dragged around the bay on a high-speed sausage. Senior citizens ply the water sedately in pedalos. If you go over to the French side there are also one or two nude beaches and topless bathing is perfectly acceptable (this is becoming more common on the Dutch side). You will find facilities of some sort on all the beaches in Dutch Sint Maarten—some hotels have a shower room, for which they make a charge. A word of warning: there has been a certain amount of theft on the beaches and so you are advised not to leave belongings unattended.

Cupecoy Beach is a series of suntraps close to the border with the French side at the western end of the island, all with a cracking view of the sunset. Coves with golden sand slope gently into the sea beneath 50ft cliffs. At the northern end of the beach nude bathing is permitted. For Sint Maarten Cupecoy is relatively secluded, though you are hardly likely to be alone. **Mullet Bay Beach** is a classic stretch of Caribbean sand in the mile-long sweep of a gently curving bay. It is also Sint Maarten's busiest, with the thousands of guests of the nearby hotels, transported by the buggy-load. All watersports are available and there are plenty of shaded retreats, palm-thatch umbrellas, where you can replace the fluids lost steaming in the sun.

There is a sign warning you that low-flying jumbos can ruin your bathing at the end of **Maho Bay**. Hotels hover above most of its length, making it another busy beach, buzzing with windsurfers and wetbikers. If the going gets too hot, you can always retreat to the terrace and watch the approach path of the incoming aeroplanes. **Simpson Bay** is a 1-mile-long half-moon sweep just south of the airport, quiet for Sint Maarten, but popular with windsurfers. One or two of Sint Maarten's smaller easy-going hotels and guest houses are located here, so you can get a drink or lunch in the unpressurized environment of a beach club.

Philipsburg itself has a reasonable strip of sand with a magnificent view of **Great Bay** and on to Saba just below Front Street. Perhaps a moment to take a walk before getting back into the shopping fray and exercising your credit card in another bout of impulse-buying. There is a fine strip of sand on the Atlantic coast of the island at **Dawn Beach**. There are a couple of hotels here, but the crowds do not usually penetrate this far and it is relatively quiet. The beach has a view of the dawn sun and of St Barts, but on a windy day the sea will be too rough for comfort.

Sailing

The island of St Maarten (both halves of it) is the sailing hub of the northeastern Caribbean. The facilities are extensive, with full repair yards, busy marinas and of course excellent provisioning in the many supermarkets (on both sides of the island). There are good possibilities for sailing around the island and then there are the islands of Anguilla and St Barts to which you can take a tour for a couple of days and more.

The busiest area on the Dutch side is in Great Bay, at the head of which lies Philipsburg, the capital of Dutch Sint Maarten. Here you will find two marinas, Bobby's Marina and the Great Bay marina. All the important **yachting services**, including sail-makers, chandleries, boatyards and workshops, are there, and the town, with its restaurants and shops, is just a short walk away. There are good **anchorages** out in the bay. Headed west, past a couple of daytime stopovers including Little Bay, there is an entrance to Simpson Bay lagoon at the eastern end of Simpson Bay itself. The lagoon is an excellent area of protected water and there are a number of marinas there, the plushest of which is Port de Plaisance; also try Island Water World in the southeast. Pelican Marina can be fun in the early evening. All yachting requisites are available: fuel, water and provisioning, and land-based activities too. Back out in the Caribbean sea you can head for the magnificent beaches that run up to the western tip and over to the French side.

You can clear **customs and immigration** in Philipsburg on the Dutch side (and in Marigot on the French side). You should also clear customs when you move from one side to the other. For major repairs go to **Marine Services** (✆ 22366) at **Bobby's Marina** in Great Bay or to **Island Water World** (✆ 45310).

Watersports

Sint Maarten's well-oiled tourist machine offers the full range of watersports. Most large hotels have snorkelling and scuba gear, windsurfers and small sailing craft on offer to their guests: more exotic sports like para-sailing and jet-skis are easily found on the busier beaches. If you are travelling independently and wish to hire sports equipment, you can use the hotels' rental companies. The main centres on the Dutch side are **Maho Watersports** (✆ 44387) and its opposite number on Simpson Bay Lagoon, **Lagoon Cruises and Watersports** (✆ 52898), **Pelican Marina** (✆ 42640) in Mullet Bay and **Ocean Explorers** (✆ 45252) in Simpson Bay.

Windsurfers can get gear at the places above, but advanced sailors will find the best winds on the French side, at Baie de l'Orient and Baie de l'Embouchure on the northeast coast. **Waterskiing** can be fixed up in the main bays and lagoons. *A half-hour outing costs around US$40.* You will get a somewhat gentler ride behind a motorboat and the added attraction of a nice view of the hotels if you opt for **para-sailing** *at around US$30 for a 15-minute flight.* And if you would like to take out a **jetski**, try **Yamaha Wave Runners** (✆ 53663) on Simpson Bay Lagoon or **Beach Boy** on Front Street in town.

Deep-sea fishing trips can be arranged with *Zing* (℃ 22167) at Great Bay Marina or the major operators above. *A half-day casting for tuna, tarpon and sailfish costs around US$400.* If you would prefer to admire the marine life in more peaceable circumstances, Sint Maarten has some good **snorkelling** grounds on the off-shore reefs. Try the rocks at the end of Little Bay and Simpson Bay, where you will see shoals of pink and yellow fish dip and dart. On the rockier east coast the reefs at Dawn Beach are good, but best of all are the small islands off the French side, Ilet Pinel and Ile Tintamarre (also called Flat Island).

Scuba divers can arrange dives and instruction with the main concessionaires as well as through **Little Bay Watersports** (℃ 22333) at the Little Bay Hotel and the **Tradewinds Dive Centre** (℃ 54387) in the Great Bay Marina in Philipsburg. Forests of coral, plied by angelfish and squirrelfish, can be found on the east coast of the island and off the south coast is the wreck of the HMS *Proselyte*, cannons and anchor encrusted, which sank in 1801. *A single tank dive costs around US$40.* There are any number of glass-bottom boats and some semi-submersibles and you can even walk on the bottom in an aerated helmet with **Ocean Explorers'** Sea Walk (℃ 45252) in Simpson Bay, if you can bear the embarrassment.

Other Sports

Activities for landlubbers include **golf** at the Mullet Bay Resort (℃ 52801), where there is an 18-hole course backing on to the lagoon. All equipment can be rented and there are pros to improve your game. *Green fees are very expensive at around US$125 in season for the 18 holes*, includes cart. Residents of the hotel pay half price and have preference in teeing off. There are about fifty **tennis** courts on the island, many floodlit. Contact the larger hotels. It is even possible to go for an early-morning dip on **horseback** through the **Crazy Acres Riding Centre** (℃ 42793).

Philipsburg

Philipsburg has just four streets, stretched out along the full length of a sand-bar that separates the Great Salt Pond from Great Bay. The Head of Town lies in the east and the Foot of Town in the west. Philipsburg is being rebuilt in concrete, but among the air-conditioned malls and modern office-blocks you will see a few old traditional gingerbread homes.

Front Street (Voor Straat) sells itself as the 'Shopping Centre of the Leewards' and the arcades and alleys (*steegjes*) manage successfully to delay most of the cruise-ship arrivals that come in safari-boats (the marine equivalent of the tourist bus), to Wathey Square, the little central square known locally as **de Ruyterplein**. Back Street (Achter Straat), where the harvested salt was once stored in vast white stacks, has the administrative buildings and churches.

There is a **museum**, *open weekdays 10–4, Sat10–12, adm*, on Front Street, set upstairs in an old town house, where island archaeology and history are revealed in pottery shards, Spanish buttons and pipes, colonial maps (reprints of historical maps are for sale), china plates and recent marine recoveries. There are also a number of galleries in the island, of which the best is probably **Greenwith Gallery**, set in an arcade off Front Street (opposite Barclay's Bank), where you will see work by artists from Sint Maarten and the rest of the Caribbean.

Behind Philipsburg is the **Great Salt Pond**, common to both nations in the 17th century, when salt was important for preserving meats that could not be frozen. Since the industry folded in 1949, land has been reclaimed to expand Philipsburg.

Much of the local life has been squeezed out of Philipsburg, but it can still be lively to hear the medley of languages—the unaccustomed stream of not-quite Spanish is Papiamento. Now people tend to live in the suburbs behind the salt pond.

Around the Island

The Sint Maarten countryside has little to offer. Much of it is as overgrown as the beaches, with houses rather than hotels. But the coast has superb views looking south to the other islands, grey stains on the horizon on a hazy day, but magnified and green if tropical rains have washed the sky. You can often see St Kitts about 45 miles away and Nevis is very occasionally visible from Cole Bay Hill. An 'international' lifestyle has taken over in most areas of the island, but in the traditional villages (like Cul de Sac and Dutch Quarter), swollen with hotel-workers now, you get an idea of Caribbean life in the raffle-ticket booths (selling tickets for the Puerto Rican and Dominican raffles as well as the Dutch Caribbean raffles) and the limers hanging around the superettes.

At the point on the western arm of Great Bay are the ruins of a fort built by the Spaniards in the 1630s. They demolished it when they abandoned the island and the remains were rebuilt by the Dutch and named **Fort Amsterdam**. The small **Zoological and Botanical Gardens**, *adm*, are on the Madame Estate behind the salt pond; there you will see Caribbean and South American animals including the racoon and the ocelot wildcat, with a special hands-on area for kids.

The route to the French side of the island leads from Cole Bay. The border is marked by a small obelisk, but there are no formalities.

Festivals

Carnival is held in April, with celebrations along traditional Caribbean carnival lines, including calypso singing and costumed parades through the streets of Philipsburg. Official holidays include Queen Juliana's birthday on

30 April (and you can always nip over to the French side on Bastille Day, 14 June). A day shared by both halves of the island is St Maarten's day on 11 November, or Concordia Day on the Dutch side.

© (599 5)–   **Where to Stay**

Many hotels in Sint Maarten have recently been built and seem to be no more than speculative investments. An infestation of condominiums encrusts the Dutch side, and literally every available area of beach space is developed. But you will find one or two small hotels with character and charm, particularly in the Simpson Bay area. Many offer 'efficiencies' (self-catering apartments). Remember that hotels usually add a 15% charge (sometimes 20%), 10% (15%) for service and the statutory government tax of 5%.

expensive–very expensive

The two most charming (and most expensive) hotels are on the island's secluded east coast: the **Dawn Beach**, PO Box 389 (© 22929, fax 24421, US © 800 351 5656), has attractive cabins lost in 16 acres of tropical grounds. They are well decorated in pastel shades with bamboo furniture and kitchenettes and balconies. Quite large with 155 rooms, but the setting is a superb beach and there is a nice central area with a pool and a restaurant. A little isolated, so you may well need a car. At the smaller **Oyster Pond Hotel**, PO Box 239 (© 22206, fax 25695, US © 800 839 3030), the rooms are arranged round a shady courtyard, looking outwards across Oyster Pond or out towards St Barts. There are 40 very comfortable rooms, with air-conditioning if you want it, but constant sea breezes, and a slightly rarefied atmosphere (no children under ten). This too is on the beach and there are watersports if you want them, also tennis courts. The **Divi Little Bay Beach Resort**, PO Box 61 (© 22333, fax 23911, US © 800 367 3484), is just outside Philipsburg on the western arm of Great Bay, overlooking Little Bay on the other side. The 220 rooms stand in lines above the pool and in mock-Spanish blocks on the point, where you will find suites of high luxury with balconies and jacuzzis. Facilities include watersports and diving, tennis and entertainment around the pool or in the discotheque. If you like a big resort, this is quieter and lower-key than most. **La Vista**, PO Box 40 (© 43005, fax 43010, US © 800 223 9815), is a purpose-built resort but it has a nice air of seclusion. It is not on the beach and it is quite a way from town, but has a pool and terraces which look over the Caribbean Sea. It has 24 junior and penthouse suites decorated in high Caribbean pastel in very comfortable cottages, with kitchenettes and all other 20th-century conveniences.

Almost invisible in the recent concrete explosion, there is a hotel with distinct old-time Caribbean style, the **Passanggrahan Royal Guest House**, PO Box 151 (℗ 23588, fax 22885, US toll free ℗ 800 223 9815), on Front Street, formerly the Government rest house. The reception area and restaurant are set in a charming green and white town house with gingerbread woodwork and louvred shutters, overlooking an overgrown palm garden. There is an old-fashioned air in the high-backed wicker chairs and the mellow portraits and it is right on the sand. Some of the 30 units are in the main house, but a new modern block has been built to take the rest. And some of the best of Sint Maarten, small and easy-going hotels and guest houses on the beach, can be found on **Simpson Bay**, a fantastic south-facing beach. **Mary's Boon**, PO Box 2078 (℗ 54235, fax 53403), is a very low-key retreat with an old-time Caribbean ambience. Guests gather in the main house, where there is a small library and a charming bar and dining room on a balcony above the waves. A colour theme of black and white runs through the buildings, which are linked to the main house by walkways through the garden of palm and flamboyant. There are 12 big rooms with white walls and wicker furniture, kitchenettes, no children under 16. Not far down the beach is the **Horny Toad**, PO Box 397 (℗ 54323, fax 53316, US reservations ℗ 617 729 3171), which has a variety of apartments scattered around a sandy garden. Eight units, some of them in the classic Caribbean main house on the beach, all with kitchenettes and private balconies. A friendly air, expensive. The pink **Residence la Chatelaine**, PO Box 2056 (℗ 54269, fax 53195), is also on Simpson Bay and the pink of its walls contrast strongly with the turquoise of the sea and the swimming pool above which it sits. There are 17 neat and plush one- and two-bedroom apartments set in a garden of palm and sea-grape. All have kitchenettes and some four-poster beds. The mellow **Trade Winds Inn**, PO Box 3038 (℗ 54206, fax 54796), has 10 quite comfortable rooms in a modern block at the other end of the beach. One- and two-bedroom suites with full kitchens and patios, pool on a deck right above the sea, moderate.

very cheap–cheap

The cheapest accommodation is in Philipsburg. Simple rooms at **Jose's Guesthouse** (℗ 22231) on Back Street, at nearby **Lucy's Guesthouse** (℗ 22995) and also at **Marcus Guesthouse** (℗ 22419) on Front Street. If you would prefer to stay in Cole Bay, on the road to the French side, you can stay at **George's Guest House** (℗ 45363), where there are 10 rooms with private baths and fan ventilation.

Sint Maarten is as cosmopolitan in cuisine as it is in languages and so you will find a bewildering selection of restaurants—anything from Mexican to Vietnamese, supported by an endless range of burger and pizza joints. Dutch food is not widely available, although Dutch East Indian is. The more upmarket restaurants are usually French or Italian, and it is not necessary to cross to the French side for really good French cooking, though there are certainly restaurants worth visiting there (*see* p.184). Reservations are advisable in season; most restaurants accept credit cards. Generally speaking, eating out in Sint Maarten is expensive and you can expect a 10–15% service charge to be added to your bill. Categories are arranged according to the price of a main course: *expensive*—US$18 and above; *moderate*—US$10–18; *cheap*—under US$10.

expensive

The most elegant evening out is at **Spartaco** (© 45379), which is set in a 200-year-old coral-rock house restored and surrounded by glass-fronted galleries which look out onto a tropical garden. The cuisine is Italian—*gamberoni Spartaco*, grilled shrimp sautéd in tomato sauce with garlic and mustard, or *sovrana di pollo primavera al marsala*, a breast of chicken sautéd in a marsala wine sauce. Another calm and stylish dining room can be found at **Le Perroquet** (© 54339) on Airport Road, where you sit among wooden parrots and tropical greenery and with a view through louvred windows on stilts. The menu is French with some concessions to the Caribbean: *filet de mérou à l'oseille*, grouper in a sorrel and white wine sauce, service brisk but friendly, closed Mon. **Le Pavillon** (© 54254) is one of the island's prettiest and most intimate restaurants, in a Bohemian setting of rough plastered walls, wooden floorboards and gold decor, right on the waterfront in Simpson Bay. French cuisine; *cassoulet de la mer*, shrimps, scallops and other seafood in a tomato broth, to follow a fine sunset view and an easy air. There are some good restaurants just above the waves on the Philipsburg waterfront; you will find another very popular Italian restaurant there, **Da Livio** (© 22690), set on a wooden terrace. *Aragosta fra diavolo* (lobster in spicy red sauce) or the *manicotti della casa* (with ricotta cheese, spinach and tomato). Wines from the Venice area. Closed Sun. The French restaurant **Antoine's** (© 22964) has a very pretty terrace setting with blue awnings above the waves. *Canard montmorency* or grouper in almonds, followed by *profiteroles* or a chocolate mousse. And if you would like the flavour of the Dutch East Indies in the Dutch West Indies, try the **Wajang Doll** (© 22687) at the foot of town on Front

Street. This is set in a pretty creole house, but the fare is Indonesian: *nasi goreng* and dragon-mouthed *sambals*, moderate to expensive.

moderate

Sint Maarten also has plenty of easy-going restaurants with a nautical setting, on a deck in the marinas or above the lagoon. The **Seafood Galley** is in Bobby's Marina, with a pub-style interior and a seafood restaurant at the side. Start with the **Raw Bar**—oysters, clams and rock crab claws—followed by creole shrimp or soft-shelled crabs in creole butter. There are a couple of very popular cafés at the entrance to the Maho Bay complex, **Orient Express** and **Chéri's Café**. You might also try the **Old Rock Café**, which stands on a huge rock and serves solidly international fare; steaks, kebabs and Caribbean fish. Good value moderate meals can be found at **Turtle Pier** on Airport Road, a deck sticking out onto the lagoon.

cheap

Among the delis in Philipsburg, you can get a pizza or some rice 'n' peas at **Ric's Place**, a sports and video bar on Front Street.

Bars and Nightlife

In town you will find a number of daytime cafés and bars along Front Street, including **Barrymore's**, where there is pool, loud music and a superb view of Saba. In Great Bay Marina you will find the **Greenhouse**, also pool tables on a breezy deck, some drinks specials and music in the evenings. **Turtle Pier**, not far down from the airport, collects a good crowd of yachties around the bar, particularly at Happy Hour between 5 and 7. In Maho Bay just up the road you will find the ever lively **Chéri's Café**, and just inside the Mullet Bay complex, looking over the golf course, is the **19th Hole**, usually crammed with tourists, all trying to be heard above the calypso music. Cheap drinks. For a quieter drink on a very pretty terrace, try **Paradise Café**, hidden away behind the Maho Bay area. A lively bar-cum-discotheque is the **News Music Café**, a rock and motorbike theme pub with black and white decor, neon signs and video screen, on the main road in Simpson Bay.

Some hotels have shows over dinner a couple of times a week. If you are one for comedy, you can see a few acts at **Coconuts Comedy Club** at the Maho Beach Hotel, where there is also a cabaret. Discotheques include **Chrysalis** in the Great Bay Beach Hotel, **Studio 7** in the Mullet Bay Resort and **La Luna** at Maho Bay. You will also find some excellent bars and places to dance on the French side (*see* Saint Martin, p.186).

There are eight casinos, in the big hotels and along Front Street in town.

the travellers tree

Sint Eustatius

Sint Eustatius is a tiny island with a glorious and glittering past. In the 18th century it was so rich that it was known as the Golden Rock; its warehouses were brimfull of silks, silver and guns from all over the world. At that time it was one of the most important places in the Caribbean, but its fortune has waned. It was also the first country in the world to recognize the United States, when Governor De Graaff saluted the merchantman *Andrea Doria* in 1776.

Statia to her friends, the island has an area of just 8 square miles and is situated close to St Kitts, about 30 miles south of Sint Maarten. Statia is of volcanic origin, and hills in the north descend to a central plain, where the capital and only town, Oranjestad, stands on the leeward coast, and then rise again in the south to the Quill (1890ft), a perfectly shaped volcano, now extinct.

The population of Statia (pronounced stay-sher) is now about 2200, a fraction of the numbers who lived and traded here in the 18th century. It is extremely quiet. If you go, remember that the glittering tradition remains in only a few dilapidated red- and yellow-brick walls. For now, Statia is the least developed island in the area, and she can only wait until the waves of Caribbean fortune favour her again.

History

Settled by the Dutch West India Company in 1636 after a failed attempt on St Croix in the Virgin Islands, Statia's beginnings were modest—small cultivations of tobacco and sugar. But the company had its eyes on trade. Only they had fleets large enough to supply the burgeoning West Indian colonies in the 17th century and over the next hundred years Oranjestad in Sint Eustatius and Willemstad in Dutch Curaçao became two of the most important markets in the New World.

It started with slaves, for whom there was ceaseless demand in the sugar-islands nearby. The Statian merchants were often paid in kind (hogsheads of sugar and puncheons of rum were accepted currency), so the warehouses filled up and Sint Eustatius became a massive entrepôt, presided over by merchants from Europe and the Americas. By 1750 the warehouses stretched all along the waterfront in Lower Town and as space ran out the merchants constructed dykes to reclaim land from the sea, so that they could build a second line of warehouses. Over the next forty years, these became so full that the doorways were blocked up and the goods were hauled in and out through holes in the roof. Strictly speaking, almost all of the trade was illegal because of monopoly trading laws imposed by the other European nations (which demanded that the colonies should trade only with the mother country). But the Dutch in Sint Eustatius recognized no trading laws and the sugar

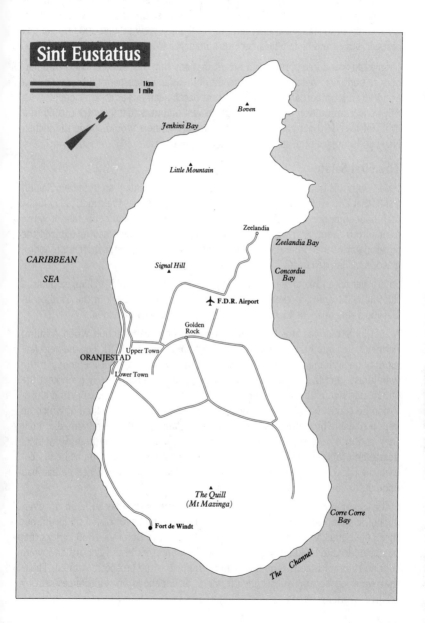

Sint Eustatius

1km
1 mile

Boven ▲

Jenkins Bay

Little Mountain ▲

Zeelandia ○

Zeelandia Bay

CARIBBEAN

SEA

Signal Hill ▲

Concordia
Bay

✈ F.D.R. Airport

Golden
Rock

Upper Town

ORANJESTAD

Lower Town

The Quill ▲
(Mt Mazinga)

Corre Corre
Bay

● Fort de Windt

The Channel

manufacturers in the West Indies knew they would get a better price and immediate payment if they sold their goods to the Sint Eustatius merchants, and so they were prepared to smuggle them there. In 1779 Statia grew around 500,000 pounds of sugar, but according to official records it managed to ship about 25 million pounds.

Oranjestad was a free port, which meant that any ship that cared to come into harbour to trade was welcome. At the height of the island's prosperity there could be a hundred ships in port at any time. The port became famous as an arms depot, with rifles and ammunition passing through in vast amounts. Gunpowder turned in a profit of over 100 per cent. American blockade-runners would dodge the British Navy and smuggle arms to the colonists in sugar-barrels.

The First Salute

It was with this trade in mind that Governor de Graaff saluted an unknown flag on a ship that arrived in harbour on 16 November 1776. It was the American colonist merchant ship, the *Andrea Doria*. Even if the gesture was not deliberate, it was a momentous event, as it was the first time that a foreign power had recognized the sovereignty of the United States. The British were furious and the Dutch apologized, recalling de Graaff.

So prosperous an island was a valuable prize and altogether Statia changed hands a ridiculous 22 times, as the different navies vied for supremacy in the Caribbean. Despite a ring of about 15 forts, Statia was never properly defended.

Maverick Statia was attacked again soon after de Graaff's action when Admiral Rodney sailed into harbour with 15 warships on 3 February 1781. For the next few months he systematically plundered the island, confiscating all the goods in the warehouses and the personal fortunes of the Statian merchants. He even kept the Dutch flag flying above the port and lured in another 150 unsuspecting ships. When he auctioned off all the goods, the profits exceeded £3 million, of which he kept a sizeable proportion for himself. Understandably, the merchants did what they could to save their riches and stories tell of an unusually high number of deaths and funerals. The coffins were loaded with gold and as soon as he discovered the trickery, Rodney promptly had them all dug up again. When he had had enough, the British abandoned the island.

Statia never really recovered, and since then the island has suffered an ever-declining spiral. As trading foundered, the plantations were started up again, but they failed quickly when slavery was abolished by the Dutch in 1863. Bricks that had been used to build the warehouses on the waterfront in the glorious days were sold on to other islands. The population dropped as the prosperity waned. Those that were left became subsistence farmers, or depended on remittances sent by relatives working abroad.

Today Statia is very quiet and has only a very small tourist industry (around a hundred rooms), although a cruise ship pier has been built recently. The government is the largest employer and the only other industry is an oil storage facility and refinery. The island has a listless and slightly tatty air, but a recent Dutch government and EC project has helped to restore some of the buildings from Statia's heyday. The present Lieutenant Governor of St Eustatius is Mr I. E. Temmer.

© (599 3)– **Getting There and Around**

Sint Eustatius is served several times a day by Winair (Windward Islands Airways) from Sint Maarten (local © 82362), sometimes via Saba. There is also a number of scheduled flights every week to the island from St Kitts. On approach, the plane often circles the volcano, the Quill, so remember to look out of the window. There is a departure tax of US$5 for travel within the Dutch Caribbean and US$10 elsewhere.

Getting around Sint Eustatius is easy enough on foot, but there are also **taxis** if you do not want to walk up the hill. The ride into town from the airport costs US$3.50. A guided tour of the island can be made, and if you spin it out to a half-day, it will cost around US$35. Taxis can be ordered at any hotel desk. There are a few **cars** for hire, at around US$35 per day. Present your driving licence to the **Avis** desk (© 82421) at the airport, **Lady Ama's Services** on Fort Orange Street (© 82451), or **Rainbow Car Rental** (© 82811). Driving is on the right.

Tourist Information

There is no tourist office for St Eustatius in the UK or the US, so you should write direct to the island. In Canada, you can get information from New Concepts, 2455 Cawthra Road, Suite 70, Mississauga, Ontario LSA 3P1 (© 905 803 0131, fax 905 803 0132).

The main **Sint Eustatius Tourist Office** (©/fax 82433) is in Upper Town, close to the entrance of Fort Oranje. Hours are 8–noon and 1–5 on weekdays. There is also a desk at the airport, open for the scheduled flights, and a small office in Lower Town. One or two books deal with Statia's famous past, including a good, if a little academic, history, *Sint Eustatius, A short history of the island and its monuments* by Ypie Attema.

In a medical **emergency**, contact the Princess Beatrix Hospital (© 82211) in Oranjestad. To telephone the island from abroad, dial **IDD code**

599 3, except from Saba and Sint Maarten where you dial (03), then follow it with the five-digit Statian number. On-island, use the five digits only.

Money

US dollars are accepted everywhere alongside the Netherlands Antilles florin (US$1 = NAFl 1.78), but credit cards are not that widely used. **Barclays Bank** (✆ 82392) is open on weekdays, 8.30–1, with an extra hour on Friday afternoons, 4–5.

Beaches and Sports

There are only a couple of beaches in Statia and they do not have the white sand for which the Caribbean is known. Off the road down to Lower Town is **Smoke Alley Beach** or **Oranje Beach**, which has an excellent view of the sunset and is popular at the weekends. Another sunning and snorkelling spot is **Crooks Castle**, beyond Lower Town. On the Atlantic side of the island is a secluded cove, **Corre Corre Bay**. Skirt round the Quill to the southeast on Mountain Road and the path down to the bay is marked. Generally, the Atlantic side is unsafe for swimming because of the undertow. The two miles of **Concordia and Zeelandia Bay** are good for walking.

Watersports are limited in Statia (you might be able to borrow a windsurfer, but there are no small sailing boats for hire and there is no waterskiing). You can snorkel at Jenkins Bay in the north and **scuba divers** have plenty of opportunity among the remains of the warehouses in the water offshore at Lower Town. After a storm, the sea still turns up 18th-century bottles, blue trading beads and the occasional ducat. About two hundred vessels are thought to have sunk off Statia. **Dive Statia** (✆ 82435) operate in the town.

On land, the Tourist Board has marked about twelve **walking** trails around the island, of which the most popular is up the slopes of the extinct volcano, the Quill, and then down into its crater. The Statians have a tradition of land-crab-hunting by torchlight in the crater at night, which is a fun way to spend an evening. A guide can be provided by the Tourist Board for an outing to the crater; if you go at night, you are advised to take one. North of Oranjestad you might see coastal tropicbirds, distinctive with their long twin tail-feathers. A floodlit **tennis court** at the Community Centre, is in the southern area of town.

Sailing

The only real **anchorage** for sailing yachts is in the broad bay off Oranjestad on the leeward coast, where you look up to the fort just as the merchantmen would have two centuries ago. There are no facilities especially for yachts, but fuel and water are available from

the dock and there are supermarkets in town. You should clear **immigration and customs** on arrival at the port office down by the cruise ship dock.

Oranjestad

Statia's only settlement, tiny **Oranjestad**, has two parts, Upper and Lower Town, which are separated by a 100ft cliff. During Statia's supremacy as a trading port, goods were kept in the warehouses down below, between the cobbled street and the waterfront and many of the traders would live up above in Upper Town. Today the Statians still live up above, in new 'gingerbread' houses that have forced aside the dark-stone 18th-century foundations and barrel-vaulted graves. Linked by an old stepped walkway built in 1803, Lower Town has now fallen into almost complete dilapidation. Just a few buildings have been restored from the old ruins of red and yellow brick. The outer rim of houses has completely disappeared since the dyke was broken by a hurricane and the sea swept back in, but on a calm day it is just possible to see the base of the walls which run between Crooks Castle and Betty Bay, below the surface of the water.

The town takes its name from **Fort Oranje**, which was built by the Dutch in 1636 on the site of an earlier French fort. Even though the island was attacked so often, the fort saw little action. Poised precariously on the crest of the hill, Fort Oranje has an attractive view across Lower Town. Among its monuments, the most significant commemorates the firing of the salute to the *Andrea Doria* on 16 November 1776.

The **Sint Eustatius Museum**, *open weekdays 9–5, adm*, is located in Simon Doncker House (also known as de Graaff House after the Governor) just off the Wilheminaweg and central square. Admiral Rodney made it his headquarters when he ransacked the island in 1781. The exhibition has an Amerindian section with old Indian pottery and artefacts from the extensive archeological programmes that have taken place in Statia; there are two very attractive period rooms, restored to the time of Statia's prosperity, including impressive antique furniture and a planter's tea service, and a more recent room, 'Granny Statia', exhibiting life on Statia within the last hundred years. Also on view are some small china pieces from the Nanking cargo (which was on order to the Dutch West India Company in Sint Eustatius when the Dutch East India Company ship that was carrying it sank in the South China Sea); they arrived two hundred years late, but they made it.

Statia's sizeable Jewish community, who suffered most of all during Rodney's ravages in 1781 (not only was all their money taken, but they were deported), is remembered in the ruins of the **Honen Dalim Synagogue**, on the little alley, Synagoogpad. On the Kerkweg, the **Dutch Reformed Church** tower, with a cemetery full of barrel-vaulted graves, has been restored and gives a fine view of the harbour.

South of Oranjestad is Statia's volcano, **the Quill**. It is perfectly shaped, with concave slopes rising to nearly 2000ft and a circular crater, from which it takes its name (*kuil* in Dutch means pit). Inside the crater, which is 900ft across and 550ft deep, is a moist and tangled rainforest, where the trees grow tall in their efforts to reach the sun and mosses infest their trunks. Some cultivation takes place in here. Its highest point is Mt Mazinga.

There are thought to have been about 19 forts dotted around Statia's barren coastline; a few are lost without trace. At **Fort de Windt** on the southern tip of the island, a couple of cannon look south over the superb view of St Kitts.

Festivals

National holidays include **Statia Day** on 16 November, which remembers the event in 1776 when Statia saluted the young United States of America. **Carnival** is the main event in the year and takes place for ten days from late July to early August. It is similar to other Caribbean carnivals, with a pyjama jump-up in the early morning at jouvert, a Carnival Queen and a calypso competition, culminating in the burning of Momo, the spirit of the Carnival.

© (599 3)–   ### Where to Stay

The island has only a few hotels, two in Lower Town and one beyond the airport. There are one or two guest houses and it is possible to rent cottages through the Tourist Board. There is a 7% government tax on rooms and an energy tax of 5%. Expect a 10% service charge on your bill.

The Old Gin House, PO Box 172 (© 82319, fax 82555), has been rebuilt in the small red bricks of the old Statian warehouses. Two centuries after the mercantilist mayhem they have taken on a rust of stateliness, festooned on the outside with tropical growth and a traveller's palm. There are 20 rooms, all neatly dressed up with antique furniture, some overlooking the sea, others tucked under the cliff, looking into the garden and pool. The restaurant, the Mooshay Publick House, takes advantage of the rarefied 18th-century atmosphere for candlelit dinners. More relaxed is the Terrace Restaurant across the road, overlooking the sea. Accommodation moderate to expensive. **La Maison sur la Plage**, PO Box 157 (© 82256), is a collection of cottages set beneath a hill above the isolated Zeelandia Bay, a 2-mile strip of brown sand dashed by Atlantic waves (swimming is not recommended because of the undertow). The main house has a bar looking out to the bay and the Quill volcano in the distance, and good dining on a trellis-work terrace with a rush-matting ceiling. On a small island this is a secluded retreat, with good trails all around. Cheap to moderate. The **Golden Era Hotel**, PO Box 109 (© 82345), on the waterfront in Lower Town, is a modern construction that has none of the atmosphere of old-time Statia. However, it is in town, just a minute's walk from the Old Gin House or a stumble down the hill from the bars of Upper Town. The dining room serves West Indian and international fare. Moderate. **Talk of the Town Hotel** (© 82236, fax 82640) is situated in town and has 18 rooms in the modern main house and around the pool. Comfortable rooms with air-conditioning, cable TV and phones. Cheap to moderate.

You can get a cheap and comfortable room at the **Country Inn** (©/fax 82484), which has just six secluded apartments, set far away from the hustle of Oranjestad in Concordia, or at the **King's Well Inn** (©/fax 82538) where there are four rooms in a modern villa about halfway down the Lower Town. The **Airport View Apartments** (© 82299) are just next to the airport and **guest houses** include **Daniel's** (© 82358) on Rose Mary Laan Road, and **Brice's** place, both very cheap.

Eating Out

 There are not many independent restaurants in Statia and so you may find yourself depending on the **hotels**. Each of these has a dining room with a standard and price roughly equivalent to the rooms. **The Old Gin House** has the best food (expensive) but you will find good fare at **La Maison sur la Plage** (moderate) and at **Kingswell Inn** and **Talk of the Town**, both moderate.

Restaurant categories below are arranged according to the price of a main course: *expensive*—US$15 and above; *moderate*—US$8–15; *cheap*—under US$8.

L'Etoile (℡ 82299), up the hill on Heilgerweg, serves local fare. Start with a callaloo soup and follow with creole catch of the day, moderate. **The Stone Oven** (℡ 82543) on Faeschweg has wooden tables and bright table-cloths and serves fish and chicken, moderate. If you feel like a Chinese meal, then you can catch a chicken noodle soup and *chow mein* or a roti at **Sonny's Place** on Fort Oranje Straat.

Nightlife

Nightlife in Statia is limited to the hotels and the local bars, of which the best is **Kool Corner**, where the Statians can be found 'limin' at all hours. At **Franky's** on the Ruyterweg you can get simple meals—burgers and a fry fish or chicken—or simply have a beer when the band is playing. Make sure to finish off with one of Franky's ice-creams. There is a disco, **Largo Heights**, in the Mall. **The Stone Oven** also holds dances, with DJs playing the best Caribbean music.

Saba

Saba is impossibly steep, a mountainous pimple just 5 square miles in area, a central cone surrounded by little lieutenants. Standing about 30 miles to the south of Sint Maarten, the volcanic island of Saba is the final peak in the chain of volcanic islands that runs in an arc from Grenada in the far south. Mount Scenery (2885ft), the island peak smothered in rainforest, is the highest point in the Kingdom of the Netherlands. Near the summit, Saba can seem like a tropical Gormenghast—clouds swirl through the dripping greenery and the gnarled branches of ancient trees are clad in creeping diabolic green mosses.

Besides the capital, The Bottom, there are three main villages on the island's slopes (Windwardside, St John's and Hell's Gate). They appear almost alpine with their stepped alleys, switchbacks and steep retaining walls (the base of one house perched on the roof of the one below) and their spectacular views. There is a certain pastoral calm about the place as well.

Saba (pronounced as in sabre, the sword) is incredibly neat. Tidy gardens tamed from the tropical jungle nestle behind white wooden picket fences; fluorescent blooms stand out against the whitewashed clapboard walls of the houses with their horseshoe-shaped chimney-pots. Curiously, every single roof in Saba is painted red.

You have a good chance of getting a person's name right in Saba if you call them Mr or Mrs Hassell (about a quarter of the population are called Hassell). However, beware, because you might just come across a member of the two rival Saban dynasties, a Johnson or a Simmons. The population is just 1200 (mostly of British descent) and it is untypical in the Caribbean for being roughly half white and half black. With few plantations, most slaves on Saba were domestic servants and their numbers never exceeded those of the white population. Though the islanders all know each other, there are unspoken rules concerning skin colour (as there are in many Caribbean islands) and even today, there is little intermarriage between the races. And as with many small islands, much of the youth has left in search of work and adventure. The population appears to be mainly grandparents and infant grandchildren. Relatively speaking there is a large population of about 250 expatriates.

Saba is quiet, calm, sedate and very stable. It is certainly not a place for a wild time, or for a beach-bound resort holiday. However, if you

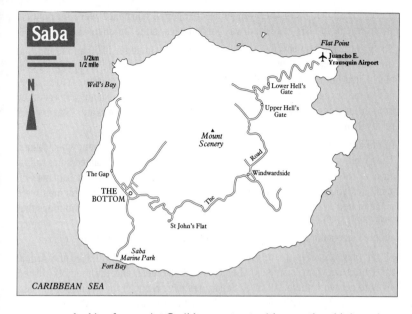

are looking for a quiet Caribbean retreat with a gentle, old-time air, then Saba is a satisfying and very pleasant place to stay.

History

A stream of famous visitors passed by the island in the 16th century, among them Sir Walter Raleigh and Piet Heyn, the Dutch privateer, but most thought better of trying to land. Somebody must have done so, however, because in 1632 a ship-wrecked crew of Englishmen found a plentiful supply of fruit on the trees but no inhabitants. (It was a tradition that sailors would plant food-bearing trees for just this sort of occasion.) The first permanent settlement of Saba was made by Dutchmen from nearby Sint Eustatius in about 1640, and they were joined by a succession of misfits, many of them English speakers. In 1665 an English pirate named Morgan paused to capture the island and he promptly deported everyone who wasn't English.

Saba was almost impregnable. There are few easy landing sites and the terrain is so precipitous that storming the island presented quite a problem. For their part, the Sabians supposedly defended themselves by man-made avalanches. They constructed platforms at the top of the ravines and loaded them with boulders; on the approach of an enemy, they simply knocked out the supports. In 1689 the French had a go after successfully capturing Sint Eustatius, but decided in the end to leave the island alone. From then on, most changes of allegiance were by political arrangement. In 1816 the island was handed back to the Dutch for the last time.

The great Caribbean rover, Père Labat, dropped by in about 1700 and found that the islanders' principal trade was in boots and shoes. Even the parson was a cobbler. Labat bought six pairs. Since then Sabians have been in many trades. They had some success growing sugar in the fertile parts of the island. For this they brought in some Africans, whose descendants are still on the island. Slavery was relatively benign here compared with other islands.

In the 19th century the Sabian men took to the sea and became renowned sailors. They were much in demand by the shipping lines and they captained ships sailing all over the Americas. (Give them a bit of encouragement and old Sabians will gladly tell you of the days when 'the boats were made of wood and the men were made of iron'.) The economy of the island was supported by the contributions that they sent back to their families. At home, with no men around, the Sabian women adopted lacemaking, or drawn-thread work, an industry that continues today.

As shipping waned in the thirties, the oil industry boomed in Curaçao and Aruba, the Dutch Leeward Islands off the coast of Venezuela, and the menfolk rushed away to get work there. All these departures have reduced the population of Saba from around 2500 to its present level. Today the 'remittance money' sent home by Sabians abroad has dwindled but returns from tourism have increased. Saba also receives grants from the Central Government of the Netherlands Antilles in Curaçao, to which they send one elected senator.

© (599 4)–   **Getting There**

The only scheduled flights that go to Saba are with **Winair** (© 62255). They originate in Sint Maarten and sometimes touch down at Sint Eustatius. You can also get to Saba by the power-yacht *The Edge* (© 42640), which departs three times a week from Pelican Marina in Sint Maarten.

There are a number of organized **tours** on offer from Sint Maarten, both by sea and by air, which come for a day's sightseeing. There is a departure tax of US$2 if you are travelling to Sint Eustatius or to Sint Maarten and US$5 for elsewhere.

Flying into Saba is a novel experience. Juancho E. Yrausquin airport is on Flat Point—named so because it is one of the only flat places on the island (even if there is a 130ft cliff at either end). At 1312ft, this strip is one of the shortest in the world (this includes most aircraft carriers), and as you look at it from the air, it seems impossible that anything could land on it. But be reassured, the STOL Twin Otters can land on a sixpence and they usually take only half the runway.

Getting Around

With no buses, getting around Saba is limited to **taxis** and hitching, which works well. There is only one road, so you can't go wrong. It is usually enough to sit on the wall at the edge of town for someone to pick you up. The taxi-fare from one end of the island to the other costs around US$12.

Taxi-drivers are willing to give a tour of the island, taking in the historical sights and views and a stop for lunch. They know about catching the last plane out, though it would probably not go without you anyway. A day's tour for two comes to around US$40, with a small charge for extra people.

A few **hire cars** are available and they can be rented for about US$40–45 per day. Remember to drive on the right, and that Saba's only petrol station is in Fort Bay (© 63272), on the coast below The Bottom. Cars can be hired from **Doc's Car Rental** (© 62271), **Hardiana** (© 62205) and **Johnson's Car Rental** (© 62469).

Tourist Information

The **Saba Tourist Office** (© 62231, fax 62350) is in Windwardside, on the road down to the Bottom. The staff are helpful and are in the office on weekdays, 8–noon and 1–5. They will also send information abroad. Books about the island can be found at the Artisan Foundation in The Bottom.

Not so many years ago, isolated Saba had only a weekly mail service, but now communications are rather easier. To **telephone** the island from abroad, dial 599–4 and then the five-digit Saban number. If phoning within the island, dial the last five digits only. In case of a medical **emergency**, contact the M A Edwards Medical Centre (© 63288) in The Bottom.

Money

Barclays Bank (© 62216) operates in Windwardside, 8.30am to 1.30pm on weekdays. Places accustomed to tourists, for instance hotels and dive-shops, will accept credit cards. Others will not. US dollars are accepted everywhere alongside the Netherlands florin (US$1 = NAFl 1.78).

Sailing

Saba is not frequented much by yachts—it is quite a long haul south of Sint Maarten and the anchorages are limited. But for divers and those simply curious enough to want to see such an extraordinary island, it is well worth the visit. The only areas with reliable **anchorages** are on the western shore, around Ladder Bay, and at Fort Bay in the southwest, the main dock for ships. There are no facilities specifically for yachts (though there are a few mooring buoys available), but you can load fuel and water in Fort Bay. Saba is almost entirely surrounded by Marine Park and there are restrictions on anchoring and strict rules with respect to marine life. You can clear **customs** in Fort Bay in the Harbourmaster's office. There are mooring charges in Saba which vary according to the size of your yacht.

Beaches and Sports

Saba has no 'beaches' as beaches are generally thought of in the Caribbean. However, a patch of migratory grey volcanic sand returns annually to the north coast of the island in the spring, staying over the summer until about November. This is at **Well's Bay**, at the end of the road from The Bottom. On a calm day, it makes a good picnic spot. The other place occasionally referred to as the 'beach' is the concrete ramp down into the water at Fort Bay. There is not much in the way of watersports but sunset cruises around the island can be arranged through either of the three dive shops.

Saba does have a name as a **scuba-diving** destination. The island's slopes descend as steeply beneath the water as above and the coral growth there is as lush as the flora on land. There is a great variety in a small area, with caves, pinnacles and lava flows and good visibility, often as much as 100ft. The fish life is abundant; you might see a turtle or a migrating humpback whale or even a formation of flying gurnards. Expect patrols of sergeantfish (striped) and soldierfish to dart around the coral forests and sponges. The Saba Marine Park was established in 1986 to protect the marine life, and has placed mooring sites in the seabed (the coastline is so rough that all dives are made from boats). Spearfishing is illegal, as is the removal of any coral. There are three **dive** operators on the island: **Saba Deep**, which works from Fort Bay (© 63347, fax 62389) and offers instruction (NAUI and PADI), **Sea Saba** (© 62246, fax 62377), in Windwardside (offering PADI certification) and **Wilson's Dive Shop** (© 63410). Saba has a four-person decompression chamber. *A one-tank dive costs around US$40.* For a look at marine life without getting wet, a slide show is staged at Juliana's Recreation Room every Tuesday by the manager of the Marine Park.

Walking

All over the island you will see the stone walls of old-time Saba, when the villages of the island were linked in a network of stepped pathways (before the arrival of cars in 1947). People would walk or ride a donkey to get around. Any older Sabian will tell you about the morning rush-hour (a crowded ¾-hour's walk) over the hills from Windwardside to The Bottom, and how the islanders used to arrive at parties in their walking boots. A few of the ingenious old paths remain and they make good walking trails.

A favourite walk is up to Saba's summit, **Mount Scenery**, best when the peak is not engulfed in cloud. A sign on the road at the start (past the tourist office) fore-warns you that there are 1064 steps. It is hot work and a good 1½-hour hike, though you can miss the first bit out by taking the upper road. Cable and Wireless (who operate the radio mast on the summit and have to climb the hill quite often) have the right idea, and they have erected a shelter on the way up. The flora is fairly typical of the steep volcanic islands, with whole hillsides of elephant ears on the lower slopes and an ever-thickening rainforest with its profuse growth that eventually gives over to elfin woodland. Gnarled trees are covered with mosses that creep, tangles of lianas hang suspended and cycads and bromeliads explode from their perches in the trees. Perhaps you will see a trembler or a garnet-throated hummingbird in the upper woodland.

There are a number of trails in the northern part of the island, between Well's Bay and Hell's Gate, where there are a couple of abandoned villages. In these remoter areas you may come across sea-birds like terns and brown noddies as well as shear-waters and tropicbirds. Further details of walks on the island, and a guide if you would like one, are available from the Tourist Office in Windwardside.

'The Road that Could Not Be Built'

Before the construction of The Road, anything from a bean to a grand piano had to be carried around on the pathways and so the Sabians decided that they needed a road. On seeking expert advice in the thirties, they were simply told that they shouldn't bother to try. But the Hassells and the Johnsons were made of sterner stuff than that and so Josephus Lambert Hassell, the architect of The Road, decided to take a correspondence course in civil engineering. In 1938 work began at Fort Bay, slowly winding its way uphill for the next five years to The Bottom. In 1947 the first car arrived and by 1951 it could drive to Windwardside. The 19 miles of The Road cling to the mountainside, climbing to 1800ft as it winds from village to village, so you get some unexpected and stunning views as you drive around. To the builders' credit, The Road was repaired for the first time in the late 1980s.

The Bottom

The Bottom is the capital of Saba and despite its name sits at an altitude of 850ft. It is a jumble of white walls, red roofs and green shutters set in neat little gardens, sit-ting in the bottom of a bowl (hence the name) thought to be the crater of Saba's extinct volcano. The evening shade comes early to The Bottom as it is towered over by vast forested escarpments. The Dutch and Saban flags fly alongside one another in front of the Lieutenant Governor's residence at the southern end of the town, a gingerbread house defended by a couple of fearsome cannon (at least four-ouncers). The present Lieutenant Governor is Mr Sydney Sorton.

Close by is the road that leads down through the 'chicane' to **Fort Bay**. This is the island's main port, and all goods have been brought in here since the pier was constructed in 1972. Before that, landing was a skilled technique which involved beaching the row-boat on one wave and scrambling out before the next one broke over you. At the other end of town, 520 steps lead down to **Ladder Bay**, the other main port, off the new road to Wells Bay. These steps have seen everything from shoes to the kitchen sink transported up them in their time. You might also see a charcoal-burner's pit on the way down.

The Road passes by way of St John's to **Windwardside**, Saba's second settlement, *open on weekdays 10–3, adm: a suggested donation of US$1*, which is scattered over the mountainside at around 2000ft and occasionally disappears in the clouds. More white picket fences, barrel graves/cisterns and steep alleys. In one of the many neat houses, you will find the **Saba Museum**, dressed up as it was in its prime 150 years ago. It exhibits Saban memorabilia from Indian axe-heads to a Victorian mahogany four-poster bed with pineapple motifs. Outside the museum is a bust of 'El Libertador', Simon Bolivar, who recruited men here in 1816 for his struggle against the Spanish authorities in South America. There is a fantastic view across to Statia from the Lookout, just up the hill from Windwardside.

windwardside village saba

From Windwardside, The Road switchbacks its way through terraced cultivation to the alpine village of Hell's Gate (a curious adaptation of the original name of Zion's Hill), where each house is held in place and prevented from tumbling down the hill by the one above. The church was constructed only in 1962. From here The Road makes its nineteen curves to get down to Flat Point, where the airstrip is situated.

Festivals

Saba's **Summer Festival** runs for a week in July, following traditional Caribbean carnival lines with calypso shows, a festival parade in the streets and the usual jump-ups in the evenings.

© (599 4)–

Where to Stay

There are a surprising number of places to stay on Saba. Each has the cosy and friendly atmosphere for which the island is known. There are about 20 villas for hire—more details can be obtained from the Tourist Board or through Johnson's Real Estate (©/fax 62209). There is a government hotel tax of 5% and hotels also add a service charge of 10% or 15%.

moderate–expensive

The **Captain's Quarters** (© 62201, fax 62377), in Windwardside at the foot of the hill, has the best in old-time Saban charm. Twenty very comfortable rooms stand in small blocks; some in the charming central house which has wooden floors, a small library, four-posters and louvred windows. From the balconies you look over banana trees to the sea 1500ft below. The dining room is on a terrace beneath the main house, decorated as the sea captain's home that it once was. The bar is a popular gathering point after dark, prices moderate. The **Queen's Garden Resort** (© 62236, fax 62450) stands high above The Bottom, on a hillside smothered in rainforest, with sea views. The rooms are very comfortable and have cable TV.

cheap–moderate

The **Gate House** (© 62416, fax 62415, US © 708 354 9641) is set in a classic Saban house with triple pointed gables and shuttered windows in the village of Hell's Gate, with views over the islands to the north. Comfortable friendly atmosphere, brightly decorated rooms, some with kitchens. In Windwardside, looking southwest from the top of the ridge in town, is **Scout's Place** (© 62205, fax 62388), with 15 simple rooms, overlooking the attractive roofs and jungle-like greenery. There is a lively open-air bar, where the Sabians stop off on their way home from work and the dining room is presided over by Dianna Medero, who is something of a local celebrity. **Juliana's** (© 62269, fax 62389), also in Windwardside, has ten private rooms with balconies facing the sea. There is a dining room and a pool. **Cranston's Antique Inn** (© 63203) is the former Lieutenant Governor's residence in The Bottom. As the name implies, the Inn basks in fading Saban glory, a pretty wooden creole house painted white with green shutters behind a picket fence. Some of the six rooms have four-poster beds, others share a bathroom, cheap, includes breakfast. Nearby is the **Caribe Guest House** (©/fax 63259) with six rooms with private baths; although there is no restaurant, the kitchen is for the use of guests; cheap.

© (599 4)– ## Eating Out

Most hotel dining rooms (book in season) will serve local dishes— callaloo followed by fry chicken—alongside standard American fare. Try the **Captain's Quarters**, on a veranda, **Willards of Saba**, **Tropics** at Juliana's and **Scout's Place**, on a veranda. Categories are arranged according to the price of a main course: *expensive*—US$15 and above; *moderate*—US$8–15; *cheap*—under US$8.

Outside the hotels you will find good seafood and creole fare at **Brigadoon** (© 62380) in Windwardside. Try a lobster in butter or a creole or Cajun fish, moderate to expensive. If you feel like a Chinese meal, try the **Saba Chinese Restaurant** (© 62268), set in a modern house, where there is a huge selection, moderate. And there is also an Italian restaurant, **Guido's** (© 62230), with burgers as well as pizzas and pastas, cheap to moderate. If you are feeling peckish in the daytime, the **Deli and Gourmet Shop** can fix you a sandwich, cheap. In The Bottom you will get classic local cuisine at **Queenie's Serving Spoon** (© 63225) —pumpkin soup or callaloo, followed by a curry goat and a fruit ice cream to finish, cheap to moderate. **Lollipops** is another local bar and restaurant; try fish or chicken with local vegetables, cheap to moderate. By the harbour in Fort Bay you will find **In Two Deep**, a daytime bar and restaurant. 'Fast food and libations', cheap.

Nightlife

When Père Labat visited in 1701, he wrote: 'The settlers live as it were in a large club and frequently entertain each other.' It is much the same today, except that they congregate in the bars around the island, many in the hotels and restaurants. There are a few local bars in The Bottom, including **Midway Bar** and **Sunset Bar**, occasionally some entertainment in Scout's Place and if you want to dance, the **Mountain High Club** is open at weekends at Guido's Pizzeria.

Saint Martin

French Saint Martin shares an island with Sint Maarten, a member of the Netherlands Antilles (*see* pp.137–52) and it is the smallest island in the world to be shared by two nations. The French half in the north is divided from the Dutch side by an imaginary line, marked only by an obelisk and a Bienvenue/Welkom sign.

Saint Martin looks across to British Anguilla in the north of the Lesser Antilles and is about 20 square miles (53sq km) in area (the Dutch half is around 17 square miles/44sq km). Its beaches are supreme and inland the yellow-green scrubland rises to hills of 1200ft. About 13 miles (21km) southeast is the other French island 'commune' of St Barthélémy.

Saint Martin is fairly crowded. It has lost its air of a building site slightly, and is now getting on with the tourist business in hand. Everything is right there for a trusty French break in the tropics, with windsurfers zipping across the bay and waterfront bistros ideal for lingering and watching a lunch-time fashion-show. And in the gourmet restaurants, of which there are plenty, the food is served with customary French flair.

Beyond the seaside screen of beach chairs and palm trees, though, you will find a few pockets of real French West Indian life, with local markets and games of *pétanque*. Zouk, the music of the French islands of Martinique and Guadeloupe, is heard in the local clubs.

If anything, over the past few years, Saint Martin has become more French than it was, as large numbers of investors and immigrants from France have come to the island. The population has rocketed with the tourist industry, now by far the largest income generator. There is a certain French exclusivity in the language, but it is possible to get by in English. The other major contributor is the French Government. Saint Martin is a *commune* in the Région of Guadeloupe and it is administered by a *sous-préfet* appointed from Paris. The islanders vote members on to the Conseil Général that sits in Basse-Terre, Guadeloupe, and directly in the French elections.

History

Although the two communities on either side of Saint Martin avoided each other most of the time (a road between the two was not built until earlier this century), it was not always possible: their pasts were occasionally linked and anyway quite similar. Saint Martin's history is included under Sint Maarten (*see* p.140).

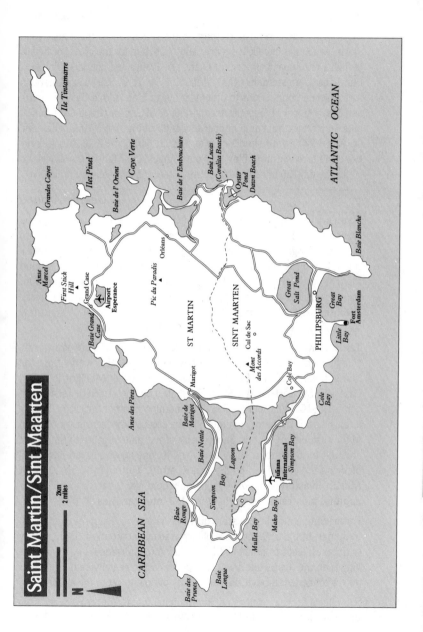

Saint Martin/Sint Maarten

CARIBBEAN SEA

ATLANTIC OCEAN

Ile Tintamarre

Grandes Cayes

Ilet Pinel

Caye Verte

Baie de l'Orient

Baie de l'Embouchure

Baie Lucas (Cordula Beach)

Oyster Pond

Dawn Beach

Baie Blanche

Anse Marcel

First Stick Hill

Grand Case

Airport Esperance

Orléans

Pic du Paradis

ST MARTIN

SINT MAARTEN

Cul de Sac

Great Salt Pond

PHILIPSBURG

Great Bay

Fort Amsterdam

Little Bay

Baie Grand Case

Anse des Pères

Marigot

Baie de Marigot

Mont des Accords

Cole Bay

Cole Bay

Baie Nettle

Lagoon

Juliana International

Simpson Bay

Simpson Bay

Baie Rouge

Mullet Bay

Maho Bay

Baie Longue

Baie des Prunes

2km
2 miles

N

175

Getting There

Most flights arrive at Juliana airport on the Dutch side of the island (code SXM), which has excellent services and is the hub for the area. For details of flights into Juliana airport from Paris (Air France and charters), Frankfurt (Lufthansa), Amsterdam (KLM), Miami, New York, San Juan (American Airlines) and connections to other Caribbean islands, *see* Getting There, Sint Maarten, p.141. Espérance airport (code SFG) near Grand Case cannot take jet aircraft, but some hopper flights do put in here: Air Guadeloupe (© 87 53 74) from Pointe-à-Pitre and Air St Barts (© 87 73 46). A **ferry boat** will take you from Blowing Point, Anguilla to Marigot if you wish to go for the day (20 min; US$20 return). There is a departure tax of US$10.

Getting Around

If you arrive at the airport on the Dutch side, the easiest way up to the French half is by taxi as hardly any **buses** run past the airport. Buses do run from Marigot down to Philipsburg and up to Grand Case with the occasional link on to Orléans. They leave from the rue de Hollande behind Marigot (fare to Philipsburg about US$1.50) from early in the morning for the workers and they run until about 10pm (not so late to outlying areas). **Hitch-hiking** is the normal lottery; there are hundreds of cars but few seem to stop, so you may need a fair amount of patience.

Taxis, however, come two a penny (except in price) and are easily available at both airports and at the hotels. A taxi rank also works from the Marigot waterfront (© 87 56 54). Sample prices are: **Marigot** to Grand Case—US$9, east coast US$15–20, Baie Longue—US$10, Juliana airport—US$10, Philipsburg—US$12. A morning's tour of the island is easily arranged, though there is not much to see except views across Saint Martin to the surrounding islands. Shopping stops and time to pause in the bistros are built in to the tour. Hotel desks will fix one for you (safari buses will pick you up) or you can go through **R. and J. Tours** (© 87 56 20) or **St Martin Evasion** (© 87 73 01). If you would like to take a tour by **helicopter**, Sint Maarten offers that too: **Héli-inter caraïbes** (© 87 37 37).

For maximum mobility, to score duty-free bargains in Philipsburg or go out to dinner, hire a car. There are plenty available at around US$45 per day with taxes, jeeps from about US$55. Any foreign licence is valid and driving is on the right. Hotels will arrange for cars to be delivered. The towns do get congested, though, so leave plenty of time to get to the airport.

Some local firms as well as big international rental companies work from the Dutch side (*see* Sint Maarten, p.142) and **Avis** has an outlet in Marigot

(© 87 54 36). Local French hire-companies include **Sandyg** (© 87 88 25) in Sandy Ground, **Island Trans** (© 87 91 32) in Marigot and **Express Rent A Car** (© 87 70 98). If you are fond of scams and are prepared to spend a couple of hours being given the hard sell about 'investment in vacationing' in a condominium complex, you can sometimes score a '$50 off your rental bill' voucher. And if you want a scooter or a bicycle, contact **Location 2 Roues** at Galerie Commerciale in Baie Nettlé.

Tourist Information

There are Tourist Information Offices in: **France** 96 rue de Rivoli, 75004 Paris (© 1 42 77 91 70, fax 1 44 59 22 75) and the **USA** 10 East 21st Street, Suite 600, New York, NY 10010 (© 212 529 8484, fax 212 460 8287).

There is a small Tourist Information Office (© 87 57 23, fax 87 56 43) on the waterfront in Marigot. Open on weekdays 8.30–1 and 2.30–5, Sat 8 to noon. If you think you might be spending time on the beach, remember to make a selection from the superabundance of tourist literature that litters the airport when you arrive. Of all the magazines, the most revealing and best informed is the joint publication *Discover*, which has some features alongside the normal tourist advice. *Reflets* is the official Tourist Board publication and there are a number of dining guides.

To **telephone** Saint Martin from abroad, the **IDD code** is 590 followed by the six-digit local number. Within Saint Martin, dial just the six digits. Phoning from the French to the Dutch side, dial 3 and then the five-digit number, and from the Dutch to the French side dial 06 followed by the six digits. There are no coin-boxes on the French side and so you will need to buy a *télécarte* from the post office or the few newsagents that stock them. In a medical **emergency**, there is a hospital in Marigot (© 87 50 07).

Money

The official currency of Saint Martin is the French franc (US$ = Fr5.5 approx). However, with so many visitors from America, the greenback is accepted everywhere. In local shops and eateries you may receive your change in francs and centimes. Netherlands Antilles guilders or florins (the currency of the Dutch side) are not accepted, though credit cards are (all over the island). There are three **banks** in Marigot with different opening hours, so you can usually find somewhere to change money during the day. Hotels are always willing to change money, but the rate is not so good.

Shopping hours are as they are in France: 9–1 and 3–7. In Marigot you might try **Oro de Sol** for watches and **Cartier** for jewellery.

Beaches

There are excellent beaches on both sides of the island (*see also* Sint Maarten, p.144). Those nearest the hotels are usually active and lively, but there are some more secluded ones too. Topless bathing is perfectly acceptable here and there are a few nude beaches (Baie de l'Orient is the only official one, but it has been known to happen at Baie Rouge and Baie Longue). Unlike the Dutch side, where hotels often have a shower room you can use, the beaches on the French side tend to be without changing facilities. On the larger beaches there are often concessionaires who will hire out snorkelling and windsurfing equipment. You may see the word *anse* on the French side; it means cove and there are one or two delightful ones to visit. There have been thefts on beaches all over the island and so do not leave belongings unattended.

Probably the best beach on the island is **Baie Longue** (Long Bay), a cracking mile of soft golden sand on the west of the French side. The best swimming is at the bottom end (near the Samanna Hotel). Take food and drinks. Just around the corner is the **Baie des Prunes** (Plum Bay), an afternoon suntrap with good snorkelling (but watch out for the rocks when swimming). **Baie Rouge** is a lively beach, a fantastic stretch of golden sand with crystalline water that looks north toward Anguilla. Huts have snorkelling gear for hire and drinks for sale. From the eastern end you can swim round to an idyllic smaller cove, **Crique Lune de Miel** (Honeymoon Cove).

Nettle Bay or Marigot Bay is the built-up strip to the north of Simpson Lagoon that runs into Marigot. The sand is all right and most watersports can be arranged here. There are two small isolated coves between Marigot and Grand Case—**Anse des Pères** (Friars Bay), where you will find a rasta beach bar and **Happy Bay**. The town of Grand Case itself has some small hotels and guest houses along its strip of sand: sports equipment is available and there are plenty of bistros to retreat to at the height of the sun. **Anse Marcel** has recently been built up and so the valley is dominated by an infestation of mock-classical gingerbread, but the beach has brilliant white sand enclosed by enormous headlands. A short walk round the western point takes you to the tiny and secluded **Duck Beach**.

Some of the island's best beaches are on the eastern Atlantic coast, even though the sea is a little rougher there. **Baie de l'Orient** is a stunning mile of fine white sand and clear blue water. It is very active at the northern end, with lines of beach chairs and sports on offer. Officially it is a nudist beach and so the odd naturist might wander by, but they stick mainly to the southern end. To the south of here there are two other strips of sand before you come to the Dutch side, **Baie de l'Embouchure** or Galion Bay, a sweeping curve where windsurfing is popular and **Baie Lucas**, also known as Coralita Beach, which has excellent snorkelling, with ocean winds and the full brunt of the morning sun (a dangerous combination). Both beaches have a hotel where you can get lunch and a drink to cool you down.

There are a few off-shore islands in the northeast of Saint Martin, where you can go for a day's seclusion on your own strip of sand (remember to take a picnic and plenty to drink and arrange to be picked up again). The two most popular for their beaches are **Ilet Pinel** and **Ile Tintamarre**.

Beach Bars

There are a number of free and easy haunts above the waves in St Martin where you can linger over a beer after a dip. On Orient Bay you will find a whole string of bars, including **Waikiki, Bikini** (*Tapas not topless! Bikini or not...*—the bar sees some spillover from the nudist section of the beach), **Kakao** and **Kontiki**, which has a covered terrace and tables scattered around a sandy garden; salads, grills and some creole dishes. On the secluded Friar's Bay you will find **Kali's**, another hip spot, where you might spend hours admiring the colours of the sea and the sunset to the tune of reggae and dub or just the susurration of the waves. Run by a rastaman, there is some food, but you also get standard West Indian chicken and fish, served on the wooden deck above the sand. Full moon party.

Sailing

The French side of St Martin offers excellent sailing among the off-shore cays in the tortuous indentations of its shoreline. And its facilities, both in matters of technical assistance and repair, and the more vital matters of self-indulgence (i.e. French restaurants) mean that it is the hub of the northeastern Caribbean. Services on the north side are complemented by those of the Dutch side of the island to the south.

St Martin is mostly quite recently rebuilt, but Marigot has settled into its routine of receiving boatborne visitors like a pro. The broad bay has **anchorages** offshore, a short dinghy ride to the action of the market and waterfront, and a marina, the Port la Royale, inside the lagoon. There are good **services** including chandleries and of course supermarkets and there is technical support out in the Sandy Ground area (the entrance to the lagoon). Heading northeast there are stopovers worth exploring at Grande Case, where you will find excellent bars and restaurants, and Anse Marcel, where there are calm anchorages and a marina for supplies. Finally there are good day cruises on the east coast of the island, where you can make stops among the offshore islands. You can put in to the northwestern side of Tintamarre, or go closer into Ilet Pinel or Green Cay. Finally, close to the border with the Dutch side, you will find a protected harbour with a marina at Oyster Pond.

There are **immigration** offices in Marigot and you should clear on arrival (even from the Dutch side) and departure. For major **repairs** you can go to SGP (© 87 74 77) in Marigot or the workshop at Mendol (© 87 05 94).

Yacht charter companies include **Stardust** (© 87 40 30) with yachts and pleasure craft for hire and **Star Voyages** (© 87 39 36). **Sunsail** (© 87 83 41) are based at the **Port Royale Marina** on the lagoon in Marigot and the **Moorings** are at Captain Oliver's Marina on the east coast (© 87 32 55).

Watersports

Windsurfing is very popular on the French side of the island and it is marginally cheaper there. You can get a board in Nettle Bay or Grand Case, but the winds are best on the east coast, where Baie de l'Embouchure is a good place to learn because of the gentler sea and onshore winds, and Orient Bay is the one to head for if you like speed sailing. Try **Orient Watersports** (© 87 33 85) and **Windsurfing Club Nathalie Simon** (© 87 32 04), who can help all standards of windsurfers. Most hotels have sailing dinghies for hire and they will usually lend to somebody from outside. General watersports operators in Nettle Bay include **Caribbean Watersports** (© 87 58 66) and **Laguna Watersports** (© 87 91 75).

Deep-sea fishing trips can be arranged (*about US$700 for a full day*) at the marinas. There are good fishing grounds off the Anguillan islands, where you can cast for bonito and spiked-back wahoo. Contact **CSB** (© 87 89 38) in Port la Royale Marina.

Snorkellers will find excellent corals (do not pick any or use a spear-gun against the fish, though, as they are protected) in places off Saint Martin, particularly off the northeast of the island, where there is a reserve. The best beaches are Baie Rouge near the western point of the island and Green Cay opposite Orient Beach on the Atlantic side (also Ilet Pinel and Tintamarre). There is a large glass-bottom boat, *Karib 1* (© 87 89 73). If you would like to **scuba dive**, you will see the reefs patrolled by sergeant-major fish and trumpetfish off the bay of Grandes Cayes on the shoreline and offshore round the islands in the northeast. Dives and instruction (PADI and NAUI) are available through **Blue Ocean Dive Centre** (© 87 89 73) at the Pirate hotel in Marigot and in Anse Marcel and **Lou Scuba Club** (© 87 22 58) on Baie Nettlé. *A single-tank dive costs around US$45.*

Other Sports

A number of walking trails have been cut into the Saint Martin scrub, taking in the Mont des Accords and the Pic Paradis, both of which give cracking views of the surrounding islands and lowlands like the salt ponds. The island's limited **flora** and **fauna** ranges from soldier crabs in their conical shells to the mournful white cattle egret on land and the yellowlegs who scurry around the mangrove swamps. Try the path leading over First Stick Hill from behind the airport, an hour's walk ending up in Anse Marcel, or the flatland on the east coast near Oyster Pond. More details can be found at the tourist office and they will arrange a guide if you want one. An early-morning dip on horseback can be arranged through **Sea Fun Caraïbes** (✆ 87 33 33) in Anse Marcel or **OK Corral** in Oyster Pond on (✆ 87 40 72).

There is a **golf** course on the Dutch side, at the Mullet Bay Resort (✆ 42081). *The green fees are very high at around US$125 for the 18 holes*, and residents of the hotel have preference in teeing off. There are about fifty **tennis** courts on the island, many of them lit for night-play. Contact any of the larger hotels.

Marigot

Like its Dutch counterpart Philipsburg, Marigot has four streets, clustered between the sea and a salt-pond, but where the Dutch town looks inwards to its shops, Marigot looks out across the water.

The old warehouses of the esplanade, boulevard de France, are now fitted out with bistros and streetfront awnings and parasols, where it is possible to linger all day, with a few distractions between meals—a stroll around the marina on the lagoon or a visit to the waterfront market (*best Wed and Sat mornings*), watching fishing boats land their catch and sloops off-load their cargoes. Behind, the few streets have recently been restored and you will see the old wrought-iron balustrades of the town-houses and municipal buildings among the pastel-fronted shopping arcades. The marina Port la Royale is another area with lively restaurants and bars.

The town first grew up in the 1680s, when the danger of raids that had forced the islanders inland to Orléans was passed. In the 1760s the fear revived; this time it

Marigot architecture

was navies on the rampage rather than marauding boatloads of pirates, and so **Fort St Louis** was constructed on the heights above the town. It is overgrown and littered with just a few cannon, but it has a fine view of Anguilla, from where the old adversaries would nip over at the first sniff of war. The path to the fort leads past the church, with its fresco of a black Virgin in a Caribbean scene, the hospital and the Sous-préfecture, the residence of the island administrator.

The **Saint Martin Museum**, *open daily except Sun, 9–1, 3–6, adm expensive*, on the waterfront in Marigot gives an illustration of island history with Arawak ceramics and shells and other tools like the wicker squeezer used to extract the poisonous juice from cassava. Also old-time pictures of the island.

Around the Island

The road leading north out of Marigot leads beneath the **Pic du Paradis**, the island's highest point, from where on a clear day there are fantastic views of islands as far away as Nevis (about 60 miles). **Grand Case** is really a single shoreside street lined with old and new houses and festooned in tropical greenery, set on the wide sweep of the magnificent Grand Case bay. There is a friendly feel to the place as crowds of tourists come to its excellent restaurants and bars. But there is also something of a local West Indian life here and you might even see a cock-fight in a pit at the western end of the village. Other spectator sports include watching the planes come in over the rooftops to land at the airstrip just behind the town. On Sundays there is often a jump-up on the beach, with a disco set up on the pier and braziers cooking chicken legs and soldier crabs in their shells.

Orléans, or French Quarter as it is sometimes called, a collection of villas and one or two shops, was the capital of the French half of the island in the early days.

Festivals

Carnival is celebrated at the beginning of Lent with street parades in Marigot and Grand Case on Mardi Gras and Mercredi des Cendres (on the Dutch side, Carnival is at Easter) and in May there is the **Saint Martin Food Festival** in which island crafts, recipes and drinks are displayed (and offered for tasting) to steel band and 'old-time' band music. Bastille Day (14 July) sees fireworks and on Schoelcher Day (21 July) there are boat races. Grand Case also holds a special day in July, with sailing races in traditional island vessels and a general blow-out. **St Martin's Day** is celebrated on 11 November, which brings joint ceremonies with the Dutch side.

Until recently it was the Dutch side that had the block resort hotels, thrown up by speculators as an investment, but they have arrived in Saint Martin too. However there are a few more stylish places to stay, such as the French West Indian inns dotted around the island. Except in guest houses, the rates quoted usually include breakfast. A small government tax (US$3) is added to your bill and service is 10% or 15%.

luxury

La Samanna, PO Box 4077, 97064 St Martin Cedex (© 87 51 22, fax 87 86, US © 800 854 2252), is an enclave of super-luxury set above the magnificent sweep of Long Bay in the west of the island. The main house, with its palm-thatched dining room with wicker chairs, stands on a bluff above the pool and sea, and the 80 extremely elegant and comfortable rooms and suites are ranged in villas set in a tropical garden and giving on to the sand. A theme of stark white and royal blue, the colour of the sea on a bright day, runs through the resort. Top-notch service and comfort and a superb sunset. Certainly the most elegant place to stay as well as the most expensive.

expensive–very expensive

At the top of Orient Beach, the **Esmeralda Resort**, PO Box 5141, 97071 St Martin (© 87 36 36, fax 87 35 18) has 54 units set in pretty terraced villas that echo the best of old Caribbean style with louvres, verandas and gently sloping roofs. The rooms, which look onto their own pool, have all you need in the way of 20th-century comfort with wicker furnishings, king-sized beds and televisions. Sports on offer right on the sand, but a fine place to sit and relax on an old-time veranda. Surrounded by all the activity of the marina at Oyster Pond, **Captain Oliver's**, PO Box 645 (© 87 40 26, fax 87 40 84) has an easy, nautical feel. All the rooms, brightly decorated with white tiles and pastel colours, have balconies overlooking the marina or the offshore islands towards St Barts. Kitchenettes in the rooms. It is not on the beach, but there is a boat taxi across to Dawn Beach. Watersports and sailing, expensive. **La Belle Créole**, PO Box 578 (© 87 66 00, fax 87 56 66), is set on its own beach at the western end of Nettle Bay. The hotel is quite large with over 150 rooms, but there is a certain atmospheric grandeur in the Mediterranean interior and the tiled and stepped courtyard set with tables. Plenty of watersports and tennis, expensive. If you like a large and active resort try the **Nettle Bay Beach Club**, PO Box 4081 (© 87 95 24, fax 87 21 51), where horseshoes of cottages and villas stand around pools on a windy waterfront. Comfortable suites and rooms, some with kitchenettes, decorated with tile floors and bamboo furniture; watersports available and tennis courts, some evening entertainment, expensive.

moderate

Another beach hotel with the advantage of being just off Orient Beach is **St Tropez Caribe** (© 87 42 01, fax 87 41 69). There are 86 rooms in villas altogether, comfortable and cool in white and bright pastel colours with watersports close by. Moderate to expensive. Grand Case has a number of small mid-range hotels and guest houses. Most do not have pools, but they are right above the waves. Many have kitchenettes. The most comfortable and friendly is the **Hévéa Hotel**, 163 boulevard de Grand Case (© 87 56 85, fax 87 83 88), which is set in an old colonial house across the road from the beach. A good dining room and just eight rooms and suites redone in old West Indian style—muslin bed-netting and dark wooden furniture. **Chez Martine**, PO Box 637, Grand Case (© 87 51 59, fax 87 87 30) has just six large and comfortable rooms giving on to a large terrace in a modern house, with a restaurant above the waves. Hotel **Pavillon Beach**, PO Box 313 (© 87 96 46, fax 87 71 04, US reservations © 800 373 6246) is a little farther along the bay. It has 16 studios and suites with kitchenettes and a pretty terrace with balustrade from which to admire the sea.

cheap

If you are happy to explore from a base that is quite isolated in the Quartier d'Orléans on the east coast, then you will find a friendly reception at **Gracie Mansion** (© 87 41 56). Set in a modern block at the roadside, the studios and suites are comfortable and breezy and overlook the sea to the offshore islands from a terrace. Some kitchenettes. **Ma Chance's** has a couple of simple air-conditioned rooms in a family house in Grand Case (© 87 50 45). Otherwise try **Rosely's** (© 87 70 17, fax 87 70 20) in Concordia, where there are 48 comfortable rooms. Also **Fleming's Corner** (© 87 70 25). There are some cheapish places to stay on the Dutch side.

© (590)–
Eating Out

Eating out is something of a pastime in Saint Martin and there are some excellent restaurants on the island, offering both classical French cuisine and its creole counterpart. So if you are one for a gastronomic steeplechase, there is plenty to occupy you here. Grand Case calls itself the 'gourmet capital of Saint Martin' and there is a string of pretty restaurants along the waterfront (and in Marigot too). There is no real need to dress up, but most restaurants would prefer you not to go in shorts. Prices are not cheap, but service is *compris*.

Categories are arranged according to the price of a main course: *expensive*—US$20 and above; *moderate*—US$10–20; *cheap*—under US$10. There are also good restaurants on the Dutch side (*see* p.151).

expensive

Ever popular, **La Vie en Rose** (℗ 87 54 42) has a commanding view over the waterfront square in Marigot from the first floor balcony with white and pink awnings and a smart pink dining room, which is tended by lightning waiters. Classical French cuisine—try *magret de canard aux grains de cassis et pommes fondantes* or *filet de vivaneau dans son feuilletage et beurre rouge*. A rose for the lady at the end of dinner and an impressively large bill. **Le Poisson d'Or** (℗ 87 72 45) is slightly farther down the waterfront, in an old stone warehouse, restored with arches and beams. You dine on the terrace to piano accompaniment. French cuisine: their red snapper is superb, wrapped in puff pastry with caviar and *beurre blanc*. In Grand Case, **Le Tastevin** (℗ 87 55 45), has a charming waterfront setting under palm trees. French cuisine and some creative concessions to Caribbean flavours—*magret de canard à la banane et au citron vert*, and *croustillant de mérou au gingembre* (crispy grouper in a ginger sauce). Another charming restaurant where you dine on the waterfront veranda is **L'Escapade** (℗ 87 75 04). Friendly and family run, the cuisine is mainly French. Try red snapper filet in a champagne cream sauce and a fruit ice-cream for pudding.

moderate

Two slightly less expensive French restaurants, still with excellent fare and in charming settings, are **La Maison sur le Port** (℗ 87 56 38), where you dine on a pretty veranda with the lights of the Marigot waterfront ahead of you (duck in a mango sauce and light spicy chicken in mustard); and in Grand Case **l'Auberge Gourmande** (℗ 87 73 37), set in a charming stone town house with louvred windows and doors opening onto the street. Friendly and intimate dining room to go with a delicious *mérou à la fondue de poireau*, grouper in a leek sauce. There are a number of excellent restaurants serving **creole** food. For a waterfront setting of antique stone arches, flaming torches and waves lapping beneath you, try **Le Jardin Créole** (℗ 87 99 56) at the end of Eagle Road in Sandy Ground. Start with *petits boudins des Antilles* (creole sausage with nutmeg) and the best of Anguillan rock lobster in island thyme with a creole sauce or coraline butter. One of the most original settings is that of **Le Bistrot Nu** (℗ 87 97 09), which is in an old wooden chattel house hidden in an alley in the backstreets of Marigot (on the left as you leave Marigot to the north, opposite the school). Paysanne salad and provençale scallops. It is fun but small, so you have to be flexible about when you eat. Another good bet is **La Rhumerie** (✆ 87 56 98) in the valley of Colombier, which serves French and creole food on a small veranda surrounded by the encroaching jungle and the ringing of tree frogs.You can get a good *boudin créole* followed by *blanquette pêcheur*. Then comes a volley of flavoured rums (in keeping with the name of the restaurant)—*maracudja* (passion fruit), *cajou* (cashew) and *quenette* (guinep). Finally **Chez Yvette** (✆ 82 32 03) is hidden away in the Quartier d'Orléans, serving excellent West Indian cuisine.

cheap

In Marigot you can eat quite cheaply in all the cafés along the waterfront. Outside the town you'll find a good French creole meal in an old Caribbean clapboard house at **Lila's Restaurant Chez Bruno** (✆ 87 80 05), up the hill on the road to Grand Case. Tables are laid with plastic tablecloths and flowers; try *brochette gambasse* (shrimp kebab), *ragout de cabrit* (stew goat) and other Haitian dishes. Grand Case has some pleasant places to eat for a (relatively) cheaper meal. **Les Arts Café** is set in a creole house on the road and **Chez Lolotte et Jojo** has local blaffs and court-bouillon fish. At the **Cha Cha Cha** Caribbean Café there is a tapas garden with tables set around a sea almond tree. But one of the best places to eat is at **Les Lolos**, where the food is cooked in front of you on flaming roadside grills. Grilled chicken, ribs, lobster, shrimp and stuffed crab, take away or sit in at the easy-going waterfront bars. There are more 'Lolos' in Marigot by the stadium on the road out to Grand Case.

Bars and Nightlife

In the old trading warehouses in downtown Marigot you will find a couple of cocktail bars patronised by a trendy crowd—the **Bar de la Mer** and **Sturgis Café**, often with live music. Along the waterfront is **La Fiesta**, an open lounge dressed up in pink, around a central bar. Music every night in season and a cocktail list as long as your arm. On the **Terrase des Naufrages** (shipwreck terrace) in Port Royale marina there are endless cafés where you can linger over an ice cream, but at the end you will find a favourite haunt of washed-up sailors at **Le Lafayette**. **Le Circus** in Nettle Bay is a video bar with a stray car in the dining room—pizzas and beer, rock music. In Grand Case you can start at **Surf Club South**, a rock and roll bar in a neat shack under the trees in the middle of town, and go on to the **Blue Moon**. There are discotheques, including **Caribe Club** and **Macumba** in Sandy Ground, which play Caribbean music, and **Night Fever**, just by the turning to Colombier, where you can flex your legs with the locals (weekends).

Saint Barthélémy

Saint Barthélémy is one of the most chic, civilized and least-known parts of France. Here bronzed beauties cruise by on the beaches in just a nuance of a bathing costume and out in the bay the water whistles with windsurfers in red, white and blue; Dior, Chanel, Lacroix, jazz, restaurants to linger in, haute cuisine and Veuve Cliquot champagne. It is a chi-chi 20th-century playground, as only the French could conceive. Even the tourist brochures are stylish and sexy in St Barts.

Southeast of Saint Martin in the Leewards by 15 miles (24km), St Barts is a crooked island 6 miles (10km) long—folds of volcanic lava and rubble that have been pushed up from beneath the ocean and sprouted a mantle of scrub. The fragmented coastline has some lovely coves, many of them culminating in perfect strands. St Barthélémy (pronounced 'San Bar-tailer-mee' in French) is the island's formal name, but it is hardly used. It is usually known as Saint Barth in French, St Barts in English. There are 5050 islanders.

Strangely, for much of the 19th century, St Barts belonged to Sweden and it was turned into a successful trading outpost. Despite their interlude as Swedes, the St Barthéléminois (sic) are mostly descended from French settlers and you might see a traditional bonnet or hear a snatch of a strange French dialect in one of the original villages. The population has always been white as there were never many slaves. As the tourist industry has steadily grown in the last thirty years, St Barts has turned from one of the quietest islands in the area to a trusted home-from-home for expatriate French. It is a little *snob* at times, but is generally friendly. It has taken on an overlay of the République—there is practically no recognizable West Indian culture outside the cultivated prettiness of the tropical gardens—and it has gained a reputation as an exclusive tropical resort. It is the favoured haunt of transient millionaires on a crusade against winter.

History

St Barts was not seen by Columbus, but later travellers called the island after his brother, Bartolomeo, who went with him to the New World. Like the rest of the Leewards it was given a wide berth by the Spanish colonists for their first hundred years because *Ouanalao*, as the Caribs knew the island, was cannibal country.

Settlers came in 1659, eking a living out of the ground with such crops as tobacco and indigo, but the main source of income for the next hundred years really lay in

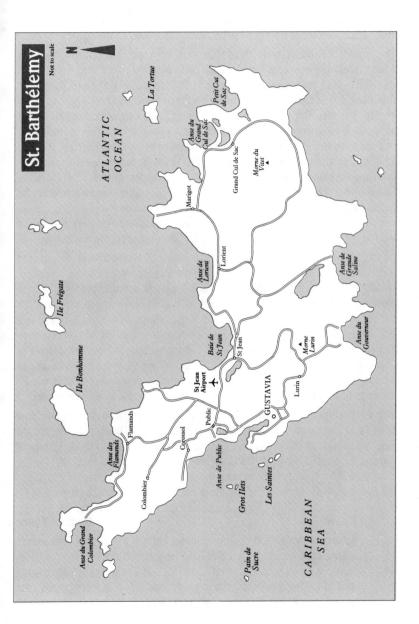

St. Barthélemy

Not to scale

N

ATLANTIC
OCEAN

La Tortue

Petit Cul
de Sac

Anse du
Grand
Cul de Sac

Grand Cul de Sac

Morne du
Vitet

Île Frégate

Marigot

Lorient

Anse de
Lorient

Anse de
Grande
Saline

Île Bonhomme

Baie de
St Jean

St Jean

Anse du
Gouverneur

Morne
Lurin

Anse des
Flamands

Flamands

St Jean
Airport

Colombier

Corossol

Public

GUSTAVIA

Lurin

Anse du Grand
Colombier

Anse de Public

Gros Îlets

Les Saintes

Pain de
Sucre

CARIBBEAN
SEA

189

the island's position and in its well-protected coves. Smugglers and pirates, *en route* from South America to the Bahamas, would use the bays to repair their ships, and the islanders made a profit by selling them the provisions they needed to refit.

The original St Barthians were Frenchmen from Normandy and Brittany. They had a few slaves, domestic ones only because there were no plantations. Even late in the 18th century there were still less than 1000 inhabitants on St Barts. Then, on 1 July 1784, the St Barthians woke to find that their island was no longer owned by France, but that they were on lease to Sweden. The King of France had simply swapped it for a warehouse in Gothenburg and for trading rights in the Baltic, without even consulting them. St Barts was Sweden's only colony in the Caribbean and little remains of their influence except the old stone warehouses on the waterfront and the street names in Gustavia, the capital. The Swedish reign benefited the St Barthians, however. King Gustav promptly declared the island a free port and before long St Barts was prospering as a market on the trade routes from Europe to the burgeoning United States. While the other islands were held to ransom in the wars at the turn of the 18th century, St Barts continued to rake in the money.

As soon as peace came to the Caribbean in the early 19th century and the seaborne trade waned, the island fell into decline and the Swedish venture failed. The population, which had reached 5000, began to fall, particularly after the Swedish king emancipated the island's slaves in 1847. There was no land for freed slaves to settle so they emigrated, mostly to the American Virgin Islands. In the end, King Oscar II put sovereignty to a referendum, and the islanders voted 351 to 1 to return to French rule. On 16 March 1878 St Barts was handed back to France. Appended to Guadeloupe once again, the decline continued. When Guadeloupe was made an overseas département of France in 1946, St Barts became one of its *communes*, under its financial control. St Barts retains its duty-free status since Swedish days.

Today it is administered, along with nearby Saint Martin, by a *sous-préfet* appointed from Paris. The islanders vote members on to the Conseil Général and the Conseil Régional, which sit in Basse-Terre, Guadeloupe, and directly in the French elections. Like Saint Martin, St Barts receives some assistance from the French Government via Guadeloupe for roads and large municipal projects. Tourism is the big earner now and the island maintains an exclusive and luxurious style.

✆ (590)–   **Getting There**

St Barts cannot take international flights but it is well served from islands nearby, of which the best is Sint Maarten (most flights and good connections), or possibly San Juan in Puerto Rico or Guadeloupe. Air St Barth (✆ 27 71 90) has eight flights a day to Juliana airport in Sint Maarten, four a week from Puerto Rico and three from Guadeloupe. Winair (✆ 35 42 30

Sint Maarten, 27 61 01 St Barts) has ten a day to Juliana. Air Guadeloupe (© 27 61 90) flies from Saint Martin (Grand Case), Guadeloupe, Puerto Rico and St Thomas in the USVI. Air St Thomas (© 27 71 76) also fly from Puerto Rico and St Thomas.

The airstrip on St Barts, situated on the Plaine de la Tourmente(!), is one of the most sporting in the Caribbean. The main problem is that at whichever end you make your approach, there is a hill just where you should be lining up. And so from one end passengers get a close inspection of some hillside forest and the roof of a hotel and from the other they drop close enough to the road to read car-drivers' T-shirts. If you look over the pilot's shoulder, it may seem that he is going to miss the runway, but the small planes are so manoeuvrable that they can turn on a sixpence. The runway closes at dusk, but you can usually make connections the same day from Europe and the USA. If this all sounds a bit much, there is a seaborne link from Saint Martin (both Marigot and Philipsburg) on the powerboat *St Barth Express*. It departs daily from Marigot (4.30pm) and returns to Saint Martin in the morning. There are only 12 seats, so book in advance (© 27 77 24).

If you just want a day trip to the island from Saint Martin, then there are plenty of yachts and launches that make an early start from Philipsburg. Try *White Octopus*, which leaves from Bobby's Marina (© 599 5 23170). For a trip to one of the other islands, contact **St Barth Voyages** on rue Duquesne in Gustavia (© 27 79 79). There are also helicopters available; contact **Héli–Inter** (© 27 71 14).

Getting Around

Taxis are readily available at the airport and on the main quay in Gustavia. You can also order them through a hotel or through the central number (© 27 66 31). Gustavia to the airport will set you back US$6. There is no bus service, but hitching is quite a dependable way to get around.

Car hire is expensive across the board, though it gives you much more flexibilty. The island favourite is the mini-moke and its Volkswagen equivalent, the Gurgel, and most recently the Suzuki jeep—they can just about cope with St Barts' many hills. Some of the big international names operate out of the airport and many hotels keep cars for their guests. If you will want one during the high season, you should order it in advance. A foreign driving licence is valid, credit cards are usually accepted, driving is mostly on the right and many companies will deliver to your hotel. The minimum price in season is about US$35 a day plus taxes. Some rental companies are: **Budget** (© 27 66 30) and **Hertz** (© 27 71 14) in St Jean and **Turbe**

Car Rental (✆ 27 71 42) at the airport. **Scooters** are also easily available for hire, though they are less likely to get you up the steep hills. Try **Chez Béranger** (✆ 27 89 00) or **Rent Some Fun** (✆ 27 70 59), the exclusive Harley Davidson dealer (if there are any on island) for scooters and bigger bikes, or **St Barth Motos** (✆ 27 67 89).

Tourist Information

The **Office du Tourisme** (✆ 27 87 27, fax 27 74 47) is on the Quai Général de Gaulle in Gustavia, open weekdays 8.30–6, Sat 9–12. An information bureau at the airport keeps the same hours. There is an annual glossy magazine *Tropical St Barth* with features about the island and some advice on sports, shopping and restaurants and the annual *Ti Gourmet* will give hints about restaurants.

In a medical **emergency**, the Gustavia Hospital is on the seaward arm of the town, on the rue Jean Bart (✆ 27 60 00). The **IDD code** for St Barts is 590 followed by the the the six-digit number. If you are calling within the island, dial just the six digits. There are no coin boxes and to use a public phone you need a *télécarte*, bought in advance at the post office.

Money

Generally speaking, St Barts is very expensive. Though the official currency is the French franc, the US dollar is accepted universally (US$1 = Fr5.5 approx). If you are one to watch exchange rates, then you might find that you can get a marginally better deal in francs than in dollars. Credit cards are accepted by all shops, restaurants and hotels. Service is *compris* in restaurants, and hotels add 10–15% to your bill. **Banks** are open on weekdays until mid-afternoon. BFC opposite the airport is open on Saturday mornings and Crédit Agricole in town has a hole-in-the-wall machine. **Shops** keep hours of 8.30–noon and 2–5. St Barts has been allowed to keep its tax-free status from Swedish days.

Beaches

St Barts has magnificent beaches, mounds of golden sand tucked away in coves, cut into the coastline and protected on both sides by mountainous headlands. Topless bathing is accepted and happens everywhere, but surprisingly on a French island, nudity is against the rules. All beaches are public, though you may have to get permission to cross somebody's land (ask if they stop you). *Anse* means cove.

The island's two best beaches are on the south coast—**Anse du Gouverneur** and the **Anse de Grande Saline**. Both have stacks of bright white sand that shelve gently into the sea in their own deep bays, with views of the volcanic peaks of Saba, St Eustatius and St Kitts. Both are popular, as you will see by the hundred-yard line of mini-mokes and jeeplets, but as there are no beach bars, you will need to take all you need in the way of water and food. Anse du Gouverneur is approached via Lurin (south out of Gustavia) and Anse de Grande Saline from St Jean.

St Jean itself is the island's busiest beach; a calm double curve of perfect sand where the tanned scooter-brigade congregate, exercising their windsurfers or taking a dip. Beach bars include **Le Pélican**, **Chez Francine**, a pretty veranda retreat and for real beachfront *dégustation*, **Le Filao** (a member of 'Relais et Châteaux').

In the northwest of the island are two cracking suntraps lined with talcum-powder sand: **Anse des Flamands** is 600 yards of gentle waves, with a stunning view of the deserted Ile Bonhomme. **La Frégate** is a charming spot to retreat to when the sun and sizzling becomes too much; and **Anse du Grand Colombier**, a walk off the beaten track from Petit Morne, palm-shaded and usually very secluded (take water and a picnic). **Lorient** is less known by tourists than by fishermen, but has a magnificent curve of white sand. It is quiet, and good for those with children.

The **Anse du Grand Cul-de-Sac** receives winds straight off the Atlantic, but the bay is protected by a reef and so it is good for swimming and windsurfing. There are a couple of hotels here, where you can get a drink and a meal or borrow water-sports equipment. If you are feeling chic and wealthy, you might take lunch at **Le Lafayette Club**, winter haunt of the stars. The **Petit Cul de Sac** is a smaller secluded cove bordered by mangrove. Ten minutes' walk out of Gustavia is the **Anse de Grand Galet** where shells are washed up in piles of pink and orange on the soft light-brown sand—good for a walk. Beyond the town travelling north is another suntrap beneath the hills, in the fishing village of **Corossol**. Just down from the nets and the boats there is a strip of beige sand so soft that you sink up to your shins and a cracking sunset view.

Sailing

St Barts is surrounded by offshore cays which make attractive stopovers, but the island itself also has superb coves and calm anchorages for those who like slithering overboard and swimming up to the sand before retiring to further inactivity. The main **anchorage** is the port of Gustavia, which has excellent shoreside restaurants and simple requirements such as water and fully stocked supermarkets. Inside the harbour it can get quite crowded. Technical support and fuel are available at the commercial dock just out of the town. You can also anchor overnight beyond here in Anse du Corossol and even Anse du Colombier near the northwestern tip of the island. The most popular beaches for a daytime stopover are on the south coast, the steep-sided coves of Anse du Gouverneur and Anse de Grande Saline. A good anchorage offshore is on Ile Fourche, where there is a protected bight and good snorkelling.

Customs are in the main port office on the eastern side of the bay. You will be charged a cruising fee which varies according to the size of your yacht.

Bareboat charters can be arranged through **Marine Service** (© 27 70 36, fax 27 70 34), or you could try the many fleets in St Martin. Crewed yachts are available from **Stardust Marine** (© 27 79 81, fax 27 79 82). For **repairs** contact **St Barts Ship Services** (© 27 77 38).

Sports

Windsurfers and small **sailing** boats are available for hire at two main beaches: on the **Baie de St Jean**, try the **St Barts Wind School** (© 27 71 22) for Mistral and BIC boards; on the **Anse du Grand Cul-de-Sac** at the eastern end of the island, you will find **Wind Wave Power** (© 27 82 57). Lessons available. Most hotels also have boards for hire. **Marine Service** (© 27 70 34) have boats if you would like to spend a day **deep-sea fishing** (*pêche à gros*), casting for marlin and kingfish, *six people for a half-day for about US$400.*

Snorkellers will find the water around St Barts rewarding. Try the reefs at Petite Anse beyond Anse des Flamands, Anse Maréchal and the Grand or Petit Cul-de-Sac. Alternatively some hotels and the companies above offer snorkelling trips. **La Plongée** (scuba diving) on the off-shore reefs and islands is also easily arranged. Expect to see striped sergeant-major fish gliding by followed by grunts, and long-spined urchins lurking in among the seafans and staghorn coral. Reefs include the off-shore rocks of Les Saintes, Gros Ilets and Pain de Sucre. *A one-tank dive costs from US$45.* In Gustavia contact the **St Barth Diving Centre** at Marine Service (© 27 70 34) which is PADI certified. **La Bulle** (© 27 68 93) and **Rainbow Dive** (© 27 31 29) work from Gustavia. Certification courses available. If you would like to look at the corals in the dry, then contact **Aquascope** at Marine Service.

On land there is little in the way of sports other than **tennis**. There are courts at many of the hotels—Guanahani and the St Barth Beach Hotel—as well as the Sports Club of Colombier (© 27 61 07). If you would like to explore the island on horseback, contact **Ranch des Flammands** (© 27 80 72).

Gustavia

Only hints of a Swedish heritage remain in St Barts' capital after a hundred years and the recent tourist redevelopment. Almost all the original town was destroyed by hurricane and a fire in 1850, and only a couple of houses remain in use (on the rue Sadi

Carnot and the rue Jeanne d'Arc). But streetnames—Vikingagatan, Hwarfsgatan, Ostra- and Westra-Strandgatan—on the waterfront give an unusual impression for the Caribbean. The name Gustavia is taken from the enlightened despot King Gustav III who leased St Barts from France and gave the island free-port status, enabling it to prosper.

Swedish Belfry

Today the population of Gustavia is a few hundred, a fraction of what it was two hundred years ago when the harbour was filled with merchants and the warehouses were overflowing. Sailing craft are filling the harbour once again, though—the waterfront is given over almost entirely to marina space in season—as they cruise between the Virgin Islands to Antigua. And the port maintains its mercantile tradition with chic-looking mannequins displaying Christian Lacroix and Gucci clothes at duty-free prices. But it is no longer Swedish in atmosphere: with endless bistros and police wearing *képis*, the ambience is now distinctly French.

At the four points around the harbour stand the tired old fortresses that once guarded Gustavia. It is possible to visit Fort Gustave on the road out of town, from where there is a magnificent view of the harbour. Another remaining Swedish feature of Gustavia is the distinctive triangular-roofed clock-tower known as the Swedish belfry. It stands high above the town next to the **sous-préfecture** (formerly the island prison) and was originally built as a church-tower. The **English anchor** at the head of the harbour is about two hundred years old, but it has only been in St Barts since 1981 when it was dragged here by mistake from St Thomas in the Virgin Islands. It was left on the quay and has become part of the furniture.

The **Municipal Museum**, *open Mon–Thurs 8–noon, 1.30–5.30, Fri 1.30–5, Sat 8–noon, adm*, can be found near the point of the bay (and will be installed in the Wall House when that is restored). On display you will see prints and pictures of old-time St Barts, alongside mock-ups of the traditional cottages and some rush-work articles made of the *latanier* palm.

Around the Island

For an island with no peak over 1000ft, St Barts is extremely hilly and rough. There is little rain, not much cultivation, and the hills are infested with scrub, tall torch cactus and the distinctive St Barts palm tree, the *latanier*. For centuries the villagers were completely isolated from one another and would meet only in church after walking for hours along tortuous paths hacked out of the undergrowth. Nowadays the island is cut and crossed with impossibly steep and windy roads and the furthest reaches are occupied by holiday villas. In the narrow valleys you will see mournful white cattle egrets waiting for food while their companions graze.

You might catch snatches of a strange language in the country, the old speech of the islanders' Norman ancestors (the communities were so isolated that people living just 5 miles from one another spoke with a different accent). And you may just still see the womenfolk wearing their traditional frilled bonnets, or *calèches*— starched and prim white hats that keep the islanders' Norman skin protected from the sun. They are nicknamed *quichenottes*, supposedly a corruption of 'kiss-me-not', because it is rather difficult to get another face underneath them.

North of Gustavia the sea road cuts inland to St Barts' small industrial estate at **Public** and then emerges on the coast again at **Corossol**, a charming fishing village, where the houses clutter the slopes of a valley that opens on to the beach. In Corossol they wear the *calèche à platine*, with multiple hems, a frilly border and little chance of scoring a kiss. Farther up the coast in Colombier and in Flamands traditionally they wear the *calèche à batons*, strengthened with wooden slats. There is a private sea-shell collection on view in the town at the **Inter Oceans Museum** (© 27 62 97), *open daily 9–5, adm*, where you can see giant clams with wavy lips and some miniature creations of incredible intricacy.

All over this area you will see the *latanier* with its smooth trunk, a tangled confusion of stubs and then a series of fronds that grow like scratchy fans. When dried these leaves are very skilfully woven by the local women into hats, bags and table mats. Corossol is probably the best place to buy them.

East of Gustavia, **St Jean**, the site of the earliest settlement on the island, has become the centre of the tourist industry in St Barts—the old town has been almost swallowed by recent development. As you go east the villas thin out on the hills and old St Barts begins to appear—dry-stone walls and distinctive houses with red roofs and sloping plastered walls. A few fishermen still work out of Lorient Bay. Boobies nest on the clifftops and in the mangroves you may see a pelican digesting a meal in the sun. The road rings the eastern end of the island, around St Barts highest peak, Morne de Vitet (about 930ft), emerging on the southern coast, with views as far as Statia and St Kitts, and then returning to the north coast at St Jean.

Festivals

St Barts stages a number of traditional French and Caribbean events as well as get-togethers for interested sportsmen and wine-drinkers. **Carnaval** takes place around Mardi Gras, with dances at the weekend culminating on Ash Wednesday with the black and white parades and the burning of *Vaval*, the spirit of the French Caribbean carnival; on their **Saint's Days**, Gustavia (14 August) and St Barthélémy (24 August), St Louis (25 August) and the eastern towns (27 and 28 August) come alive in trusted Caribbean style—jump-ups in the street. Mid-January sees the **St Barts Music Festival**, with performances of chamber music, dance music and jazz by top international musicians. In mid-May there are celebrations around the arrival of yachts from Lorient in France; the **St Barts Regatta**, also usually held in May, stages traditional boat races. In December, the St Barts Yacht Club organizes the **Route du Rosé**, a race for yachts of 65ft and above to bring a case of rosé wine from St Tropez, followed by the usual partying.

© (590)– **Where to Stay**

St Barts has some extremely expensive and sumptuous hotels (none larger than about 60 rooms). And they are particular in the Caribbean for being set in delightful tropical gardens. Service is usually charged at 10%. There are also many villas to rent on the island; contact **Sibarth**, PO Box 55 Gustavia, 97098 Cedex, St Barthélémy (© 590 27 62 38, fax 27 60 52); US PO Box 1461 Newport, Rhode Island 02840 (© 401 849 8012, fax 847 6290, US toll free © 800 932 3222), UK toll free (© 0800 898 318), France (© 05 90 16 20), Germany (© 01 30 81 57 30).

very expensive–luxury

Perhaps the most elegant and comfortable hotel on St Barts is **Le Toiny** (© 27 88 88, fax 27 89 30) in the southeast of the island. Just 12 villas make up the resort, which stands on the hillside, looking over the Anse de Toiny to St Kitts (there is no beach there, but each villa has a pool). The villas are decorated in colonial style—wooden parquet floors, mahogany furniture and four poster beds—but have all the 20th-century luxuries too, down to the video recorder and satellite television and a shower in the open air. There are kitchenettes, but also room service and an excellent restaurant. Car necessary, luxury. If you prefer to be on the beach, the **Hotel Manapany**, PO Box 114 (© 27 66 55, fax 27 75 28) has 52 rooms and suites located in 32 cottages, some fronting on to the sand, each with its own large veranda. All have video recorders, and room service at mealtimes. There are tennis courts and watersports, with two restaurants above the pool, very expensive. The Hotel **Ile de France** (© 27 61 81, fax 27 86 83) also proffers beach-front sumptuousness on the Baie des Flamands on the north coast. The mock-classical main house stands majestically above the sand, with 12 huge rooms, marble floors, English antiques and private jacuzzis in outsize bathrooms. Across the road there are 17 slightly smaller rooms, suites and bungalows in the *latanier* garden, where you will also find the other facilities including the restaurant and sports room, luxury. Next door at the end of the beach is the fashionable and idiosyncratic **Taïwana** (© 27 65 01, fax 27 63 82). Difficult to recommend personally as guide-book writers (along with anyone else they do not like the look of) are booted out, but the place seems to have an easy exclusivity about it. On offer is pretty much everything you might want; from helicopter transfer from Sint Maarten and champagne breakfasts to famous acquaintances in the next-door cottage, and of course privacy (from riff-raff). Absurdly expensive. The **François Plantation** (© 27 78 82, fax 27 61 26) stands high on the hillside above Colombier. The estate house has the old-time ambience of a plantation; an antique drawing room and dining room on a breezy terrace, where you dine on classical French cuisine. Rooms are furnished in dark-stained tropical wood, each with its own terrace. Quiet and reserved, very expensive. A hip spot, beautifully set in a garden of tropical profusion, is **Club la Banane**, in Quartier Lorient (© 27 68 25, fax 27 68 44). Just nine rooms in suitably eclectic style; antique furniture, colourful tiles and louvres on the windows. The bathrooms are part outdoor and overgrown with tropical flora. Also worth going for the evening show— champagne bottles decorked with a cutlass and very OTT. Very expensive.

expensive

El Sereno Hotel (© 27 64 80, fax 27 75 47, US reservations © 800 373 6246) is a marginally less expensive resort, on the beach in Grand Cul de Sac. Comfortable rooms are lost in an explosion of greenery, with brightly painted garden walls for privacy, and each room has a hammock. The waterfront restaurant, La Tocque Lyonnaise, serves French and exotic creole cuisine. Close by is the **St Barth Beach Hotel** (© 27 62 73, fax 27 75 57), 36 comfortable rooms in a block above the beach. In Gustavia is **L'Hibiscus** (© 27 64 82, fax 27 73 04) which has a fantastic view of the harbour. The 11 rooms, set in bungalows on the hillside, are very comfortable if a little small, but they have their own terraces. The Hotel **Baie des Anges**, PO Box 162 (© 27 63 61, fax 27 83 44), has just nine rooms and kitchenettes overlooking a well-tended garden in Anse des Flammands.

moderate–cheap

Nearby is **l'Auberge de la Petite Anse**, PO Box 117 (© 27 64 60, fax 27 72 30), which stands on the clifftop at the end of the Anse des Flamands, with rooms in the 16 bungalows, moderate. In Colombier you will find

Le P'tit Morne, PO Box 14 (© 27 62 64, fax 27 84 63); 14 apartments and a pool, moderate. There are three cheaper places to stay: **La Presqu'ile** (© 27 64 60, fax 27 72 30) in Gustavia, the **Hotel Normandie** (© 27 61 66) in Lorient and nearby the slightly cheaper **Manoir de Lorient** (© 27 79 27). There are *chambres d'hôtes* in Anse des Cayes (© 27 75 20).

© *(590)–*   ## Eating Out

There are some excellent restaurants in St Barts, from hotel dining rooms (Filao Beach in St Jean, François Plantation, La Tocque Lyonnaise at El Sereno and le Gaïac at Le Toiny) to water-front bistros and converted hilltop homes. Cuisine is sometimes heavyweight classical French, but you will find concessions to the climate—lighter sauces and exotic ingredients—in *nouvelle cuisine créole*. It is expensive, but all part of the experience. Categories reflect the price of a main course: *expensive*—Fr130 and above; *moderate*—Fr70–130; *cheap*—under Fr70. There are often set menus and service is *compris.*

expensive

Perhaps the most elegant setting is at **Le Sapotillier** (© 27 60 28) in a stone house in the heart of Gustavia. You dine inside or in the walled garden beneath the branches of a huge sasparilla tree. The menu is mainly French—*escalope de fois gras de canard au genièvre et choux vert*, duck fois gras in juniper served on green cabbage, or *le couscous de gambas à la créole.* Stylish, attentive service. At **Chez Adam** (© 27 93 22) you dine on the large gallery of an old Caribbean house looking down through a lit garden to an inland lagoon. The cuisine is French—*croustillant de saumon et légumes parfumés au pistou*, with some concessions to the Caribbean—*filet mignon de porc au coco et curry.* Ever-popular and chic is **Chez Maya** (© 27 73 61), where you sit on a deck festooned with greenery or under a flamboyant tree above the waterfront in Public, a short drive from town. It serves fish and creole specialities including chicken in *sauce chien.*

moderate

A very pleasant evening out in town can be had at **Au Port** (© 27 62 36), where you dine upstairs, perhaps on the veranda, in a pretty old creole town house. A mix of traditional French dishes and some creative creole fare with Caribbean fruits—*aiguilletes de poulet au rhum blanc et baies roses*, chicken filet in white rum and pink pepper. **La Marine** (© 27 68 91), towered over by yachts on the western arm of Gustavia bay, special-izes in seafood and fish as the name suggests. Fish-net decor and brisk service, *escalope de saumon à l'oseille* (salmon in sorrel). There is also simple fare at the popular **L'Escale** (℗ 27 81 06), next door. Pizzas and pasta in comfortable white wicker arm-chairs on the bay, moderate to cheap. Across the road is **L'Entrepont** (℗ 27 90 60), an Italian restaurant set in a pretty tropical garden with tables under sea almond trees and palms. For something more West Indian you can try the creole restaurant **New Born** (℗ 27 67 07). Curried or creole fish grilled over a wood fire, smoked shark and blood pudding, followed by local fruit-flavoured rums. The **Marigot Bay Club** (℗ 27 75 45) serves French and creole fare on a shoreside deck brushed by coconut palms in Marigot Bay—*farandole des trois boudins créoles* (lobster conch and fish sausages), or *christophine farcie à la langouste* (christophine with a lobster stuffing), moderate to expensive. **Chez Francine** (℗ 27 60 49) is a popular spot in St Jean; French and creole fare. Back in town there are a string of easy-going haunts with reliable food. **Eddy's Ghetto** has a tamed rustic feel with pretty wicker chairs surrounded by palms and greenery. Salads, grilled fish and ribs are specialities, with reggae music to boot. **Les Lauriers** (℗ 27 64 12), on the rue Victor Hugo, is a quiet creole restaurant in a garden dining room with bamboo walls. Try the court bouillon of fish with spices or the Caribbean curried chicken. At **Côte Jardin** (℗ 27 70 47), just off rue Gambetta, you eat Italian food on a veranda, settled in canvas deck chairs.

cheap

Chez Joe has the simplest menu in town, with hamburgers, salads or a steak and frites; **Entre'Acte** also serves simple meals, as does **Le Créole** in St Jean. **Le Santa Fé** has burgers and the sunset to compliment video and billiards.

Nightlife

St Barts has a low-key attitude to entertainment. In town the **Carl Gustaf Hotel** is a great place for a cocktail with a view and **l'Hibiscus** will give you a jazz accompaniment to your drink. There is sometimes a singer at **Manapany**. You will get a lively evening out at the dinner and show at **Club La Banane** (℗ 27 68 25). Tanned windsurfers collect in the garden at **Le Select** in the centre of town. If you prefer to watch than be watched, you might retreat across the road to the balcony of the **Bar de l'Oubli**. The **American Bar** is on the waterfront on the seaward arm of Gustavia Bay. Decor of all-American heroes to go with American rock and a lively crowd late on. In St Jean you can try the **Pelican**, a bar and jazz haunt on a beachfront terrace set with palms at tipsy angles. Not far off is **Topolino**, a video bar. Nightclubs include **Le Petit Club**, **La Licorne**, a local disco in Lorient and **Why Not** in Lurin.

The British Virgin Islands

The Virgin Islands must have been a nightmare for early cartographers—more than a hundred islands scattered over 1000 square miles; forested volcanic colossi that soar from the water and tiny cays that barely make it above the surf. To sail among them is a glorious sight, as stunning as it was five hundred years ago when Columbus himself passed through. He was so awestruck by their beauty that he compared them to St Ursula and her 11,000 virgins—a name which has remained ever since.

The British Virgin Islands—fifty or so reefs, rocks and raging volcanic towers—are sprinkled across the sea to the northeast of the USVI. They run in two lines about 3 miles apart, enclosing the Sir Francis Drake Channel. The bays make magnificent anchorages, as good now for hiding out as when the pirates caroused and careened their ships here. The British Virgin Islands are some of the best sailing grounds in the world, hiding some great places on which to be marooned (particularly in five-star luxury).

The British Virgins are undeveloped in comparison with their American counterparts. There is none of the hustle and bustle of St Thomas. Tortola is changing though, as the tourism industry develops. Construction has recently broken the green continuity of the hillside scrub as the islanders build themselves larger homes and outsiders build vacation villas. There is an increasingly upbeat air in Tortola. In Virgin Gorda, though, life continues at a dozier, more typical Caribbean pace.

There are about 17,000 inhabitants in the BVI, most of whom live on Tortola. However, for generations they have been travelling to the USVI and so there is probably a larger number than this living in the American Virgin Islands. They benefit from their special status as belongers and from having the dollar as their currency, but they talk fearfully of how the USVI has been over-developed and of the crime level there. In the BVI the policemen carry truncheons rather than guns. Some islanders claim that the very word 'British' adds a stability of sorts.

In times past the BVI have looked east to the Leeward Islands, and they still do in some matters such as sport, carnival and music, which is mostly calypso. However, most BVIers admit that American influence will inevitably increase and the old British ways recede. There is continual American investment and most consumer goods

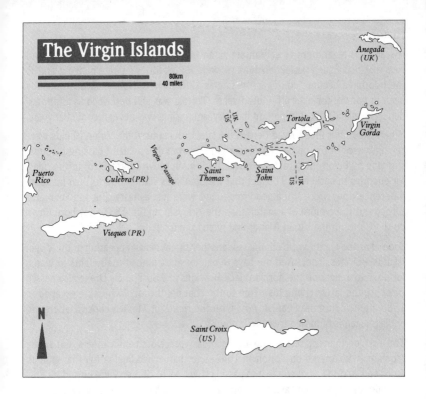

The Virgin Islands

Anegada (UK)

80km
40 miles

UK US

Tortola

Virgin Gorda

Virgin Passage

Puerto Rico

Culebra (PR)

Saint Thomas

Saint John

UK US

Vieques (PR)

N

Saint Croix (US)

originate in the USA anyway. It is probably only a matter of time before softball overtakes cricket in popularity.

About 200,000 tourists visit the BVI each year, of which the majority come for the sailing. The BVI have angled their tourism at the upper end of the market, setting themselves out as a sophisticated Caribbean playground. They do it pretty well. The BVI are hardly cheap, but the islanders are friendly and easy-going and there is a lower hustle factor than elsewhere in the islands. You can get a very good tropical break here and for a price you can get luxurious seclusion on a tropical island resort.

Most people who come to the Virgin Islands will spend time on the water: on a ferry, belly-flopping over the sea in a seaplane or in snorkelling gear, or cruising in a yacht between secluded coves and beach bars. The cartographer's nightmare is a sailor's paradise.

History

History and legend are closely intertwined in the Virgin Islands—the coves and bays that make such perfect anchorages were for centuries a pirate hangout and so the two have become confused. As late as 1792, when the British had officially been in control for over a hundred years, Tortola was still described as a 'pirates' den'. The islands' most important industry, smuggling, was never recorded anyway.

When Columbus first arrived here in the late 15th century, the Virgin Islands were seeing waves of the belligerent Carib Indians from down-island passing through, stopping by before they raided Arawak Borinquen (now Puerto Rico) in the quest for enemies to barbecue. The fact that the Spaniards settled Puerto Rico made no difference, they were still a good target and were just as tasty. But the Spaniards turned out to be more of a match than the Arawaks and in 1555 they bore down on the Caribs in the Virgin Islands and wiped them out.

Soon after the Caribs were eliminated, another threat began appearing in the Virgin Islands—pirates. They used the bays to anchor and climbed the heights to watch for a sail to appear on the horizon. Jack Hawkins and Sir Francis Drake also passed through, the latter giving his name to the channel through which he escaped in 1585 after raiding the Spanish *flota* with the riches of Mexico aboard. There are endless legends of buried treasure in the BVI.

The first permanent settlers on the islands were Dutch buccaneers and cattle ranchers, who arrived on Tortola in 1648. They barbecued beef rather than human limbs and sold the smoked meat to passing ships. In 1672 they were ousted by English buccaneers and the eastern Virgin Islands were taken over by England. Despite the official status, the smuggling continued as the buccaneers became settled.

Although the islands are not particularly fertile, they were able to grow cotton and experienced some prosperity at the height of the sugar era during the 18th century. Slaves were brought here and the steep hillsides were terraced and planted with cotton and cane. Quakers who came to the islands had a hand in freeing some of the slaves (they thought slavery immoral and rallied against it) and the plantations folded quickly, even before emancipation in 1838. As they failed, so the white population left. In 1805 the population was about 10,500 (9000 slaves) and a century later there were 5000, of whom two were white. The islanders became subsistence farmers on the land abandoned by the white settlers. This has only changed in the last few years with the advent of the tourist industry.

Early on the British Virgin Islands were governed by an elected council, but in 1867 this was abolished and the islands were simply appended to the Leeward Island Federation as a 'Presidency'. The British Virgin Islands are still a Crown Colony of Britain and are nominally administered by a Governor appointed in

London, but since the Second World War the Virgin Islands have steadily taken on internal self-government. There is a 12-member elected council with a ministerial system. The Chief Minister is the Hon H. Lavity Stoutt of the Virgin Islands Party.

Lying so close to their American counterparts, the British Virgin Islands have often considered political union with the USVI. In the fifties, as the other British Caribbean countries moved together in federation, the British Virgins turned away and seemed to be on the point of making the link. There were even rumours in the 1960s that the British Government had offered to sell the islands to the United States. But no union was formed and most islanders feel that it was the right decision.

The biggest foreign exchange earner is tourism: of the 200,000 visitors each year, there are 80,000 cruise ship arrivals and of the rest 60 per cent come for the sailing. Other industries include construction (the scars of quarrying and building plots are visible in the hillsides), some light manufacturing and an expanding off-shore finance sector.

© (809 49)–
Getting There

By Air: The BVI are still relatively remote and you will have to make a connection to get there (the biggest aircraft that can land in the BVI is a 49-seater). The main hub in the area is San Juan in Puerto Rico and plenty of airlines make the onward connections—LIAT (local *©* 52577), Sunaire Express (*©* 52840), American Eagle (*©* 52559), Four Star Aviation (*©* 54389) and GAS (Gorda Air Services) (*©* 52271). Airstrips on the islands include Beef Island (for Tortola), Virgin Gorda and Anegada. There is a departure tax of $8 if you are leaving by air and $5 if you are departing on a boat or a ferry.

By Air from the UK: British Airways has a couple of flights a week to San Juan, arriving early enough to make the connection the same day. It is perhaps preferable to fly via Antigua, where LIAT connects with BA and BWIA flights from the UK and Europe.

By Air from the USA: Connecting flights can be arranged via San Juan, Puerto Rico (e.g. American Airlines and Delta from Atlanta) and through the USVI (*see* p.235).

By Air from other Caribbean Islands: There are flights to Tortola from St Thomas, Puerto Rico, Antigua, Anguilla and Sint Maarten. Services to Virgin Gorda are more limited, though there are direct links from San Juan. Charter companies include GAS and Fly BVI (*©* 809 49 51747).

Ferries between the USVI and the BVI: There are plenty of ferries from **St Thomas**, USVI to **Tortola** in the BVI. Most depart from the Charlotte Amalie waterfront, touching West End on Tortola and then continuing to

Road Town. The crossing takes about an hour with customs. Companies include Native Son Inc (© 809 495 4617) and Smith's Ferry Services (© 809 494 4430). Speedy's (© 809 495 5240) runs a service three times a week from St Thomas to Virgin Gorda, a two-hour ride through Sir Francis Drake Channel, return fare about $40. St John also has links to West End on Tortola (usually three a day) and an occasional sailing to Jost van Dyke and Virgin Gorda.

© (809 49)– **Getting Around**

With so many islands, boats are a good way to get around. There are some scheduled flights (with GAS from Tortola to Virgin Gorda and to Anegada) but the islands are also well served with regular ferries. The main terminals are at West End and Road Town on Tortola, Beef Island (for the airport) and at the Valley and North Sound in Virgin Gorda. There are five or six sailings each day between Road Town and the Valley, on Speedy's (© 55240) and Smith's (© 44430). The North Sound Express (© 42746) meets flights in Beef Island if you want to go to the northern end of Virgin Gorda (Leverick Bay and Bitter End), about four trips a day. The boats are sleek and fun to ride as they skim across the water with a sonorous rumble. There is also a link from Beef Island to the Valley in Virgin Gorda on the Virgin Gorda Ferry Service (© 55240).

There are three or four daily sailings from West End to Jost van Dyke on the Jost van Dyke Ferry Service (© 42997). Peter Island is served by the Peter Island boat, which departs from the CSY marina in Road Town; about six crossings a day. There are no actual ferries to Anegada, so if you want to visit by sea your best bet is to take one of the many day cruises. Up-to-the-minute ferry schedules can be found in the BVI *Welcome* tourist magazine. An alternative way of travelling in the Virgin Islands is to go to the marinas and talk somebody into taking you on their yacht.

Tourist Information

The BVI Tourist Board has offices in:

UK: 110 St Martin's Lane, London WC2N 4DY (© 071 240 4259, fax 071 240 4270).

USA: 370 Lexington Ave, Suite 511, New York, NY 10017 (© 212 696 0400, toll free © 800 835 8530), or 1686 Union Street, San Francisco, CA 94123 (© 415 775 0344, toll free © 800 232 7770).

Germany: Sophienstraße 4, D 65189 Wiesbaden (© 0611 30 02 62, fax 0611 30 07 66).

In the **BVI** itself, the main Tourist Board is in the Social Security building in Road Town on Tortola, PO Box 134, Road Town (✆ 43134, fax 43866). The Virgin Gorda Tourist Board is in the Virgin Gorda Yacht Harbour (✆ 55181). The Tourist Board put out the quarterly *Welcome Tourist Guide*, in which you will find plenty of useful information about current events and the latest investment opportunities. The weekly *Limin' Times* gives an up-to-the-minute breakdown of boozing opportunities.

In a medical **emergency**, dial 998 or contact the Peebles Hospital in Road Town (✆ 43497), Tortola. On Virgin Gorda there are clinics in Spanish Town (✆ 55337) and at North Sound (✆ 57310).

The **IDD code** for the BVI is 809 49 followed by five digits. On island, you dial just the last five figures of the number.

Money

The currency of the BVI is the US dollar (adopted in 1967). You will find that major credit cards are widely accepted in hotels, restaurants and shops. **Banking** hours are weekdays 9–2.30 with an extra couple of hours on Friday afternoons until 5. Shops generally keep hours of 9–5, Mon–Sat.

Festivals

The highlight of the BVI calendar is **carnival**, which builds up in July and culminates in early August. There are bands and calypso competitions at the Carnival Village in Road Town and then the carnival bands parade through the town. Go if you get the chance. Many **regattas** are held each year, of which the main events are the three days of the Spring Regatta in April. Another fun event is the HIHO (Hook in, Hold on) Windsurfing Challenge held in June. Definitely worth a look are the huge party at New Year at Foxy's in Jost van Dyke and Foxy's Wooden Boat Regatta, held in August or September.

Sailing and Charters

Cruising Sir Francis Drake Channel is one of the best experiences the Caribbean can offer. The islands lie like sleeping animals around you, set between a fantastic blue sea and sky; close at hand small cays move with you as you sail and on the horizon the volcanic colossi do not budge. You can moor in coves where headlands enclose a horseshoe of white sand and a few palms and where the water is so clear that the boat seems to be suspended in the air. When it gets too hot on board, swim to the beach. At sunset there is nothing better to do than to watch for the Green Flash, as the sun vanishes below the seaward horizon.

The Virgin Islands offer some of the best sailing in the world—the waters are safe and sheltered by the large islands, but there are constant breezes. Anchorages are good, the distances between them are short and the sailing itself is relatively easy (with the exception of Anegada, there are few reefs) and so the area is ideal for bareboat chartering.

You will find perfect Caribbean bays all around the Virgin Islands; half-moon curves fringed with palms, where talcum-powder sand is washed by a crystal-clear sea. But you will also find by far the best collection of beach bars of anywhere in the Caribbean. The area is large and varied enough for a leisurely two-week tour.

The BVI imposes strict rules within its Marine Park, particularly regarding fishing, rubbish and protection of the coral life. Many of the popular anchorages will have moorings which you can use, though they can become occupied early in the day in season. The facilities in the Virgin Islands are excellent, with large and efficient marinas, boatyards, workshops, sail lofts and chandleries, most of which are located in the bays along the tortuous southern coastline of Tortola. **Customs and immigration** offices can be found in West End and in Road Town in Tortola, (also Beef Island at the airport within airport hours), at the main harbour on Virgin Gorda and in Great Bay on Jost van Dyke.

The two largest **bareboat** charter operators are the **Moorings** and **Sunsail**, both in Tortola. The Moorings are based at Wickham's Cay II in Road Town, PO Box 139 (℗ 42331, fax 42226, US ℗ 800 535 7289). Sunsail are based at Soper's Hole at the West End (℗ 54740, fax 54301, UK ℗ 0705 219848, US ℗ 800 327 2276). Smaller charter operators include **North South Yacht Vacations** at Nanny Cay, PO Box 281, Tortola (℗ 40096, fax 57543, US ℗ 800 387 4964).

These companies give a briefing before you set out and will provision your yacht if requested. They have some yachts with skippers who will help you out for a couple of days and then leave you to get on with it. The Moorings and Sunsail have other outlets elsewhere in the eastern Caribbean and so you can sail to other islands down the chain if you wish.

The BVI has a large number of more traditional **crewed** yachts for hire. Many of these are owner-operated and so they can give a more personal touch. Unlike the bareboats, which can be ordered directly from the charter operator, for a crewed yacht you should contact a yachting broker in your country; names are available through the Tourist Boards. For charter companies based in St Thomas, *see* p.241.

Tortola and Beef Island

Tortola (the Turtle Dove) is the largest of the British Virgins (21 square miles), and set in a huge bay on its south coast is the BVI capital, Road Town. The island is irregularly shaped, long and thin, 10 miles by 3, but it is so mountainous that you cannot cross over from one side to the other without ascending to about 1200ft. Mount Sage, whose upper slopes are covered with lush and explosive greenery that is almost rainforest, is the highest point in all the Virgins (1780ft). It is worth exploring the heights, if only for the magnificent views of the other islands. About 10,000 of the 17,000 population live on Tortola.

Tortola has become noticeably busier recently and there has been plenty of building (much of it painted in a worrying colour-scheme of obscure colours, like lavender, fuchsia and magenta). There is quite a positive air about the island and it seems to have ridden the recession quite well. The islanders are very easy-going and, with the exception of a few sports cars which have appeared, life still proceeds at a fairly gentle pace.

Getting Around

There is a rudimentary **bus service** that runs along the south coast of Tortola (fares $1–3, timings unpredictable). Catch it if you can find it. Hitch-hiking is possible and about as haphazard as anywhere else. The most reliable method of travel is via **taxi** and these are easily found in town and the airport/ferry terminals. Fix the price beforehand. Rates are pretty high, about US$14 from **Road Town** to West End, Cane Garden Bay or Beef Island. You can order one through the **BVI Taxi Association** (✆ 42322). There are also safari bus tours around the island arranged for the cruise-ship arrivals. Price around US$45 for an island tour, up to four people. Contact the Taxi Association or Turtle Dove Taxi Stand (✆ 46274). You can always sight-see by plane with FLY BVI (✆/fax 51747).

Maximum flexibility comes with your own **hire car**, but at a price (from $42 per day plus taxes in winter, less in summer). If you wish to drive, you must obtain a BVI temporary driving licence (from the car rental agency or traffic department on production of $10 and a valid licence from else-where). There is often a hefty deposit (credit cards OK). Driving is on the left and the speed limit is supposedly 30mph in the country and either 10 or 15mph in town. Rental firms include **Avis** (✆ 43322), **Island Suzuki** near Nanny Cay (✆ 43666) and **Budget Rent-a-Car** (✆ 42639) at Wickhams Cay II in Road Town. Many of these also offer jeeps.

Beaches

Tortola's best beaches are along the north coast, secluded and protected by the massive volcanic shoulders that lumber down from the mountainous heights. If there is a busy beach then it will be there. On the south coast the sand is not so good, but you will have winds for windsurfing and sailing in the channel.

The most popular beach is **Cane Garden Bay**, up over the hill from Road Town, where there is a little collection of houses and a couple of hotels and a cracking view of Jost van Dyke. You can hire watersports equipment here when frying in coconut oil loses its appeal. Travelling west of Cane Garden Bay you come to **Apple Bay** and **Carrot Bay**, which have only thin stretches of sand, and then over the hill to **Long Bay**, which is worth a visit for the mounded sand.

Perhaps the best beach on the island is **Smuggler's Cove** (or Lower Belmont Bay) in the far west. It is a perfect curve of palm-backed sand, one of the most secluded on the island; good snorkelling. Off the incredibly steep road from Cane Garden Bay over to town there is a jeep-trail down to **Brewer's Bay**, which is secluded and has a campsite. Further east are **Trunk Bay** and **Josiah's Bay**, which have excellent sand. **Lambert Long Bay** and **Elizabeth Beach** both have charming strips of sand and crystalline water and are usually deserted.

There is another **Long Bay** on Tortola, or at least on Beef Island just close to the airport. Looking across to Great and Little Camanoe, this Long Bay arches in a stunning half-mile strip of soft white sand and shelves gently into calm translucent sea. The snorkelling on the Camanoes and Scrub Island is excellent.

Beach Bars

The BVI has some classic beach bars, of which Tortola's best is **Bomba's Surfside Shack** on Apple Bay. True to its name it is a shack, made of driftwood (Bomba's was one of the few places to benefit from Hurricane Hugo; the flotsam became an extension). It's a great spot for chilling out, particularly at the monthly full moon party, famous for its jars of unusual drinks additives. Who knows, perhaps you too will feel like decorating the walls with your knickers after a heavy evening's liming. You can surf when the waves are up.

Cane Garden Bay has bars almost shoulder to shoulder, right on the sand, where you can retreat for a beer and a chicken or fish platter in the heat of the day and watch the yachts run over to Jost van Dyke. They also are worth visiting at night, when there are often live bands and big crowds. **Quito's Gazebo** gets very busy on Tuesdays and at weekend evenings, but it is also a good spot for chilling out by day, with drinks and snacks. You can have a game of darts to go with your Red

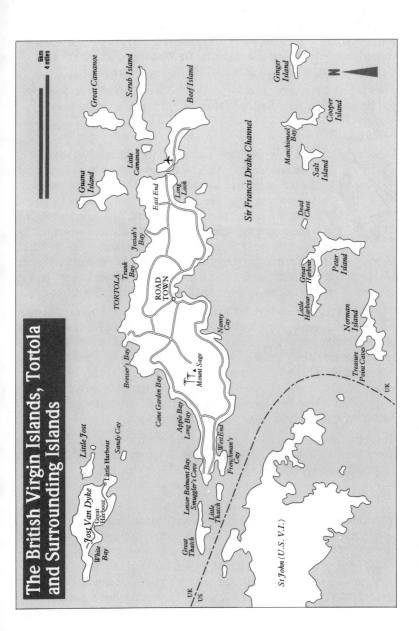

The British Virgin Islands, Tortola and Surrounding Islands

6km
4 miles

Great Camanoe

Scrub Island

Beef Island

Guana
Island

Little
Camanoe

East End

Long
Look

Ginger
Island

Cooper
Island

Manchioneel
Bay

Salt
Island

Josiah's
Bay

Trunk
Bay

Dead
Chest

Sir Francis Drake Channel

TORTOLA

ROAD
TOWN

Brewer's
Bay

Nanny
Cay

Great
Harbour

Little
Harbour

Peter
Island

Cane Garden Bay

Mount Sage

Little Jost

Sandy Cay

Little Harbour

Jost Van Dyke

Great
Harbour

White
Bay

Apple Bay
Long Bay

West End

Frenchman's
Cay

Norman
Island

Lower Belmont Bay
Smuggler's Cove

Little
Thatch

Treasure
Point Caves

Great
Thatch

UK

UK
US

St.John (U.S. V.I.)

N

211

Stripe at **Paradise Club**, or follow more Caribbean pursuits (just the Red Stripe) at **Stanley's Welcome Bar** and **Rhymers**. **Myett's** is an octagonal gazebo where you eat upstairs with a fine view of the beach. At the far end of the beach is the curiously named bright orange and blue bar **De Wedding**, quiet and isolated.

There are a couple of stopovers on Brewer's Bay: the **Bamboo Bar** hides in a forest of palms behind the curve of soft brown sand. If you are in Trellis Bay on Beef Island, you can stop for a snack at **De Loose Mongoose**, a friendly bar on the beach.

Sailing

Tortola is the gravitational centre of Virgin Islands sailing and most of the marinas, boatyards and charter companies are based here, along the southern coast, in calm and protected bays. You are quite likely to pick up your yacht here. West End has good facilities for yachts, with a large and busy marina and boatyard, with supermarkets and laundry, and most importantly a number of lively bars, set around the excellent anchorage of Soper's Hole. You can of course take on water, ice and fuel. Nanny Cay has a number of facilities, as does the Prospect Reef Resort, but the biggest and busiest marina area is in Road Town, where you will find all conceivable yachting facilities at Wickhams Cay and Wickhams Cay II.

Beyond here things are quieter and you will find secluded anchorages and daytime beach-side stopovers among the islands of the East End: Trellis Bay (with a couple of bars a dinghy ride away), off the leeward side of Marina Cay (where there is a restaurant) and Great Camanoe and off Guana Island (a private island hotel, but with an excellent beach). The north coast of Tortola is mostly windy and unsettled except for the magnificent Cane Garden Bay, where you are protected by massive mountains in a huge bay. There is a whole string of beach bars which are often wild at night. A daytime stopover nearby is Brewer's Bay.

There are chandleries and boatyards, many of them in the marines. Try **Tortola Yacht Services** (*©* 42124) at Wickham's Cay II in town, the **Nanny Cay Resort** (*©* 42512), and **Soper's Hole Marina** (*©* 54553) at West End.

Watersports

Windsurfers will find equipment and lessons at **Boardsailing BVI**, who have operations at Nanny Cay (*©* 40420), which is good for learners, and Trellis Bay (*©* 52447) in the northeast, where the onshore winds are fun-nelled between the islands into the bay, which itself remains calm. *Hire costs around $20 per hour, $55 per day.* If you would like to test out the Virgin Islands winds and waters, but would rather not take out a 50ft yacht, many of the hotels have small sailing boats. You can get instruction at the **Treasure Isle Offshore Sailing School** (✆ 45119). There are plenty of options if you would like to take a **day's sailing** excursion, usually a trip to an offshore island with picnic and snorkelling stops. The catamaran *Kuralu* (✆ 54381) goes to Jost van Dyke and *Ppalu* (✆ 57500) goes to Anegada and Virgin Gorda. *White Squall II* is a traditional schooner which goes to Virgin Gorda.

The BVI have some good reefs for **scuba diving**, where staghorn and elkhorn stand tall by sponges and seafans and patrols of sergeant majors and triggerfish follow wrasses, grunts and groupers. Spiked sea urchins and spiny lobster lurk in the crevices and depths. The most renowned dive is the *RMS Rhone*, a Royal Mail ship that sank off Salt Island in a hurricane in 1867. Some of it lies in 30ft of water; other bits of this 310ft vessel are at 90ft.

For all the islands that soar to 1000ft from the sandy bed there are also plenty of coral-clad pinnacles that do not quite make the surface, and these make good diving grounds. Try **Blonde Rock** and **Painted Walls** between Dead Chest and Salt Island; the **Indians** near Norman Island and the **Dogs** off Virgin Gorda. Other dive-sites include the *Chikuzen*, a ship in 70ft of water, 6 miles north of Beef Island. Anegada in the north, the only coral-based island in the group, has the richest marine life of all. *There is a park fee of $1 to dive.*

Dive companies include **Underwater Safaris** (✆ 43235) at the Moorings in town, **Baskin in the Sun**, who also offer lessons (✆ 42858), or **Blue Water Divers** (✆ 42847) at Nanny Cay Marine Centre. *Single tank dives cost upwards of $50.*

You can find deep water for **sport-fishing** close to the BVI, so if you wish to cruise after wahoo, marlin and kingfish, go to *Miss Robbie* (✆ 43311) at the Prospect Reef Hotel, *where a day's outing will cost around $650, including tackle and bait.* The BVI Yacht Club arranges about five tournaments in the year.

Other Sports

There are **tennis courts** in many of the hotels on the island and at the **Tortola Tennis Club** in Road Town (✆ 43733). If you would like to explore the island on **horseback**, contact **Shadows Stables** (✆ 42262), based in the Ridge Road near Skyworld, who will take you through the hills and down to Cane Garden Bay.

Around the Island

Strung along the water's edge, **Road Town** takes its name from the bay on which it sits, Road Harbour (a 'road' was an open anchorage in the 17th century), and it is the centre of government and most business activity. It is a pretty ugly town. Much of it is modern, built haphazardly on reclaimed land. The seaborne activity still continues in the town, though, in the marinas and the ferry dock, and this gives the place a pleasant nautical air.

The grandiose government building, with its line of slender arches, dominates the waterfront. Not far inland, on the original shoreline, you will find Main Street, where there is a clutch of older BVI buildings, clapboard wooden houses with shingle tiles, some of which contain shops. The **BVI Folk Museum**, *open Mon–Thurs, 9.30–12.30*, is worth a quick look. It is set in a pretty blue and white town house with wooden shutters and contains a small exhibit of natural life and human history in Amerindian pottery and plantation artefacts. There is also some crockery from the *RMS Rhone*, which sank off Salt Island in 1867. Continuing on Main Street, you come to a string of island institutions to detain you: the prison wedged between the Episcopal Anglican and the Methodist Church.

Just off Main Street farther inland, the small **Botanical Gardens**, *open Mon–Sat, 9.30–5.30 and Sun, noon–5*, give an excellent exposure to the diverse tropical flora of the Caribbean. Around a short alley of royal palms are laid out cactus gardens, a lily pond and a fern house and of course endless tropical flowers. There are some medicinal plants, and occasional benches to rest the feet.

Roads lead out of the town in both directions along the wiggly coastline to Tortola's other small settlements, West End and Long Look (in the east), where many 'belongers' have returned to build their homes. If you want to get to Cane Garden Bay (a popular north-coast bay), head inland and up. The **ridge road** runs along the backbone of Tortola and gives some superb views of the other islands.

In the **Sage Mountain National Park** trails are cut through the small patch of (almost) rainforest, where hanging vines grapple you as you pass and the ferns and philodendrons quiver on the breeze. Since the 1960s, the park has been allowed to grow naturally and the vegetation, which has some lusher growth like that on the bigger Windward Islands, is thought to be similar to the island's original growth, before the land was cleared for planting. There are some lookouts, from which the views are superb.

Frenchman's Cay is at the western end of the island. Once it was a favoured pirate hideout—it was easily defended and had good look-outs. In **Soper's Hole** there is still a working boatyard with a collection of pretty pastel boutiques and bars. Opposite, **West End** is the ferry terminal for the USVI and Jost van Dyke.

Heading east from town you eventually come to the old toll bridge over to **Beef Island**, the site of the airport. The island takes its name from its former use as a cattle ranch by buccaneers, but now all there is to see are a few goats and guest houses, private villas and the occasional 48-seater plane pitching and reeling as it comes in to land.

Great Camanoe and **Scrub Island** also lie off the northeast tip of the island and they have a few private homes. To visit them, take a boat from Beef Island. **Guana Island** is private and is devoted to a hotel, a classic island retreat (*see* below).

The BVI's smartest hotels are mostly on Virgin Gorda or on their own island, but there are some comfortable spots on Tortola as well as some cheaper places to stay. There are also some good villas on the island, which can be arranged through **Rockview Holiday Homes** (© 42550, US © 800 782 4304). A government tax of 7% will be added to all bills.

expensive–luxury

The **Guana Island Club**, PO Box 32 (© 42354, fax 52900, US © 800 624 8262) offers some of the best in Virgin Islands luxury and seclusion, on a private island of 850 acres just north of Beef Island. Tennis, watersports—windsurfing, sailing, fishing trips and seven beaches—and even croquet are there, but the club is most special for its gracious atmosphere amid superb hillside settings. Each room has a terrace, almost Greek in style with white stucco and coloured shutters. From solitude in one of the very comfortable rooms, which are simple and elegant, you can venture to the company of the main house (relative company anyway because there is a maximum of 30 guests), with dining room and of course library, or to the beach for the watersports. Afternoon tea, honour bar and a friendly communal dining room on a veranda with a view—luxury. The **Long Bay Beach Resort**, PO Box 433 (© 54252, US © 800 729 9599), uses the best of its setting in Long Bay, a quiet spot in the west of the island. Its 62 rooms (cabanas, studios and villas) stand in the seagrape just behind the excellent sandy bay and high on the hillside, very comfortable with bright decor and all mod cons. The grounds are large and there are sports for the active in body. Breakfast terrace by the pool, dinner in the very elegant tropical dining room in the main house on the hillside. Position relative to the superb beach determines the price of the rooms.

The **Sugar Mill**, PO Box 425 (© 54355, fax 54696, US © 800 462 8834), retains something of the planters' West Indies, set in restored estate buildings. The 22 rooms (one two-bedroom apartment) are white and bright, each with a wonderful view of Jost van Dyke from the balcony, over the arched gazebo, the pool and seaside beach deck and restaurant (for lighter, daytime meals). Set in the antique stone walls of the old boiling house is the main dining room, where you are guaranteed fine cuisine to the tune of water falling into copper kettles. The set menu combines classical ideas and techniques with Caribbean fruits and spices (quite expensive). Rooms expensive to very expensive. The **Frenchman's Cay Resort Hotel**, PO Box 1054, West End (© 54844, fax 54056, US © 800 235 4077), has a small number of one- and two-bedroom villas (kitchens and living rooms) in a pretty hillside garden, with views along Sir Francis Drake Channel to islands from St John to Peter Island. Hammocks in the garden around the octagonal main house, small beach with snorkelling, tennis. Quiet, but near the West End bars. If you want a comfortable spot in town, you might try **Treasure Isle**, PO Box 68 (℡ 42501, fax 42507, US ℡ 800 334 2435), which stands above the marinas on the hillside, with a pool and a restaurant on a deck. Just 40 rooms and suites, typical Caribbean comfort with television and air-conditioning.

moderate

There is a friendly guest house in Trellis Bay, the **Beef Island Guest House**, PO Box 494 (℡ 52303). Just four rooms in an older Caribbean style, but a fun spot with seclusion or activity just a short walk away. If you would like to be at the centre of the action in Cane Garden Bay, you can try **Ole Works Inn** (℡ 54837, fax 59618) in a recently renovated island house, now with an almost Alpine wooden superstructure. Rooms quite simple, air-conditioned and a little enclosed, but comfortable.

cheap

The **Cane Garden Bay Beach Hotel**, better known as Rhymer's, PO Box 570 (℡ 54639, fax 54820), sits right on the beach, painted in a not exactly delicate shade of pink. There are 24 rooms, all with air-conditioning and televisions and some kitchen equipment, quite simple, also in the centre of the action. It is worth asking around in Cane Garden Bay and then bargaining. Just beyond Government House in town there are cheap and simple rooms at the **Sea View Hotel**, PO Box 59 (℡ 42483, fax 44952). The **Wayside Inn** (℡ 43606) in the back of town has some very simple rooms at **very cheap** prices, share baths, fan ventilation. There is a **campground** in Brewer's Bay on the north coast, with showers, loos and a concessionary shop hidden among the seagrape and palms; fixed sites and bare sites, also very cheap.

℡ *(809 49)–*   ### *Eating Out*

Most of the restaurants and hotel dining rooms in Tortola are 'international' in style, though there are one or two other nationalities represented besides West Indian fare, which features in some good local haunts. It is worth bearing in mind all the beach bars, some of which can be reached by land as well as by sea—many have charming settings on a waterfront deck. Generally speaking, eating out in the BVI is expensive. Most restaurants charge service at 10%. The waterfront restaurants can usually be contacted, and a dinner ordered, on the VHF radio, channel 16 or 68. Categories are arranged according to the price of a main course: *expensive*—US$20 and above; *moderate*—US$10–20; *cheap*—US$10 and under.

expensive

The most elegant restaurant in Tortola is **Brandywine Bay** (✆ 52301), which has an excellent setting in an open tropical house on a headland east of Road Town, towards Beef Island. Start with a cocktail on the terrace and move to the stone-built dining room hanging with greenery. The menu is international with a twist of Florentine fare, often grilled and then served with artistic attention to detail: home-made mozzarella and *pomodori* or beef *carpaccio* flavoured with lime and olives, *bistecca alla fiorentina* and nightly pastas; good Italian wine list. Hotel dining rooms that are well thought of are the **Sugar Mill** (✆ 54355), which has a set Caribbean and international menu and set price (see where to stay), the **Long Bay Beach Hotel** (✆ 54252) and in town **Fort Burt** (✆ 42587).

moderate

In Road Town the **Captain's Table** (✆ 43885) has a very pleasant air, its dining room overlooking the yachts of the Inner Harbour marina from a terrace festooned with greenery and with outhanging awnings. There is a nightly-changing French and international menu—shrimp sautéd in pernod and garlic butter or blackened fresh catch, followed by crêpes suzette. Next door is the **Hungry Sailor**, which serves simpler meals in a pretty garden setting under palm thatch (cheap to moderate). Not far off is the **Fishtrap** (✆ 43626) where you dine on an open-air terrace on a wooden deck. An international menu of prawns *provençale* and teriyaki chicken, barbecues at the weekends. You will find the old-time nautical feel, stained wood and wicker chairs with maquettes of sailing ships and figureheads, set to 20th-century comfort at **Pusser's Outpost** (✆ 44199), where the international menu includes tenderloin in flaky pastry and the Pusser's Fisherman's Platter, a variety of fresh fish. The best in West Indian food can be found at **C & F Bar and Restaurant** (✆ 44941) just out of Road Town in Purcell Estate. Classic setting on a porch with plastic tablecloths and waiters watching the telly. Delicious shrimp in lemon butter and a tonnage of ground provision. Go east from town, left at the roundabout, left again and it's at the next turning right. Alternatively you might try **Mrs Scatliffe's** Restaurant (✆ 54556), set on the tin-roofed veranda of her home in Carrot Bay, where you will be fed a set menu, callaloo with home-made bread, pot-roast pork or chicken and coconut, and superb ice-creams; sometimes a scratch-band, or just the cooks singing in the kitchen while they work.

The **Apple** (℡ 54337) restaurant is situated in Little Apple Bay and is also popular for local fare; seafood speciality including whelks and conch as well as fish. The **Last Resort** (℡ 52520) is a final exotic spot for dinner in Trellis Bay—open veranda with barrel chairs and a donkey that wanders among the tables. Pumpkin soup followed by chicken in curry and honey (or roast beef and Yorkshire pudding) and particularly noted for a show in which the owner takes the mickey out of life, the universe and yachtsmen.

cheap

In town the café **Carpaccio** has true Italian style for a bit of loitering over a cappuccino opposite the ferry pier. Daytime salads and sandwiches. If you are feeling a little home-sick for the NBA or for Guinness on tap, the **Virgin Queen**, upstairs just near the roundabout in town, has a television constantly going and English pub food, cheap to moderate. The **Midtown** restaurant on Main Street has plastic tablecloths in an air-conditioned dining room setting with classic West Indian fare—curry goat and fry fish. Finally you might try the **Roti Palace** close by, on Abbott Road in town, for a roti—a spicy envelope of bread with chicken or beef. And if you would like a late-night goatwater or a chicken leg you can take away at **Nito's**, in a grounded van at the roundabout in town.

Bars

There is always a lively drinking crowd out in Tortola. There are plenty of tourist bars, with the pretty mock-nautical setting of the Pusser's Pubs, but there are classic West Indian rumshacks too. The national drink of the BVI (for the tourists anyway) is the Painkiller, usually mixed with local Pusser's Rum—cream of coconut, orange juice, pineapple juice and rum, topped with nutmeg, but there are endless other exotic cocktails.

In town an ever-popular haunt is the **Pusser's Store and Pub,** just across from the ferry terminal in Road Town, where the nauticalia and dark-stained wood and brass give it a British naval theme pub feel. Next door is the **Tavern in the Town**, where you can get English beers in a tropical garden. Also try the **Virgin Queen**. A more traditionally Caribbean waterfront bar is the **Paradise Pub**, set around a covered courtyard; darts and rowdy drinking games, dancing at the weekends.

The **West End** has some good bars—**Pusser's Landing** on Frenchman's Cay is pink and ever-popular, and across the bay, garish in even more outrageous lavender and fuschia is the **Jolly Roger**, which has seen some riotous excesses in its time, as the name would suggest. And the **beach**

bars in Apple Bay and Cane Garden Bay are of course lively; **Quito's Gazebo** and **Myett's** have live music a couple of times a week. Finally, if you want a cocktail and a fantastic view you can go to **Skyworld**. Many of the bars and beach bars have live music in season—ask around. **Bomba's** full moon party is not to be missed. More regular discotheques include **Pegleg Landing** at Nanny Cay and **Flex** and the **Paradise Pub** in town.

Jost van Dyke

The little island of Jost van Dyke lies about 4 miles off Tortola's West End. It is a perfect place to be marooned; there is a sleepy, very Caribbean air and it is less developed than the other islands. There is hardly anything there—just a couple of square miles of scrub, idyllic beaches and bars to retreat to and about 120 inhabitants, who cluster around the two main settlements of Great Harbour and Little Harbour at the east end of the island. A dirt track leads between the two, but there are hardly any vehicles. The island has only just received electricity and telephones and some of the traditional West Indian life remains here—there are endless cattle and goats wandering around, dragging their tethers, and you might see a charcoal bonfire smoking away. There is nothing to see above the waterline. Industry includes a little sand-mining and building.

And yet Jost van Dyke, supposedly named after a Dutch pirate, used to be cultivated from shoreline to hilltops (highest 1070ft), terraced to grow cotton and sugar-cane. In those days this barren outcrop was quite prosperous. It is also the birthplace of two famous men. Dr John Lettsom was born to a Quaker planter family in 1744 and eventually became the founder of the London (later British) Medical Society and the Royal Humane Society. He is remembered in the rhyme:

> *I, John Lettsom,*
> *blisters, bleeds and sweats 'em*
> *If, after that, they please to die*
> *I, John Lettsom.*

His fellow Quaker, born on the island in 1759, was William Thornton, another medical doctor, who campaigned against slavery in the islands. He became a US citizen and won the competition to design the Capitol in Washington, later serving as the first superintendent of the US Patent Office.

Beaches

There are two fantastic bays on the south coast: **Great Harbour** and **White Bay**, where the snorkelling is particularly good. And off the east end of the island there are other superb strips of sand. **Sandy Cay** is a blip with a fine beach and good snorkelling and **Sandy Spit**, off Green Cay, is the archetypal sandy spit with nothing but a few palm trees and luscious, foot-deep sand. There is a small watersports shop, **Wendell's**, in Great Bay.

Sailing

Jost van Dyke is a little off the main trail, but it makes a thoroughly rewarding visit. Facilities are few; they are just a couple of hours' sail away on Tortola. Instead, Jost offers seclusion and small island seduction. In the west, White Bay has magnificent sand and a couple of beach bars. The approach is a little difficult, between two reefs. The main **anchorages** are in Great Harbour (a port of entry), a well-protected cove, where you will find endless beach bars along the shoreline, and Little Harbour, with a couple of waterfront bars. Offshore at the eastern end you will find ideal anchorages on the leeward side of Little Jost van Dyke and Green Cay. Sandy Cay makes the ultimate daytime stopover, just sand and palms.

© (809 49)–
Where to Stay

There are few places to stay on Jost van Dyke. The **Sandcastle** is a Caribbean dream, with four breezy cottages lost in a garden of palm trees on White Bay, a stunning white-sand cove with absurdly blue water. Very secluded and low-key—hammocks, watersports if you want them, an honour bar and a library to keep you busy; occasional crowd of yachtsmen dropping in for dinner by candle-light (there is no electricity); the dining room serves fine continental fare with Cajun seasoning. Rooms quite simple, but few settings like it, expensive to very expensive. Contact address: Suite 237, Red Hook Plaza, St Thomas, USVI 00802 (USVI © 809 775 5262, fax 809 775 3590, direct © 809 496 0496). **Rudy's Mariner Inn**, Great Harbour (© 59282 or 775 3558) has just three rooms with kitchenettes; simple but moderate prices. Over in Little Harbour you can get a cheap room at **Harris's Place** or a cheap tent for two at **Tula's N. & N. Campground**, bare sites very cheap (both © 59566, fax 59296).

© (809 49)–
Eating Out and Bars

All the restaurants in Jost van Dyke double as bars and some of them have entertainment and a barbecue in the week. If you arrive mid-afternoon, you may have to wake up the barman. Alternatively come up on the radio, channels 16 or 68. You can have a candlelit dinner above the surf at the **Sandcastle**—black bean soup followed by Cajun blackened fresh local fish in a pineapple raisin chutney and vegetables. Reserve on channel 16 by 4pm, expensive. If you are stopping by for a drink, try **Gertrude's** oversized bar next door.

Great Harbour is really one long string of beach bars where you can also get a meal. The large and pre-fab **Club Paradise** will fix you a soup and a salad or a fish, moderate, along with a game of darts. **Ali Baba's** is a covered terrace on the sand with an attractive wooden bar. At the eastern end of the bay, beyond **Happy Laurry's** (also worth a stop) is **Foxy's** (reserve Channel 16 or ℂ 59258), a riotous place with multiple decks under rush and tin roofing on the waterfront. Endless visiting cards, nautical flags and the odd hammock under the palms. Foxy himself will occasionally sing to you over the barbecue and in season he has live music a couple of times a week, but the highlight of the year is the New Year's Eve party, which attracts as many as 2500 people from 300 yachts. All the bars along the waterfront have bands and there is drinking and jumping up until near dawn. Also very popular is Foxy's wooden boat regatta in August or September.

There are also a number of bars in Little Harbour: **Abe's by the Sea**, a covered terrace on the waterfront festooned with fishnets and fan coral, has plenty of happy punters to judge by the photographs they leave. West Indian fare and fish, some specials. At **Sidney's Peace and Love**, which is decorated in a serious shade of yellow, they leave their T-shirts as a memento instead; local fare. Close by is the purple and pink **Harris's**, a sandy terrace with drinks and simple meals.

Virgin Gorda

Virgin Gorda lies within sight of Tortola across Sir Francis Drake Channel, and when you get there Road Town seems almost like an uncaring metropolis. Life proceeds at an even more sedate pace and you will find that the people all greet each other here. Come to that, they may all know each other anyway, because there are only 1500 of them. There is a charming and slow life West Indian life here, with some older wooden houses in among the newer encrustations of concrete. Most of the hotels don't have locks on the room doors on Virgin Gorda, for good reason.

Virgin Gorda was the 'fat Virgin' according to the Spaniards, because they thought its shape from the south was like a pregnant woman reclining. For a while Virgin Gorda was the capital island among the British Virgins, but in 1741 Tortola took over. The island is 8 square miles in area and, like Tortola, it is long and irregularly shaped, rising from plains in the south to 1370ft at Gorda Peak in the north. Generally speaking, the island is furred with scrub and cactus, inhabited by lizards and geckos. Supposedly there is also a very rare 5ft iguana that lives in the hills. Birds include warblers and the usual cattle egrets on the plains and you may find that the odd cheeky bananaquit takes a fancy to your lunch.

The island splits quite neatly into two, with settlements at each end, barely connected by the hilly scrubland between. To the south is Spanish Town, or the Valley as it is known, the closest thing to a town; its few houses are scattered over the plain. In the north is the North Sound, a huge bay almost enclosed by islands and reefs.

The south of the island is best known for the curious assembly of vast rocks called **the Baths**, a giant's playground of granite boulders at the southwest tip of the island. These smooth rocks, which hardly seem to belong in the Caribbean, are buried to their necks in sand and jumbled on one another, creating caverns where the waves crash and race and you can clamber about. They are as impressive underneath the water's surface as above and make for good snorkelling. More granite boulders like those at the Baths make up **Fallen Jerusalem** off the south coast of the island. It has this name because it looks like a ruined town crumbling into the water. The island is a National Park and so fishing is prohibited, as is collecting the corals. You are asked to be careful when anchoring a yacht or swimming near the reef. The remains of a very early copper mine can be found close by on the southeastern tip of the island. There is a small number of hotels in the southern area of Virgin Gorda, but plenty of bars and restaurants which thrive off the yachting traffic. A road leads past the airport to the northern part of the island; from here you will have a magnificent view down the Sir Francis Drake Passage.

Overlooking the **North Sound**, a huge protected bay encircled by islands and reefs, you will find Leverick Bay, a tourist development of hotels and villas, and **Gun Creek**, a local town scattered over the hillside. Opposite them are the Bitter End Yacht Club and Biras Creek and enclosing the North Sound are Mosquito and Prickly Pear Islands and tiny Saba Rock. Slightly further out are Eustatia Island, which has just a couple of houses, and **Necker Island**, a small green lump rimmed with sand set in the translucent blue. It is owned by Richard Branson, founder of Virgin Records, who has built a house and a couple of villas there in Balinese style. It is private (above the high-water mark), but can be hired, *see* p.226.

Getting Around

There is no bus service on Virgin Gorda, but hitching is no problem. Taxis will let you hop in on someone else's fare and will ask for a few dollars for the ride. There are **hire-cars** and jeeps available (for regulations and prices *see* under Tortola). Contact **Mahogany Car Rentals** (© 55469) or **Andy's** (© 55511), both in the Valley. You can get a scooter through **Honda Scooter Rental** (© 55212). Taxis can be found through both these operators and hotels often have cars available for their guests.

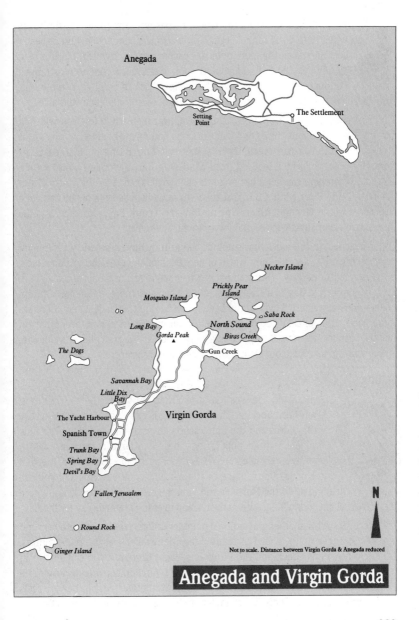

Anegada

Setting
Point

The Settlement

Necker Island

Prickly Pear
Island

Mosquito Island

Saba Rock

Long Bay

North Sound

Gorda Peak

Biras Creek

The Dogs

Gun Creek

Savannah Bay

Little Dix
Bay

The Yacht Harbour

Virgin Gorda

Spanish Town

Trunk Bay
Spring Bay
Devil's Bay

Fallen Jerusalem

Round Rock

Ginger Island

Not to scale. Distance between Virgin Gorda & Anegada reduced

N

Anegada and Virgin Gorda

Beaches

In the switchbacks of Virgin Gorda's coastline are some classic coves crowned with coral sand. Virgin Gorda also has a fine collection of beach bars. In season the more popular beaches can be crowded, but it is usually possible to find a solitary spot. Watersports have to be arranged through the hotels, though snorkelling gear can be hired at the Baths. Some beaches are a little isolated and difficult to get to from the landward side.

The most popular beaches are in the southwest, near the Baths. Here you will sink into the sand up to your ankles and you can swim among the boulders as the waves break over you. You can reach **Devil's Bay** and **The Baths** on marked paths through the scrub, which lead off from **Mad Dog Bar**, a wooden house with a veranda, where you can get a hot dog or a sandwich. Shaded by the vast rocks of the Baths is the **Poor Man's Bar**, a shack with some benches where you can get a beer and a snack. Going north are **Spring Bay** and **Trunk Bay**, also known as the Crawl, two other superb spots, often with yachts in the bay.

Other beaches on the west coast include **Savannah Bay**, a broad sweeping arc between towering volcanic hills. North of here by 2 miles, at the end of a dirt track, is the isolated **Long Bay**, a suntrap backed by mangrove and palms and a view of Tortola. **Leverick Bay** is a lively spot with a bar and some watersports equipment—you can windsurf over to the beaches on Mosquito Island, where there are some good strips of sand to collapse on to. You will find a classic beach bar on Prickly Pear Island—the **Sandbox** is a long wooden shack with seats outside, where you can take time out from the snorkelling and sizzling.

Sailing

The Baths on the west coast of Virgin Gorda are the classic Virgin Islands **anchorage**. The snorkelling is excellent among the jumble of boulders and the tight, sandy coves are magnificent. The only problem is their popularity. There is a large marina in Spanish Town, where you can provision your yacht and take on ice, fuel and water or take advantage of the bar and book exchange. If you are heading off to the North Sound, you might stop off at the Dogs, where there is excellent snorkelling. Alternatively, stop over in Savannah Bay for the day.

The North Sound is another gravitational point for sailors, where there are bars and beaches to cruise up to. There are limited facilities available at the three centres, Leverick Bay, Biras Creek and the Bitter End Yacht Club, but you can anchor in many spots around its shores, including Drake's Anchorage, Prickly Pear Cay, Eustatia Island and Saba Rock. The whole bay is well protected, but beware reefs on the way in and out. There is a chandlery in the Yacht Harbour in the Valley.

Watersports

Windsurfing and **sailing** (hire and lessons) can be fixed up through the **Nick Trotter Sailing School** at the Bitter End Yacht Club on North Sound and at Leverick Bay. Other hotels will also have equipment. There are Boston Whalers for hire for the day. For a **day's sail** you can contact **Mirage Charters** at the Biras Creek marina and **Misty Isle** (℗ 55643) in the main marina in the Valley.

Scuba diving, among the snappers and squirrelfish, can be arranged with **Dive BVI** in their shops at the Yacht Harbour near Spanish Town (℗ 55513) and in Leverick Bay (℗ 57328), or through **Kilbride's Underwater Tours**, which works off Saba Rock in North Sound, PO Box 40, Virgin Gorda (℗ 59638, fax 59369). Diving is quite expensive in Virgin Gorda. **Deep-sea fishing** can be fixed up with *Classic* at Biras Creek (℗ 43555) and *Kingfisher* (℗ 55230) at the Yacht Harbour.

The Little Dix Bay Resort keeps **horses**, if you want to explore by riding or to gallop through the surf. **Tennis** courts are also available there (℗ 55555), though the guests have priority. If you are in the north of the island, go to Biras Creek (℗ 43555) or Leverick Bay (℗ 57421).

℗ (809 49)–

Where to Stay
expensive–luxury

In the northern peninsula, **Biras Creek**, PO Box 54 (℗ 43555, fax 43557, UK reservations ℗ 0453 835801, US ℗ 800 223 1108), has been proffering high-grade, low-key luxury to returning guests for years. The 32 suites are strung out on the breezy Atlantic waterfront, where you are sent to sleep by the susurration of the waves, all stylishly decorated, with garden showers and with wind and fan ventilation. The beach is tucked in a Caribbean cove and has some watersports. The restaurant is set above the main house on the heights—guests gather for drinks before dinner, and then move to the dining room terrace, from which there is a superb view across the North Sound. An elegant air, quite strongly English. If you would prefer a busier, more club-like feel, try the **Bitter End Yacht Club**, also on the North Sound, PO Box 46 (℗ 42746, fax 44756, US ℗ 800 872 2392). Bitter End sells itself as a luxury yacht club, and has a nautical feel in the dark-stained wood and brass and pewter tableware, as well as the constant waterborne activity. And a sense of desert-island seclusion within a shout of civilization can be found in their luxurious, mock-rustic cabins on the hillside. A couple of restaurants and entertainment in season, hammocks everywhere. Expensive. **Drake's Anchorage**,

PO Box 2510 (℡ 42254, US ℡ 800 624 6651), is another idyllic island retreat overlooking the North Sound. Here there is a beach club feel, very low-key with comfortable cottages with louvred windows and fans scattered along the beachfront in a sandy palm garden, just out of earshot of one another, very expensive. People speak highly of the restaurant, where you dine in wicker chairs on a waterfront terrace, very expensive. The **Leverick Bay Resort**, PO Box 63 (℡ 57421, fax 57367, US ℡ 800 848 7081), offers the least expensive deal in this area. Rooms and villas (one- to four-bed-roomed) on the hillside above the bay. Moderate to expensive.

Necker Island (℡ 42757, fax 44396, UK ℡ 071 727 8000, fax, US toll free ℡ 800 926 0636) has to be hired as an entire island (there are prices for up to 10 and up to 20 guests), though there are occasional 'house par-ties', in which couples can join a mix. The island has beds for 20 guests in the main house and the two smaller balinese cottages (Bali Hi and Bali Lo). The open-sided main house, with its magnificent hilltop setting and views as far as Tortola, is the nerve-centre of the island. It has a snooker table and excellent sitting area with books and boardgames, video recorders and CD players, hammocks and even a weights room with a view. Pool, tennis courts and all meals included at the huge dining-room table. A statue waves you welcome and goodbye.

In the southern half of the island, **Little Dix Bay**, PO Box 70 (℡ 55555, fax 55661, US ℡ 800 223 7637), is a grand and luxurious resort set on a magnificent half-moon curve of sand backed with palms and seagrape. It is quite large (102 rooms), but it is well spread out in tropical gardens. The main dining room is under the distinctive double-pointed shingle roofs and around the central sugar mill. Watersports and tennis.

moderate

Smaller and more in the style of a West Indian inn is the **Olde Yard Inn**, PO Box 26 (℡ 55544, fax 55968, US ℡ 800 633 7411), just off the road to the north of the island. The 14 rooms, fan-ventilated (some air-conditioned if you want) overlook a charming garden, moderate to expensive. **Guavaberry Spring Bay**, PO Box 20 (℡ 55227), in the southern part of the island, is a surprising retreat: hexagonal chalets on stilts, swallowed in explosions of tropical plants and the rocks of the Baths. There are 21 rooms in one-bedroom and two-bedroom chalets, with full kitchens.

cheap

You will find cheap accommodation at the **Taddy Bay** (℡ 55618) in the Valley, just two bedrooms with a kitchen for you to use.

In the north of the island, there are really only hotel dining rooms for eating out in the evening, though by day you can always get a snack at the beach bars—try Saba Rock and Prickly Pear Island. Categories are arranged according to the price of a main course: *expensive*—US$20 and above; *moderate*—US$10–20; *cheap*—less than US$10.

Biras Creek Hotel (*see* p.225) has a magnificent setting high on the hill; *haute cuisine* and a superb wine list, and a five-course dinner for a fixed price. **Drake's Anchorage** is also renowned. If you are in Leverick Bay you might try the **Pusser's Restaurant**, bright pink and purple ginger-bread with a mock-nautical ambience, plush armchairs and painkillers; local fish and international dishes, moderate. For something a little less manicured try the **Pirate's Pub** on Saba Rock, a blip opposite the Bitter End Yacht Club. It flies the skull and crossbones and the bar is tended by washed-up yachtsmen and women. Barbecue, booze, jam sessions (on the instruments lying around) and a general riotous assembly on a good night.

In the southern half of the island try **Chez Michelle** (© 55510) if you would like to eat outside the hotels. The setting is simple and candle-lit and the menu is international with some French twists: the lobster Rémy is flambéd in cognac and served with cream and mushrooms and roast rack of lamb is cooked in Dijon mustard, garlic and honey. Be sure not to miss **Thelma's Hideout** (© 55646), which is set in a fairy-lit West Indian yard with trees and hanging plants just off the road to Little Dix Bay. Local fare: doved pork, baked chicken and curry goat; ring to reserve a table, and a dish, cheap to moderate. **Teacher Ilma's** (© 55355) also offers a good local meal in the Valley. Callaloo followed by curried chicken and local veg-etables, cheap. The shopping centre at the marina is a gathering point and the **Bath and Turtle** (© 55239) can get quite lively. Pub food, patisserie and lending library, cheap. Finally the **Sea Turtle** (a boat beached over a hundred yards inland) is an amusing spot frequented by the locals—a bar in a boat with awnings now attached. The beach bars along the southern beaches can provide a snack during the day.

Islands in the Chain

Heading southwest along the line of amoeba-shaped islets and cays on the southern side of Sir Francis Drake Channel you pass Fallen Jerusalem, a national park made of similar boulders to those at the Baths and then Round Rock. Next in line, Ginger

Island is uninhabited, but there is a small settlement set on the popular protected anchorage of Manchineel Bay in **Cooper Island**. Set in the palm-backed bay, there are just a few cottages, a boutique and dive-shop, **Underwater Safaris**, for guided dives and tank refills; there is good snorkelling on the island. Rooms (© 43721, US © 800 542 4624) are pretty, comfortable and moderate in price. There is a comfortable anchorage right offshore here, within earshot and a short dinghy ride of the bar and there is another stopover just to the south in Haulovers Bay. The **Cooper Island Beach Club** (VHF Channel 16) offers daytime and evening meals—conch fritters and chicken roti and sautéd shrimp in butter and white wine, some barbecues. It depends on the crowd, but it can get very lively. Watch out for Jazz, the despotic dog.

Next in the line is **Salt Island**, another 200 acres of scrubland that enclose a salt pond. Once the population of this island was as high as 100, mostly involved in the collection of salt, which they would sell to passing ships (the rent of the island is still set at one sack of salt a year payable to the Queen of England, but it is apparently not often demanded any more). Today the population is not usually more than about four or five, though building is just beginning on the sandy seafront at 'The Settlement'. Nowadays, most people come to Salt Island to visit one of the Caribbean's finest wrecks, the shell of the 310ft RMS *Rhone*, which lies on her side in two bits in depths from 30 to 80ft, her ribs scattered higgledy-piggledy. Snorkellers can enjoy the shallower end, playing in the exhaled bubbles of the divers below, an eerie experience. The area around the wreck is a Marine National Park and so the usual rules apply. The waters off Salt Island are rolly, making it an uncomfortable place to lie up for the night in a yacht, but all right by day.

Peter Island, which lies about 5 miles across the Channel from Road Town harbour, is almost entirely devoted to an extremely luxurious hotel. The only other inhabitant lives in a small wooden house across the bay. The **Peter Island Resort**, PO Box 211 (© 42561, fax 42313, US © 800 346 4451), has 50 rooms in all (also one villa), of which the most elegant and comfortable are on the beach on Deadman's Bay. There are two dining rooms, a drawing room with newspapers on hand-held sticks, and low-key entertainment each night in season. And there are good uncluttered beaches (Deadman's Bay, where the waves break in scallop shell shapes, is charming, and White Bay is reclusive and isolated), watersports and bicycles to get around on, very expensive to luxury prices. If you would like to go over for dinner, or for a day out on the beach (you can use the resort's facilities), the ferry sails about six times a day from the CSY marina on the eastern side of Road Town harbour. **Sailors** can put in here overnight in protected spots along the northern shore. Deadman's Bay is possible, as is the main hotel dock area. You might also try Little Harbour towards the westen end and White Bay on the south coast.

Just off the island is a cay called **Dead Chest**, a small scrub-covered lump that calls to mind the pirates who used these anchorages before today's sailors arrived. Blackbeard is supposed to have left 15 of his more rebellious sidekicks here with just a cutlass and a cask of rum. The pirates did not survive long, but the island was immortalized in the sea-shanty:

> *Fifteen men on a dead man's chest*
> *Yo ho ho and a bottle of rum.*
> *Drink and the Devil have done the rest*
> *Yo ho ho and a bottle of rum.*

The last BVI island in the chain, next to the US Virgin Island of St John, is **Norman Island**, which also features in pirate lore. Treasure has supposedly been found here. Ruins remain from past settlement, but Norman Island is home only to a few goats and seabirds today and the island's only industry is apparently smuggling. The snorkelling at the Indians and at Treasure Point caves, where there are caverns partly submerged in water, is excellent. Offshore, in the protected anchorage of the Bight, you will find one of the Caribbean's most unlikely, but sometimes most lively bars, the **William Thornton**, or the Willy T as it is familiarly known by the crowd of latterday pirates and tourists who turn up for the evening. Built as a Baltic trader in 1915, it now has a restaurant where the hatch-covers are the tables and your legs dangle in the cargo hold (reserve on channel 16, prices moderate), and a bar which is famous for body-shots (a variation on the theme of a tequila shot). Well worth a look if there is a crowd in. Look out for the remoras.

The Bight is the best place to **anchor** for the night, but there is also calm water at Banures Bay further east.

Anegada

Anegada lies out on its own about 15 miles north of the main group of the British Virgins, visible only from the mountaintops of Tortola and Virgin Gorda. It is unlike the other islands because it is not of volcanic origin. Rather it is a coral cap that just makes it above sea level (there is nothing over 28ft), rimmed with reefs and about 14 miles of beach. Anegada means 'the drowned one' in Spanish, a fitting name because it is full of lagoons and marshes and is occasionally soaked further by passing tidal waves.

At 15 square miles, Anegada is the second largest of the British islands. It is arid and scrubby and supports little life other than goats and donkeys. However, there is an ancient colony of about 400 20lb, 5ft iguanas. Once these animals lived all over the Virgin Islands, but they featured heavily in a local stew and so they are now endangered. Moves have been made to protect them by taking some to Guana Island off Tortola.

Only about 250 people live on Anegada, centred around **The Settlement**, and traditionally the islanders have depended on the sea for a living. When they were not away pirating or smuggling they fished, or looted the ships that were wrecked on the reefs.

Anegada's underwater life is superb. The coral reefs are endless forests of seafans, barrel-sponges and gorgonians, abounding with fish—parrotfish, squirrelfish and thin trumpetfish hanging upright in the water. There are an estimated 300 wrecks on Horseshoe Reef which make for good exploring. According to some estimates, there is a billion dollars of treasure on Anegada's reefs. Scuba diving and other watersports, including bone-fishing and deep-sea-fishing trips, can be arranged through the Anegada Reef Hotel.

Sailing to Anegada is difficult because of the many reefs and so most charter companies ask you not to. Those who do go will discover some of the best in easy island life, Virgin style. The best anchorage is off the Anegada Reef Hotel near the western tip of the island.

© (809 49)–   ### Where to Stay and Eating Out

The island's only hotel, the **Anegada Reef Hotel** (© 58002, fax 59362), is small and low-key in the best lazy Caribbean style, with just 10 ocean-front and six garden rooms (air-conditioned) among the casuarina pines on the island's protected southwestern shore. The restaurant prepares an excellent lobster as well as other seafood and fish on the beach barbecue, rooms expensive, some jeeps for hire. There is a campsite on the island, where a tent is very cheap and a bare site less than US$10.

Loblolly Bay beach on the north shore has excellent sand and makes a great day out. There are a couple of beach bars to retire to for a grilled fish and a beer, the **Big Bamboo** and **Flash of Beauty**. In town you can eat at **Del's** Restaurant and bar—shrimp or cracked conch, all moderate.

The US Virgin Islands

The US Virgin Islands (USVI) consist of three main islands and around seventy cays, most of which are too small to be inhabited. The largest island is St Croix (84 square miles), which lies on its own, 40 miles south of the main group. St Thomas (33 square miles) is the next largest, and the islands' capital, Charlotte Amalie, is situated on its southern shore. East of St Thomas by 4 miles is the third in the group, St John (just 16 square miles).

The islands were purchased by the USA in 1917. For 250 years before that they were Denmark's only colony in the Caribbean. Echoes of the Danes remain in the pretty waterfront towns with their warehouses and narrow stepped alleys (still with names like Raadet's Gade and Gamle Gade) and the now ruined plantation windmills out in the country. Danish was never really spoken here so the language has gone, but it seems strange that in a part of America they should still drive on the left.

Each car that cruises by in the USVI announces 'American Paradise' on its numberplate. And as somebody thrusts a rum punch into your hand as soon as you arrive at the airport, in the tropical heat, while strains of calypso fill the air, you might imagine that you are in paradise after all. It is certainly American in style—everywhere there are yellow hanging traffic lights, burger joints and cheery waitresses in shorts. You can have a good time here—there are plenty of good restaurants and bars and the islands are well organized for beach-based activity and sailing—but the paradise façade hides most of the same problems that affect the other Caribbean islands. The tourist invasion is relentless. It is big business (the USVI receive well over a million and a half visitors each year), the islands are almost completely dependent on it and development appears to proceed with more regard to the tourist playground than the needs of the islanders themselves. However, wages are far higher here than elsewhere in the Caribbean and the islanders reap the benefits.

The US Virgins (with the exception of St John, where building has been purposely held back) are among the most developed islands in the Caribbean. Hotels and condominiums cover the hillsides and there can be as many as ten cruise ships in Charlotte Amalie harbour at one time. This is tourism at its most advanced—with stateside entertainment shipped in, carefully packaged 'vacationer's investment opportunities' and plastic cards of corals and tropical fish to take underwater with you so that you can identify them.

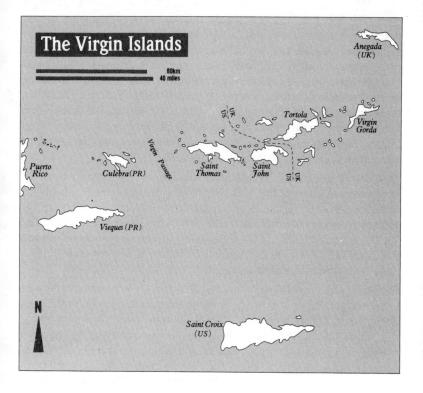

The USVI are too developed for some tastes (St John is the exception), but they remain very popular, mainly with American visitors. The setting is wonderful—the towns are as pretty as any in the West Indies and, of course, the sea, sand and sailing are impeccable.

History

At the time that Columbus arrived in the Caribbean in 1492, the Virgin Islands were seeing the first waves of attacks on the Greater Antilles by the Carib Indians. These belligerent island-hoppers, who decorated themselves with red warpaint and feathers, had come up all the way from South America over the previous centuries and had squeezed out the Arawaks as far as the Leewards. They would pass through the Virgin Islands in their vast war canoes on raids from down-island, make a lightning attack and steal a few women, and then paddle back again. The Spaniards battled successfully with them over the next century, trying to keep them away from Puerto Rico. But as the first scourge receded another arrived. Pirates began to infest the islands, taking refuge there after their raids on Spanish shipping and settlements. In the 1620s adventurers started to arrive and to plant crops—the Dutch and English and French settled in St Croix—and buccaneers took over the smaller islands, curing the meat they killed and selling it to passing sailors. These islands became stopping-off points for ships travelling up and down the island chain and for those that had just crossed the Atlantic. The Virgin Islands became known as markets and goods would be brought here for distribution all over the Caribbean. Pirates would also off-load their loot here, and then spend time ashore, revelling and waiting for another expedition.

The Danes moved in to St Thomas in 1665 and allowed the trading to continue. Business was so successful that by the end of the 17th century the British Admiral Benbow described St Thomas as 'a receptacle for thieves'. In 1724 the island was declared a freeport and it was soon on its way to being the richest port of its day. The Danes claimed St John in 1684 (though they did not settle it until 1717) and they bought St Croix from the French in 1733 for 750,000 francs. Both these islands were soon covered with sugar-cane.

The Danish islands' neutral status sheltered them from the worst effects of the wars between Spain, France and Britain. In wartime they were entrepôts and a haven against the marauding freebooters (hired by the warring nations to harry enemy and neutral shipping) and in peace they were the headquarters of the smuggling trade in the area. Slave auctions also brought in huge revenue. In the War of American Independence they shipped arms to the colonists. British objections to the trade led to two occupations in the Napoleonic Wars (1801 and 1807), but the islands were handed back to Denmark in 1815.

The Danes were the first to abolish the slave trade, in 1792, but slavery itself was not abolished until much later. In 1848 the Danish King Frederik VIII issued an edict that all slaves would be emancipated in 1859, but on hearing this the slaves revolted. When the Governor-General Peter von Scholten, a man with a mulatto mistress himself, faced the crowd on St Croix in order to make the announcement, he realized that he was unwilling to impose the law and simply announced that he was freeing them then and there. The slaves remained free and the Governor was tried for dereliction of duty, but was eventually acquitted. At about this time the islands went into financial decline: sugar failed in St Croix and St John as it did all over the West Indies, and trading in St Thomas fell off too. Eventually the islands became a burden to the Danish government and they began to look for a way of getting rid of them.

The United States first showed interest in the Islands in 1866, but at that stage the Virgin Islanders themselves vetoed the transfer. The subject came up again when the Americans were concerned about German naval movements in the Caribbean in the First World War. This time the islanders voted for cession to the United States and the Americans bought the islands for $25 million. Early on the islands were administered purely as a naval base because of their strategic position, but in 1927 the islanders were granted citizenship of the USA and in 1931 the islands were placed in civil jurisdiction.

Initially the Governor was appointed by the President in consultation with the elected Senate of the USVI, but this was changed in 1970 and since then the Governor has been chosen by the Virgin Islanders themselves in elections held every four years. Since 1972 they have sent a delegate to the House of Representatives, though he has no vote and so has more of a lobbying role. Though the islanders are US citizens and taxpayers, they do not vote in national elections. Unlike Puerto Rico, which is part of the federal banking system, taxes paid in the USVI stay within the islands. The current Governor is Mr Alexander Farrelly, with elections scheduled in late 1994.

In 1931 the American President, Herbert Hoover, described the US Virgin Islands as 'an orphanage, a poor house' and, soon after, the Virgin Islands Company was established to improve the infrastructure of the islands. The production of sugar was centralized and industry was stimulated through tax incentives. In 1966 a huge oil refinery was established on St Croix by the Hess Oil Company, capable of producing over 700,000 barrels a day. Other industries in operation today include the production of rum, some light manufacture and the assembly of parts from outside the islands. The USVI have one of the highest per capita incomes in the Caribbean. By far the largest income-generator today is the tourism industry, which reached its height in 1988 (before Hurricane Hugo and then the recession struck), when between them the islands saw 1.8 million visitors, of whom about 60 per cent arrived by cruise ship.

© (809)–   **Getting There**

The USVI have international airports on the two largest islands, St Thomas and St Croix and these have excellent connections from the States. There is no airstrip in St John.

By Air from the UK: There are no direct services from the UK or Europe to the USVI, but British Airways have twice-weekly flights from London Gatwick to San Juan, Puerto Rico, and a number of charter airlines also fly the route. Connections are easy from here. There are more daily connections through Miami on American Airlines, so this might be a better option. Lufthansa fly to San Juan from **Frankfurt** and Iberia from **Madrid**.

By Air from the USA: St Thomas and St Croix are served by numerous airlines including American Airlines, who have direct services from Miami,

New York and Raleigh/Durham; Delta from Atlanta and Orlando; US Air from Baltimore; and Continental from Newark, New Jersey. Note that many services stop first at St Thomas then continue to St Croix. From other points in the USA, passengers can either make a connection at one of those cities or fly to San Juan in Puerto Rico, from where there are endless connections.

By Air from other Caribbean Islands: San Juan, which is something of a hub for the area, has numerous shuttle services into and beyond the USVI, both St Thomas and St Croix. Going east and south, there are also direct links to Anguilla, Sint Maarten, St Kitts and Antigua.

Getting Around

There are countless island-hoppers that link St Thomas and St Croix, but the most original way to make the link is by seaplane (though service has been somewhat sporadic recently). These beasts (known as the 'Goose' and the 'Mallard' on island) bounce over the waves as they struggle to get airborne and once in the air they thrum like an outsize tuning fork; they are fun to ride. The terminal in St Croix is in the north of Christiansted and in St Thomas it is right on the waterfront in Charlotte Amalie. In St John it is in Cruz Bay. Contact the VI Seaplane Shuttle (© 773 1776).

If you would prefer not declare your body weight (needed for correct balancing of the seaplanes), then you might try Sunaire Express (© 778 9300), which flies to the Virgin and Puerto Rican islands, Air St Thomas (© 776 2722, US © 800 522 3084) or GAS (Gorda Air Services).

USVI Ferries: The link between St Thomas and St John is made by boat. Ferries depart from Red Hook at the eastern end of St Thomas every hour on the hour, 8am–midnight daily, with sailings as early as 6.30am, Mon–Fri, and arrive at Cruz Bay in St John. Crossings the other way start earlier, running 6am–11pm. The crossing takes 20 minutes, price $3. There is no reason to book as the ferries rarely reach their capacity. There is also a 30-minute ferry from Charlotte Amalie to Cruz Bay, departing six times a day, a 45-minute ride, daily, fare $7. There are no ferries from St Thomas or St John to St Croix.

Tourist Information

The United States Virgin Islands Division of Tourism has offices in:

UK: 2 Cinnamon Row, Plantation Wharf, York Place, London SW11 3TW (© 071 978 5262, fax 071 924 3171), **Germany:** Postfach 10–02–44, D-63002, Offenbach (© 069 892008, fax 069 898892) and **Italy**: Via Gheràrdina 2, 20145 Milano (© 02 33105841, fax 02 33105827).

USA: 1270 Avenue of the Americas, Suite 2108, **New York**, NY 10020 (☎ 212 332 2222, fax 332 2223); 3460 Wilshire Boulevard, Suite 412, **Los Angeles**, CA 90010 (☎ 213 739 0138, fax 739 2005); 2655 Le Jeune Road, Suite 907, Coral Gables, **Miami**, FL 33134 (☎ 305 442 7200, fax 445 9044); 900 17th St NW, Suite 500, **Washington**, DC 20006 (☎ 202 293 3707, fax 202 785 2542). There is a central freephone number (☎ 800 USVI INFO).

Canada: 33 Niagara Street, Toronto MV5 1C2 (☎ 416 362 8784, fax 416 362 9841, toll free ☎ 800 465 8784).

The Head Office of the **USVI Division of Tourism** is at PO Box 6400, Charlotte Amalie, St Thomas 00804 (☎ 77 48784, fax 77 44390). The tourist information offices are mentioned in the separate island-sections.

The **IDD code** for the USVI is 809, followed by a seven-figure number on the island. If you call within or between the islands, dial the seven figures.

Money

The currency of the Virgin Islands (USVI and BVI) is the US dollar. Credit cards are accepted in hotels and all but the smallest shops and restaurants. Tipping is the same as in mainland USA, 10–15%. **Banking hours** are 9–2.30, Mon–Fri, with an extra hour and a half on Friday afternoons, 3.30–5. **Shops** are open 9–5 every day except Sunday, though they will often open up for the cruise ship trade.

Further Reading

One of the best books to come out of the Caribbean is Herman Wouk's *Don't Stop the Carnival*, which tells the story of a statesider who comes down to the islands and sets up as a hotelier. In an unending litany of woe: every imaginable disaster befalls him in a book that is excruciatingly funny and ruthlessly tense (very unlike later books by Wouk). Budding hotel managers would be advised to read this book; the hoteliers themselves swear by it. It is rather difficult to look them in the eye after reading it. The **Dockside Bookshop** at Havensight Mall in St Thomas has an excellent selection of Caribbean books.

St Thomas

The life of St Thomas has always centred around the island's magnificent harbour—a steep-sided bowl partly closed by islands—which attracted shipping from the earliest days. The lines of 18th-century trading warehouses in Charlotte Amalie are just as busy today as they have ever been, and the harbour teems with yachts, motorboats and cruise ships.

St Thomas is one of the most developed islands in the whole Caribbean. About 50,000 people live on its 33 square miles, most of them in the extended suburb of Charlotte Amalie, the capital town in the USVI. Buildings have sprung up everywhere—villas, hotels and vacation condominiums—and there is even a rush hour. Only in the west end of the island, beyond the airport, is it less built up. In such a crowded place there is some tension (some of it racial) and it occasionally spills over into violence.

But overdeveloped as it is, the island is attractive to many for its upbeat tempo. Top entertainment acts come down to perform in the island hotels, maintaining St Thomas's tradition as the 'nightclub of the Virgin Islands' and, of course, if you want to join the fray, St Thomas has some of the best shopping in the Caribbean.

Getting Around

There is a **bus** service around St Thomas, designed primarily for locals. Services are reasonably frequent from the outskirts of Charlotte Amalie (along the waterfront and out through the suburbs) to Red Hook and then along the Smith Bay road and west out to Bordeaux, running until about 8pm. No standees, maximum fare 75c. A very small percentage of cars will stop for a hitch-hiker on St Thomas, and on an island with thousands and thousands of them it can be a pretty depressing wait.

Taxis are everywhere and work to a fixed rate (displayed in some hotels; the taxis themselves are unmetered). All the same it's best to make sure of the fare in advance. You might find that other passengers hop in along the way, which is accepted practice. The trip from **Charlotte Amalie** to the airport costs around $5, to Magen's Bay—$7, Coki Beach—$8 and to Red Hook—$9. If you don't see one on the street, taxi-drivers can always be found through the hotel lobbies. Virgin Islands Taxi Radio Dispatch is on © 774 7457 and the VI Taxi Association is on © 774 4550. Drivers will happily take you on a tour of the island—about $30 per hour for up to four people. However, this can be arranged more cheaply if you are prepared to go by safari bus. If you would prefer to go sightseeing by helicopter, that can be arranged—call **Adventure Helicopters** at Frenchman's Reef (© 775 7335).

Car hire is the best way of getting about if you are travelling around the island a lot. Cars are easily available for upwards of $40 per day, but the roads become very congested in town, so leave plenty of time. The many firms (at the airport and in town) include: **ABC Rentals** (© 776 1222),

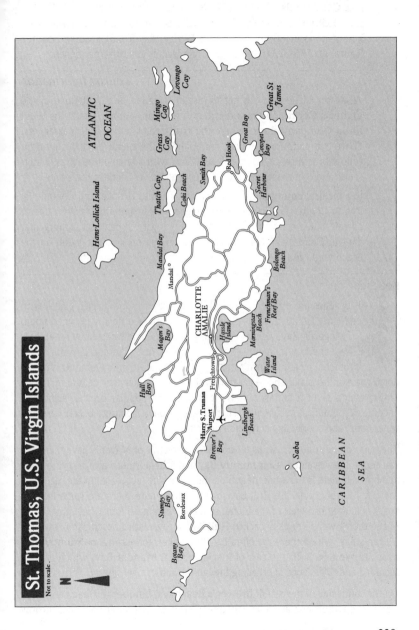

St. Thomas, U.S. Virgin Islands

Not to scale.

ATLANTIC OCEAN

CARIBBEAN SEA

Hans Lollick Island

Loango Cay
Mingo Cay
Grass Cay
Great Bay
Great St James
Coupel Bay
Secret Harbour
Red Hook
Smith Bay
Thatch Cay
Coki Beach
Mandal Bay
Mandal
Bolongo Beach
Frenchman's Reef Bay
Morningstar Beach
Hassel Island
CHARLOTTE AMALIE
Magen's Bay
Hull Bay
Frenchtown
Water Island
Harry S. Truman Airport
Lindbergh Beach
Brewer's Bay
Saba
Stumpy Bay
Bordeaux
Botany Bay

239

E–Z Car Rentals (✆ 775 6255), **Sun Island Car Rentals** (✆ 774 3333) and **Thrifty Car Rentals** (✆ 775 7282). **Scooters** are also available, with a hefty deposit ($200), for around $25 per day from **Paradise Scooter Rental** (✆ 775 2724). In the US Virgin Islands you drive on the left.

Tourist Information

While on island you can get tourist information at the **airport**, at the **Visitor's Centre** on the waterfront in Charlotte Amalie and at the **West India Company dock**, where the cruise ships let off their passengers. There is a plethora of tourist material and the island produces a bright yellow brochure, *St Thomas This Week*, with advice on beaches, watersports and other essentials like shopping and investment in real estate.

In a medical **emergency**, contact the St Thomas Hospital and Community Health Centre (✆ 776 8311). The bigger hotels sometimes have a doctor on call. You are advised to be careful with regard to personal security after dark in Charlotte Amalie and to keep an eye on belongings left on the beach while you go for a swim.

Beaches

All beaches are public in the USVI and there are one or two places with changing facilities. Topless and nude bathing is officially frowned upon. **Magen's Bay**, *adm 50c, parking $1*, the island's best-known beach, is superb, a mile-long strip of extremely fine sand and coconut palms protected by a huge arm thrusting out into the Atlantic Ocean. It is on the north coast of the island and to get there you have to go over the central mountain range, which gives a fantastic view. It is the most popular on the island and becomes crowded at weekends. There are changing facilities, beach bars and restaurants, and snorkelling equipment for hire.

There are one or two tiny strips of sand along the arms of Magen's Bay where you can sometimes be alone. **Community Bay** is on the northern arm near the point and opposite here is **Paradise Beach** on the south side (approach on the road from the E & M grocery on the Hull Bay road). Beyond here there are some isolated beaches in the northwest of the island, some of which need four-wheel drive to get to and then a walk. Try palm-backed **Hull Bay**, a cove with a beach bar just west of Magen's Bay, where there are often 6–10ft breakers for surfing, or **Stumpy Bay**, near the West End. To the east of Magen's Bay is **Mandal Bay**, which is quite secluded and offers good snorkelling,though the surf can get up.

On the south side of the island, **Brewer's Beach** and **Lindbergh Beach** are either side of the airport and are relatively free of crowds. The latter has hotels nearby where you can get a drink and a windsurfer. Out of Charlotte Amalie to the east is **Morning Star Beach** at the Frenchman's Reef Hotel, where you can hire snorkelling and windsurfing gear. Beyond here you eventually come to **Bolongo Beach** and at the eastern end, **Cowpet Bay**. Both beaches have a hotel where you can hire watersports equipment. On the Atlantic-facing east coast, try **Sapphire Beach** for the snorkelling and Sunday afternoon entertainment. **Coki Beach**, next to Coral World, gets very busy. There is some snorkelling and diving, but it is mainly a people beach—sunbathing, hair-braiding, jetskis and snackwagons.

If you want real seclusion, it is worth considering a trip to one of the off-shore islands. Recommended are **Hans Lollick** to the north of St Thomas, **Great St James** to the east and **Saba** and **Buck Island** off the south coast. Trips can be arranged through the watersports operators.

Sailing

St Thomas sees a fair few sailing yachts among the cruise ships, motor-boats and ferries. It has a number of marinas, where you will find all the requisites of sailing life. As the island is so crowded you may have to travel beyond here for seclusion, but there are some excellent harbours in the bights around the coastline. The repair and storage facilities on St Thomas are extensive. There is a port of entry at the ferry dock on the Charlotte Amalie waterfront.

There are two main marinas in Charlotte Amalie harbour: the Yacht Haven near the cruise ship dock and Crown Marina in the old Sub Base area. All the necessary facilities are on line and there are plenty of bars and restaurants a dinghy-ride or even a short walk away. Heading round to the east there is a protected anchorage and a marina complex in Jersey Bay. You might stop over at St James Island, or in Cowpet Bay directly opposite it on the mainland, but further round you will find another of the island's main anchorages in Red Hook Bay. There are repair yards and charter operators as well as other useful yachting facilities in the marina. If you are sailing around the northern shore you might put in at the huge Magen's Bay, or Hull Bay just around the point from there.

The **Virgin Islands Charteryacht League**, Homeport, USVI 00802 (✆ 774 3944, fax 776 3074) has a large number of crewed yachts and some bareboats on its books. They are based at the Yacht Haven near the Havensight Cruise Ship dock. Also try the **Charter Yacht Owners' Association** (✆ 774 3677). There are chandleries in the main marinas and the marina office will help you with your other needs. Repair and supplies can be provided by **Island Marine** (✆ 776 0088) in Charlotte Amalie and **Haulover Marine** (✆ 776 2078) at the Sub Base.

Watersports

The hotels have smaller sailing craft available if you wish to sail around the bay in a hobie cat or a sunfish. If life is more fun on a **wetbike**, again try the big hotels, or go to Coki Beach off the east end. **Parasailing**, in the comfort of a flying deck-chair and complete with stereo, can be arranged at the resorts at the eastern end of the island.

Windsurfing can be fixed up at the hotel beaches on the south and eastern sides. Any major hotel will have equipment, but for the best winds, try Sapphire Beach and Bluebeards Beach. Contact **Caribbean Boardsailing** (© 776 1730). If you would like to take a **day's sail**, with snorkelling and a picnic on an offshore cay or an isolated bay, try the trimarans *Daydreamer* (© 775 2584) and *Coconut* (© 775 5959). For a bit more old-time Caribbean authenticity you can spend the day on a wooden schooner, the *Alexander Hamilton* (© 775 6500). **Deep-sea fishing** is good off St Thomas and is easily arranged. Wahoo, skipjack, sailfish, tuna and white and blue marlin cruise the depths around the islands and there is something to catch at all times of the year. Contact *America II* (© 775 6454) and *Boobie Hatch* (© 775 0685) among the sleek chrome machines at the American Yacht Harbour in Red Hook, or *Prowler* (© 779 2515).

The Virgin Islands are surrounded by reefs and St Thomas has some excellent **snorkelling** grounds where you can hang around in a school of triggerfish or linger among the seafans. **Coki Beach** is often busy and other spots include **Sapphire Beach**, **Secret Harbour**, **Great Bay** and **Botany Bay**. Off-shore islands with good reefs include **Hans Lollick** to the north and **Lovango Cay**, **Mingo Cay** and **Grass Cay** off the east coast. A whole new world opens out for **scuba divers** around St Thomas. The crystalline water often has visibility up to 100ft, and the Virgin Island outcrops, forested above the surface, are covered in coral below. Simple dive-sites off the south coast include Cow and Calf and the shelves of St James Island, and more advanced sites are the tunnels at Thatch Cay and the spine of Sail Rock off the west coast. Once again, the hotels usually lay on equipment and often they can give instruction, but there are outside dive operators if you are travelling independently. A veteran St Thomas diver is **Joe Vogel**, PO Box 7322, St Thomas (© 775 7610), but also try the **Chris Sawyer Diving Centre** (© 775 7320) and **Caribbean Divers** (© 775 6384) at Red Hook. *Dives cost from $40 per tank.* There is a decompression chamber on the island (© 776 2686). If you would prefer not to get wet, you can still get a tame view of the fish and corals from **Coral World**, off Coki Bay (*see* p.245). Alternatively, the **Atlantis Submarine** runs excursions under the waves for a close inspection of the submarine underworld. It leaves from the Havensight Mall, near the cruise-ship dock (© 776 5650 for reservations, *price around $50*).

Other Sports

On land there are other sports to keep the body active. The 18-hole **Mahogany Run Golf Course** is on the northern side of the island, east of Magen's Bay. *Green fees $45*. There are endless **tennis** courts on the island and can be fixed through a hotel. Guests usually play for free but visitors will be charged a fee. And if you would like a trail ride on **horseback**, contact **Rosendahl Riding** (© 775 2636).

Charlotte Amalie

Charlotte Amalie is a classically pretty Caribbean town—red roofs and bursts of palm fronds that scatter the hillsides around a bay and steep alleys that lead down to the harbour. The warehouses on the waterfront are doing a roaring trade as they have on and off for over three hundred years. Even in 1700 Père Labat, the roving Dominican monk and self-confessed gastronome from Martinique, found silks from India and gold-embroidered Arabian muslin cloth. It was all off-loaded by pirates who stopped in port to spend their loot before heading seawards again for more 'cruize and plunder'. The infamous Blackbeard, Edward Teach from Bristol, was known to have hidden out here when he was not on the high seas.

Encouraged by the Danes, the trade became a little more regularized and at its height the harbour would see as many as 1300 vessels in a year. In the late 18th century, the future architect of the American Constitution, Alexander Hamilton (on the reverse of the $10 bill), decided the town was so rich that 'gold moved through the streets in wheel-barrows'.

The seaborne arrivals continue—marauding characters pour off the ships, with fists full of dollars to spend—but nowadays they race past the rum shops and load up into little safari buses instead, ready to go shopping. The wares still come from all over the world; they are just shipped in legally, that is all. It is fascinating mercantile mayhem and it gets quite frantic, so you are advised to avoid Charlotte Amalie on a busy day (when as many as ten cruise ships have been known to call in). Originally the town was known as Tap Hus (roughly translated as the rum shop), but in 1730 the Danes renamed it after the wife of their King Christian V, Charlotte Amalie. As well as the name, many Danish buildings also remain in Charlotte Amalie.

The heartland of Charlotte Amalie is the alleys of trading warehouses from the 18th century, which are still buzzing with trade. As in all West Indian islands, the main **market** in the middle of the town sells fruit and vegetables to the St Thomians who dare venture that far into town. Dark red **Fort Christian**, built in 1672 when the Danes first arrived, stands on the waterfront guarding the bay. In its time it has been the Governor's house, the garrison and recently the prison, police station and courts. It is now home to the **Virgin Islands Museum**, *open Mon–Fri, 9–noon and 1–5, adm free*, and the underground cells have displays of the simple island existence of the Arawaks and the planters' and traders' sumptuous life when St Thomas was in its prime. Over the road is the island **Legislature**, *open 8–5*, formerly the Danish barracks, a grand structure from the 1870s that is dressed up in lime-green, where the 15 US Virgin Island Senators sit.

On the hillside behind the town, aloof from all the activity on the waterfront, is **Government House**, *open during working hours, 8–noon and 1–5, adm free*, a three-storey building with wrought iron balconies built in 1867 for the Danish colonial council and now the official residence of the Islands' Governor. Inside you will see the names of the early Danish Governors and their American counterparts. Some paintings by impressionist painter Camille Pissarro are on display (he was born on the island).

Black Beard

Climbing the **99 Steps** to the top of Government Hill you come to what is known as **Blackbeard's Tower**, an fine look-out, where the pirate was supposed to have lived around 1700. He was an extremely violent man, who would occasionally shoot one of his sidekicks to keep the others on their guard and he liked to adopt an especially demonic appearance when going into battle by burning fuses in his hair. He was eventually killed in a shoot-out with the British navy in 1718.

On the western outskirts of the town you come to **Frenchtown**, the original settling point of a group of immigrants from the island of St Barthélémy in the Leewards, who first came over in 1852. Their descendants form a distinct community on the island: some remain in Frenchtown and work as fishermen, others have become very influential and own some of the most valuable land on the north side.

At the opposite end of town is **Homeport**, St Thomas's main yachting marina, and close by is the West India Company Dock, where you will find the **Havensight Mall**, another agglomeration of tourists shops in long parallel warehouses. If the hustle gets too much, you might take a ride up the hill to **Paradise Point** for a fine sunset view and and excellent banana daiquiri.

Around the Island

The island of St Thomas is highly developed all around. The hills above Charlotte Amalie are covered with homes to their summits and wherever you go on the island you are not far from a residential area. Near the top of the central range is **Drake's Seat**, the vantage point supposedly used by Sir Francis Drake in his privateering days in the 1580s. Where the old English sailor had his henchmen to give him advice and clarify the magnificent view across to the BVI, today's visitors have

T-shirt vendors. At the summit is Mountain Top, where there is another cracking view of the north coast, complete with shopping centre for when the view palls.

Worth a visit in this area is the **Estate St Peter Greathouse Botanical Gardens** (© 774 4999), containing countless examples of tropical plants, from the many different Caribbean floral regions—cacti, water-plants, tropical crops (including 20 species of bananas) and flowering trees, ornamental flowers like heliconia, Indian head ginger and an orchid jungle; 300 species in all alongside a small aviary, a nature trail and iguana and monkey habitats. The great house has been modernized and is surrounded by decks and lookouts, from where there is an excellent view of Magen's Bay.

The southeast of the island is built up with condominiums and vacation homes that take advantage of the beaches in that area. **Coral World**, *adm expensive, adults $14, children $9*, is a small underwater world complex at Coki Beach in the east of the island, with good displays—a walk-in observatory 20ft underwater, a predator tank where sharks and tarpons patrol and Reef Encounter, in which you will see over a hundred sorts of fish including filefish and barred hamlets (which need no mate to reproduce), lionfish like fans and fluorescent corals. The west end is the least developed area of St Thomas and is mainly residential.

© (809)–   **_Where to Stay_**

St Thomas has its share of large and expensive luxury beach resorts, but it also has a surprising collection of excellent small hotels in Charlotte Amalie, many of them set in charming antique townhouses on the hillside with a view of the town below. The government adds a 8% room tax to all bills and most places charge 10% for service.

Beach Hotels

very expensive–luxury

By far the most elegant and luxurious place to stay in St Thomas is the **Grand Palazzo**, Great Bay, USVI 00302 (© 775 3333, fax 775 4444, US reservations © 283 8666). The balustrades and pediments of the Italian renaissance look a little odd amid the permanent blooms of bougainvillea and luxuriant Caribbean palms, but the amphitheatrical setting of the rooms, standing in blocks above a superb bay, is magnificent. Each of the 150 rooms has a balcony taking in the cracking view and is decorated sumptuously with pink marble, Italianate furniture and leather trimmings down to the ice-buckets and waste-paper baskets. Watersports around the pool and beach, rarified atmosphere in the main house and dining rooms. Luxury. The **Morning Star Beach Resort**, PO Box 7100, St Thomas

00801 (© 776 8500, fax 774 6249, US © 800 232 2425), also has a secluded feel, just outside Charlotte Amalie. It has 96 comfortable rooms set in blocks along a private and charming waterfront and beach. Attentive service, but all the facilities of the Frenchman's Reef resort next door, very expensive. If you like a large and active beach resort try the **Stouffer Grand Beach Resort**, PO Box 8267, St Thomas 00801 (© 775 1510, fax 775 2185, US reservations 800 Hotels 1), at the eastern end of the island. About 300 rooms, air-conditioned and cable television, all the watersports, fitness centre, beauty salon, kids' programme, very expensive to luxury.

expensive

For a small and private retreat, with personal service and a friendly atmosphere, try **Pavilions and Pools**, 6400 Estate Smith Bay, St Thomas 00802 (© 775 6110, fax 775 6110 ext 215, US reservations © 800 524 2001). Each of the 25 units has a view through French windows to a private deck with a personal pool. All are air-conditioned with kitchenettes and cable televisions and have showers with garden greenery. Library and central dining room for breakfast and dinner; trails down to Lindquist Beach, all the activity of Sapphire Beach nearby; good idea to have a car.

moderate

Set in a forested tropical garden and looking out onto a very pleasant curve of sand on Lindberg Beach, quite close to the airport, is the **Island Beachcomber Hotel**, PO Box 2579, St Thomas 00803 (© 774 5250, fax 762 5615, US © 800 982 9898). It is lower-key and less expensive than the rest of St Thomas's beach hotels. The 50 rooms are in simple blocks, but the atmosphere is friendly and comfortable. Some watersports. Another informal spot, overlooking Hassel island from just beyond Frenchtown, is the **West Indies Inn**, PO Box 4976 (© 774 1376, fax 774 8010, US © 800 5448 0493). It is set around an old holiday home overlooking Hassell Island. There is an old-time Caribbean air, rooms are air-conditioned, with private veranda and cable television. A cheaper option just above the beach in Estate Nazareth at the southeastern corner of the island is the **Sea Horse Cottages**, PO Box 2312, St Thomas 00803 (© 775 9231). There are 16 units in one- and two-bedroom configurations, in cottages and a small block, each with kitchenettes, some lost in a pleasant tropical garden. Pool, small beach and snorkelling a breath off the coast. Relaxed atmosphere.

Town House Hotels

If you would like to experience some of St Thomas's antique charm, Charlotte Amalie itself has some sophisticated and tranquil retreats. The colonial echoes of the **Mark St Thomas** (© 774 5511, fax 774 8509) make it one of the most congenial places on the islands. The façade of the yellow-brick house is decorated with filigree cast-iron balustrades around its balconies and inside the rooms are fitted with original and reproduction antiques. All 20th-century comforts available too, including air-conditioning and cable television. Eight double rooms, small pool, expensive. Nearby, the **Hotel 1829**, PO Box 1567, St Thomas 00804 (© 776 1829, fax 776 4313, US © 800 524 2002), on Government Hill, is another spot with old-time island ambience. The original town house, with dark backgammon bar and balcony restaurant, has been extended behind with some rooms over-looking the courtyard garden. There are 15 suites and rooms, some a little small, moderate to expensive. The **Galleon House** is also close by, PO Box 6577, St Thomas 00804 (©/fax 774 6952, US © 800 524 2052), with cracking views of the red roofs of Charlotte Amalie. There are 14 comfortable rooms, a pool and (best of all) central dining tables on the terrace where a friendly crowd gathers to read or listen to the wind-up piano—anything from the 'Blue Danube', through ragtime to James Bond theme tunes. Cheap to moderate, good value, good home-cooking at breakfast. The **Villa Fairview Hotel**, 8 Catherinaberg, St Thomas 00802 (© 775 4795, fax 7754 8010, US reservations © 800 544 0493), is set in a very pretty red and white clapboard townhouse under a mango tree, just above the town. Fans, private baths and central sitting area with television, moderate. The **Heritage Manor Inn**, PO Box 90, St Thomas 00804 (© 774 3003, fax 776 9585, US reservations © 800 838 0757), is at 1A Snegle Gade in town, a pretty pink façade with cast-iron balustrades and white stucco. Small and friendly, just eight rooms, with fans, air-conditioning and fridges, some shared baths.

cheap

The **Miller Manor**, PO Box 1570 (© 774 1535), with the faded elegance of a town house and a fantastic view of the bay, is the cheapest deal on the island. At a pinch, if you are down to your last few dollars, go to the marina and ask a yacht owner if you can sleep in a berth on board while the yacht is not on charter; some owners are prepared to allow this in exchange for a few hours' work.

© (809)–

Eating Out

As a developed island, St Thomas has a grander variety of restaurants than others, and so you can eat anything from 'contemporary exotic' cuisine through to good local rice 'n' peas. Many menus are reliably American—burgers and steaks—but everything can be imported, so you will find fine French fare as well as Caribbean seafood and fish. Categories are arranged according to the price of a main dish: *expensive*—US$20 and above; *moderate*—between US$10 and $20; *cheap*—US$10 and below. A 10% or 15% service charge will be added to your bill, for your convenience... '*Tipping* is not a city in China...'

expensive

Some of the best local food can be found in Frenchtown, just outside Charlotte Amalie. **Café Normandie** (ℂ 774 1622) is set in an upstairs drawing room decorated with the works of local artists and presided over by hip waiters in white coats. Classical French cuisine with some light sauces. Nightly-changing five-course menu—*soupe du jour*, salad, intermezzo and sherbert, main courses including *poulet fine champagne* or veal *normandie* in mushrooms and cognac cream. Worth reserving a table in season, *prix fixe*. In town you will receive minutely attentive service and presentation on the veranda at the **Fiddle Leaf** (ℂ 775 2810) on Government Hill. Echoes of nouvelle in the contemporary exotic dishes—Caribbean *bouillabaisse* (scallops, shrimps, mussels and calamari) followed by ginger crusted snapper filet with tropical fruit chutney. Closed Mon out of season. Nearby on Back Street you will find the ever-popular **Virgilio's** (ℂ 776 4920), which serves classic Italian dishes in a comfortable dining room hung with pictures and stained-plastic windows. Egg-plant parmigiana, followed with pastas and meat and vegetarian dishes, *scampi della casa* with linguini oil and garlic. There is an extensive wine-list and it is worth going just for the cappuccino, to which is added a blend of galliano, Bailey's and Kahlua.

moderate

In Frenchtown, there is a charming restaurant at **Craig and Sally's** (ℂ 777 9949). It is set indoors, but has trelliswork walls and murals of Caribbean scenes. An eclectic menu presented with artistic flair—chicken *pignoti* (pine nuts, fresh spinach and mozzarella) or a jumbo sea scallop in passion fruit sauce—to a jazz accompaniment. Good wine list. Nearby, **Alexander's** (ℂ 776 4211) serves Italian and Austrian food in plush, black and white air-conditioned comfort—pastas, wursts and a variation on the Wiener Schnitzel (made with conch). Lunch and dinner, closed Sun. **Alex's Bar and Grill** next door serves simpler meals accompanied by music and television; grilled honey-mustard shrimp, cheap to moderate, lively crowd at the bar. In Charlotte Amalie itself is **Il Cardinale** (ℂ 775 1090), upstairs above the pleasant courtyard at Taste of Italy, a quiet and comfortable dining room where brick walls are hung with imitation Italian paintings. Authentic Italian fare; home-baked *focaccia* and a long pasta menu followed by *scaloppine di marsala*. For something a little more West Indian try **Victor's New Hideout** (© 776 9379), an overlarge dining room with a superb view, which sits on a hilltop above Sub Base. Fresh native fish, steamed with creole or butter sauce, served with a tonnage of rice 'n' peas, fungi or plantain. **Cuzzins** (© 776 9292) is on Back Street in town, an air-conditioned lounge with brick walls, popular for local food— curried and stewed meats (chicken, conch, mutton and goat) accompanied by bewildering local vegetables. Yet more local, and set in a traditional Caribbean clapboard house is **Tasha's** on Gamle Gade just above Market Square. Start with Tasha's rum punch (ingredients undeclared) and then callaloo, curry goat, fried plantain and rice 'n' peas. Just seven tables, cheap to moderate. Beyond Charlotte Amalie you will find the ever-popular and cheery **East Coast** restaurant (© 775 1919) near Red Hook. Set on a breezy wooden terrace, the fare is American and local; shrimp tempura in beer batter, followed by grilled, blackened or teriyaki fish. Some entertainment, also American-style television bar. On the north side of the island there are a number of good restaurants, usually frequented by locals. Try **Berry's Farm** (© 778 8622) on Lionel Berry Road. There is a bar crowd in the evening, but also reliable local fare on the pretty veranda festooned with greenery; fish *à la française*, sautéd in lemon, wine and fresh herbs or chicken creole. At **Ferrari's Ristorante** (© 774 6800), you get Italian food on a balcony with a superb view, and at **Bryan's Bar**, you can play pool and have a beer before you tuck in to one of the island's best lobsters.

cheap

A typically Caribbean waterfront restaurant in Frenchtown is **Hook, Line and Sinker**, where you sit on a wooden deck above the waves. Simple fare, burgers, fried fish and steaks, cheap to moderate. On the waterfront in town is **Percy's Bus Stop**, a London bus, a No.12, somehow re-routed on its journey to Piccadilly Circus; red tablecloths and simple West Indian fare, stew chicken or conch. Finally, if you do not want to spend too much and don't mind dining out of a polystyrene box on your knees, you can get an excellent batter chicken or ribs swimming in barbecue sauce, set in a lump of coleslaw, at **Bill's Texas Pit BBQ**, strategically placed snackwagons on the waterfront in downtown Charlotte Amalie and in Red Hook.

Bars and Nightlife

An excellent bar to start the evening with in Frenchtown (whether you'll eat nearby or not) is the **Epernay Champagne Bar**, where hip chicks and executives gather after work for sushi and goat cheese. Close by, **Alexander's Bar** is also a lively gathering point. Otherwise you might try one of the small town hotels—**Blackbeard's**, **the Mark St George** or **1829**, where the bars often have piano players.

Downtown there are lively pub-style bars at **Coconuts** on Paradise Alley and straight opposite, **Rosie O'Grady's**. You could even try the **Hard Rock Café** (much in the style of other worldwide Hard Rocks), if that's your thing. A little more West Indian in decor is **Calico Jack's Courtyard Inne**, which can be lively till late. You can catch a game of pool or air-hockey with a few locals at **Wet Willie's** at the eastern end of town.

There are also bars in the Sub Base area, another yachties' hangout, so it gets quite lively. Try **Barnacle Bill's**, which you will spot by the outsize lobster on the roof, or by the noise of a band playing (watch out for talent-night, Limelight Monday). Heading east of town **For the Birds** on Scott Bay is a lively dining room and bar, with dancing some nights; **Puzzles** is a piano lounge on a double-decker riverboat, with puzzles to keep you amused if the drinking palls; in Red Hook the bar at **East Coast** can be fun and there is often a rumbustious white crowd at the **Warehouse**—'A Poor Man's Bar'; pool, pinball, loud rock music and a load of beer. Often there is an evening's **jazz** on offer (check the papers and tourist magazines). And if you want to go dancing, there are places open, usually at weekends. **Club Z** is worth the climb up the hill; beyond Charlotte Amalie, try **For the Birds** and **Sib's Mountain Bar**, where there is a young crowd at weekends.

Shopping

St Thomas (particularly) and the other Virgin Islands offer some of the Caribbean's finest hunting grounds for shoppers. As you step off the cruise ship, the dockside warehouses are ranged in front of you and there is literally no manufactured accessory you cannot find. In St Thomas prices will occasionally be marked at about 60 per cent of their stateside price. American citizens are encouraged to spend with special tax concessions when they return home—their duty-free limit is doubled from $400 worth of goods to $800, with yet more concessions on drink (USVI rum).

There are two main areas on St Thomas, the **Havensight Mall**, by the West India cruise ship dock, where three lines of air-conditioned glass-fronted boutiques jostle for business, and downtown Charlotte Amalie, which has been involved with trade for over 300 years and is really an out-size emporium. It is a network of alleyways and streets with everything on sale from Swiss watches and jewellery from the world over to Chanel perfumes and the *chic*-est French modes. There is a small mall at Mountain

Top, so you can shop with a view if you want. The new mall at Paradise Point (just a cable-car ride above Havensight Mall) has an artisan's gallery.

You can try La Romana for Italian clothes, A. H. Riise or Little Switzerland for jewellery purchases and Tropicana for perfumes. Gucci have just one shop for leather clothes and you can try Louis Vuitton for leather goods.

St John

First appearances are enough to show that St John is altogether different from St Thomas. Unlike its larger neighbour, where houses dot the hillsides to their very summits, St John is almost entirely green and forested. As you make the short crossing over the Pillsbury Sound, the pressurized tempo of St Thomas will evaporate and low-key St John will welcome you with a nonchalant calm.

Since 1956 St John has taken a different path from the other Virgin islands. Laurence Rockefeller and his Jackson Hole Preserve Corporation granted two-thirds of the island to the National Parks. St John has remained undeveloped since then and much of the land has now returned to second-generation forest. The National Park has opened up the forests with walking trails and holds seminars on the wildlife.

St John feels almost pastoral and of the three USVI it is the most similar to the BVI. Its capital, Cruz Bay, has just a few streets and the only other settlement consists of a few houses in Coral Bay at the east end. It is not hard to imagine how life was fifty years ago when the islanders travelled everywhere by donkey on small trails cut out of the forest. The island now boasts a bank, a post office and a petrol station.

All may be quiet today, but once St John was as much a hive of plantation activity as the rest of the Caribbean islands. Two hundred years ago the slopes were cut with terraces for the sugar-cane. In 1733 St John saw one of the Caribbean's most successful slave rebellions, in which the Africans revolted and held out for over nine months, successfully beating off attempts by Danish and British troops to put them down. When they were eventually defeated by French soldiers brought in from Martinique, many preferred to commit suicide by jumping off the cliffs at Mary's Point rather than allow themselves to be returned to slavery. Just a few plantation ruins remain, throttled by the jungle.

Like all the islands, the vast majority of St John's income derives from tourism and that has been developing too. Around Cruz Bay, it has a feeling of the modern Caribbean playground—neat and tidy with little complexes of shops and restaurants and day-trippers shifted around in little safari buses—but out east, in the Coral Bay area, you will find some cool and easy waterfront haunts. The island has a pleasant holiday spirit about it and goes out of its way to provide a nature-based holiday for those who want it (the campsites are often booked up well in advance).

Today's population of 4500 is less than that in the island's plantation heyday. Nowadays the island is tranquil, favoured by campers and a few writers and recluses. The desperation suffered by the rebellious slaves seems as far away as the mercantile mayhem of St Thomas.

Getting Around

There is no **bus service** in St John and so if you do not want to pay for a taxi, you will have to hitch a ride, which is not that easy, or walk.

Taxi rates: **Cruz Bay** to Trunk Bay—$5, Cinnamon Bay—$6, Annaberg—$10 (these prices are for one person, and so people will sometimes team up because that brings the price down). You may find that somebody hops in anyway. A two-hour tour of the island by taxi will cost $30.

Cars are available for hire, though when you are out driving you should watch for safari buses and water delivery trucks on the steep bends. Jeeps are popular here and daily rates start at around $40. Companies include **Delbert Hill Jeep and Auto** (© 776 6637), **Hertz** (© 776 6695) and **Spencer's Jeep Rentals** (© 776 6628), all of them in Cruz Bay. Remember to drive on the left.

Tourist Information

There is a Tourist Information office in Cruz Bay (© 776 6450), PO Box 200, USVI 00830, opposite the ferry dock; and the **National Park Service** has a visitors' centre in Cruz Bay near Mongoose Junction (© 776 6201), for an orientation video, bookshop and aquarium. Open 8–4.30. For more information you can write to Virgin Islands National Park, PO Box 7789, St Thomas VI 00801. If you are making a day trip to St John, check in the tourist magazines to see when the fewest cruise ships will be in dock.

In a **medical** emergency, contact the DeCastro Clinic in Cruz Bay (© 776 6252).

St John National Park

The 13,000 acres of the St John National Park are cut and crossed with about twenty **walking trails**, and you can get information on them (along with films) and maps from the Visitors' Centre in Cruz Bay, opposite Mongoose Junction. Many species of plants in the forest are marked. Some 5,600 acres of the National Park are offshore, covering reefs and marine life. The guides (with an ency-clopaedic knowledge of island flora, fauna and history) take out walks a number of times a week, which include picnics and snorkelling breaks. A popular hike leads

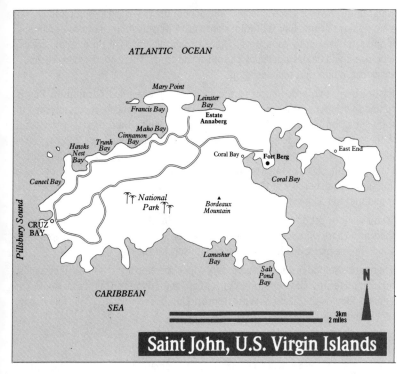

ATLANTIC OCEAN

Mary Point

Leinster Bay

Francis Bay

Estate Annaberg

Maho Bay

Cinnamon Bay

Trunk Bay

Hawks Nest Bay

Coral Bay

Fort Berg

East End

Caneel Bay

Coral Bay

Pillsbury Sound

National Park

Bordeaux Mountain

CRUZ BAY

Lameshur Bay

Salt Pond Bay

CARIBBEAN SEA

3km
2 miles

N

Saint John, U.S. Virgin Islands

from Centerline Road in the middle of the island over to Reef Bay, from where they arrange a trip back by boat to save you the walk. There are also evening slide shows in the camp grounds.

The walks and snorkelling tours (reservations on ✆ 776 6330) cover all the terrain of St John, from the mangroves on the shoreline at Leinster Bay, where you may see gallinules and a mangrove cuckoo among the leafy sprouts, and into the lusher vegetation on the upper mountainsides. On the offshore islands you can see frigatebirds and the usual boobies and pelicans. If you would prefer to hike on horseback, **Pony Express** (✆ 776 6494) will take you on guided tours through the island's blanket of forest and to hidden coves where you can ride along the sand.

Beaches

St John's beaches are mostly along the northern coast and they are more secluded than the beaches on St Thomas, although this does not prevent crowds building up on the more popular ones, particularly if a cruise ship crowd is in. Between the forested fingers of the coastline, the water in the coves is crystalline and will glow in the richest shades of turquoise on a sunny day. **Trunk Bay** is St John's answer to Magen's Bay, mounds of blinding white sand backed by palm trees. There is a snorkelling trail through the corals, where you will be surrounded by parrotfish and tangs. There are changing rooms, a snack bar, a hire shop and lifeguards.

East of here, two broad curves are cut out of the coastline: **Cinnamon Bay** is rimmed with the softest sand and has a snack bar and changing rooms attached to the Cinnamon Bay camp-site. In the next cove, **Maho Bay**, there is good sand, while the cove connected to it, **Francis Bay**, has good snorkelling. Both bays have a superb view out over the other islands. Heading back to Cruz Bay, there are a couple of thin strips of sand in **Hawksnest Bay** where you can usually be alone and many small beaches at **Caneel Bay** (you may have to swim in because you are sometimes not allowed over the hotel's private land).

If you want to get off the beaten track, try **Salt Pond Bay** and **Lameshur Bay** on the south coast, where there are few people, the water is calm and the snorkelling good. Take a picnic and drinks if you plan to stay for the day.

There are also one or two off-shore cays which are worth the visit for their sands, including **Henley Cay** (out from Caneel Bay) and **Lovango Cay** (farther out). Off Leinster Bay in the north is **Waterlemon Cay**, a short ride out of Francis Bay, where the snorkelling is good.

Sailing

Of course, when compared to St Thomas, St John's anchorages are as quiet and unassuming as the rest of St Johnian life. There are some magnificent stopovers, particularly off the beaches of the north coast and in Coral Bay at the east end of the island. There is a port of entry in Cruz Bay.

Cruz Bay is a popular and attractive anchorage and there is plenty of sheltered water (either side of the ferry channel) in which you can drop anchor. The comparative activity of the town is right there, for provisioning and entertainment. Caneel Bay is a calm and protected anchorage and then as you head further east you will find superb beach stops at Hawksnest Bay, Trunk Bay and Francis Bay. Around Mary Point is another good daytime anchorage in the protected Leinster Bay. Around the eastern point the harbours are not so pretty but they are good places to stop for the night. Coral Harbour has a few restaurants and bars; the fingers of Hurricane Hole and Round Bay are very secluded and quiet. Southeast of here there is a good anchorage in Lameshur Bay. If you need supplies you can try **Caneel Bay Ship Yard** (© 776 6111) in Cruz Bay or **Coral Bay Marine Services** (© 776 6859) at the east end.

Sports

Watersports are handled by the hotels and by a few outside operators. They will fix up windsurfing, kayaking and snorkelling gear (*see* 'Beaches', above, for the best sites). Contact **St John Watersports** (© 776 6256), **Low Key Watersports** (© 776 7048), who also arrange parasailing, and **Cinnamon Bay Watersports** (© 776 6330) in Cinnamon Bay (good for windsurfing). If you would like a day's sail, the catamaran *Jolly Mon* (© 776 6239) takes a ride around the island with snorkelling stops. A day's sail can also be fixed up through *Serenity* and sportfishing through **World Class Anglers** (both © 776 6922). And if you want a more traditional sailing yacht, complete with on-board loony dog, try the yacht *Spree* (© 771 3734). **Deep-sea fishing** trips can be arranged on *Gone Ketchin'* (© 776 7709).

Scuba divers can go to any of these companies, or at the east end of the island to **Coral Bay Watersports** (© 776 6850). Favourite dive-sites include the reefs and cays to the north of the island, Eagle Shoal to the south, Ten Fathom Pinnacle and even the steamship *Rhone* off Salt Cay in the British Virgin Islands. A tamer version of scuba is **Snuba** (© 693 8063) in Trunk Bay. You can view the corals and fish at a depth of 20ft; your air supply is fed by a hose pipe from a boat. If even this sounds outlandish, take a ride on a glass-bottom boat, the *Calypso Queen* (© 776 6922).

There are some **tennis** courts in the hotels as well as four public courts in Cruz Bay.

Cruz Bay

Cruz Bay, the miniature capital of St John, is a typically sleepy West Indian town set on a west coast bay just a few miles across the Pillsbury Sound from St Thomas. The houses scattered on the hillside tumble down to the waterfront, where a couple of pint-size pastel-painted arcades have sprung up to catch the day-trippers.

The small island **museum**, *open Mon–Fri, 9–5*, is downstairs in the public library as you go up the hill. Alongside the St Johnian schoolchildren, you can discover old-time St John through prints and the descriptions of their slave revolt in 1733.

Around the Island

In its plantation days the slopes of St John were completely covered in sugar-cane, but since the early 19th century the land has been left, and so the island is now carpeted with 50ft-high jungle. Just a few mill-ruins poke out from beneath the overgrowth. To drive along the north coast, follow the bay past Mongoose Junction, where the road starts to switchback, clambering up the slopes and sweeping down into the successive bays. On each headland there is a view of the other Virgins. At Mary Point is a ravine called Minna Neger Ghut, where the last survivors of the slave rebellion in 1733 are thought to have jumped to their deaths rather than submit themselves to slavery once more. Eventually you come to the best preserved and most accessible of the estate ruins at **Estate Annaberg**, *open in daylight hours, no guides, adm free*, a former sugar plantation with displays showing the process and describing the buildings.

Centreline Road carves a path into the forested hills, wiggling over the impossibly steep slopes and passing beneath Bordeaux Mountain, St John's highest peak. From **Coral Bay Overlook** there is a superb view of the islands to the northeast, looking along Sir Francis Drake Passage towards Virgin Gorda about 20 miles away. From here the road descends towards St John's only other settlement at Coral Bay, a light smattering of houses around the harbour with an easy-going atmosphere in the waterfront bars and restaurants. Coral Bay was the first area settled by the Danes and Fort Berg, the dilapidated fort on the point, dates from 1717, the year they arrived. Beyond the town, roads lead both south around the coast and to the eastern tip; these areas are mainly residential.

© *(809)–*   **Where to Stay**

 There is a small selection of hotels on St John, concentrated around Cruz Bay. Another option is to take a villa, of which there are plenty on the island (*see* p.257). There are also a couple of campsites, if you want to see the National Park from close up. Government tax of 8% is levied on all hotel bills.

very expensive–luxury

Caneel Bay, PO Box 720, St John 00831 (© 776 6111, fax 776 2030, 800 223 7637), is set on the magnificent sweep of Caneel Bay, with rooms ranged along the waterfront overlooking Pillsbury Sound and St Thomas. Set amid lawns and manicured gardens, lit at night by flaming torches, the restored estate buildings lend the hotel an elegant, old colonial atmosphere. Low key, high luxury enjoyed by generations of returning visitors. It has been upgraded recently to meet the demands of modern travellers. The **Hyatt Regency St John**, PO Box 8310, St John 00830 (© 693 8000, fax 779 4986, US © 800 233 1234), has a more tangibly modern beach front resort feel about it. It is large, with rooms in blocks standing around land-scaped gardens and has watersports and entertainment. The **Gallows Point** Hotel, PO Box 58 (© 776 6434, fax 776 6520, US © 800 323 7229), is a very comfortable and attractive hotel set in modern Caribbean-style build-ings on the clifftop just out of Cruz Bay (a walk or a drive from the beach). Each suite has a balcony with a fine view, a kitchenette and there is a cen-tral restaurant, expensive to very expensive, good summer rates.

There are a number of less formal hotels around Cruz Bay. The **Raintree Inn**, PO Box 566, St John 00831 (✆/fax 776 7449, US reservations ✆ 800 666 7449), is a busy spot in the heart of Cruz Bay's tiny downtown. Eight air-conditioned rooms, three apartments and the Fish Trap restaurant, set on a pretty wooden deck hung with greenery. The **Cruz Inn**, PO Box 556 (✆ 776 7688, fax 776 7449), takes a rather more aloof view from the hillside over a bay behind town. Friendly with quite simple rooms, some shared baths, cheap to moderate. Cheaper rooms can be found in the modern, pink block of the **Inn at Tamarind Court**, PO Box 350, St John 00831 (✆ 776 6378, US reservations ✆ 800 776 6378). The 20 rooms are simple but adequate and there is a charming courtyard bar and restaurant where you sit in the shade of a huge tamarind tree. You can sometimes get a very cheap room at the **St John Hostel** (✆/fax 693 5544), high on Bordeaux Mountain. Simple bedrooms with shared baths.

St John has two **campgrounds** on its forested north shore. The camping is by no means 'rustic'; you live in permanent 'tents' (raised floors with walls and netting at either end or wooden cabins with mosquito screens) connected by a lacework of paths and wooden walkways to the central area, washrooms, concessionary shops and beaches. Hikes, watersports and even environmental lectures. Try **Maho Bay Camps**, PO Box 310, St John 00830 (✆ 776 6226, fax 776 6504, US reservations ✆ 800 392 9004) in Maho Bay, the more comfortable of the two, which has cottages on the hillside, carefully hidden among the profuse greenery of the national park. Kitchenettes and balconies, watersports down below. **Cinnamon Bay**, PO Box 720 (✆ 776 6330, fax 776 6458, US reservations ✆ 223 7637), is at sea level in the forest. Cottages and tents and simple cooking facilities, and a restaurant too. Both resorts get booked up in the winter season.

St John is also an ideal place to hire a **villa**. **Windspree Vacation Home Rentals**, 6-2-1A Estate Carolina, St John 00830 (✆/fax 693 5423), has several villas in the Coral Bay area; **St John Properties**, PO Box 700, St John 00831 (✆ 776 7223, fax 776 6192), has villas and apartments around the island. Price range $100 to $400 per day for a single bedroom villa.

✆ *(809)–*

Eating Out

St John has quite a good variety of places to eat for a small island (perhaps worth investigating from St Thomas). As well as the more formal dining rooms of the big hotels, you will find lively restaurants in Cruz Bay and some easy-going haunts around Coral

Bay in the east. The larger restaurants will accept credit cards. Service charge runs at 10–15%. Categories are arranged according to the price of a main dish: *expensive*—US$20 and above; *moderate*—between US$10 and $20; *cheap*—US$10 and below.

expensive

Château Bordeaux (℃ 776 6611) has top position for cuisine and particularly for its setting, high in the central mountains with a supreme view of the east coast from an almost alpine deck. You dine at pretty tables with mock silver cutlery, on international cuisine. To start, banana, papaya, conch fritters or baby wild greens with goat cheese tossed in a raspberry walnut vinaigrette, followed by veal in white wine and lemon basil sauce.

moderate

In Cruz Bay is a charming and very lively restaurant where you will find excellent food, **Morgan's Mango** (℃ 693 8141), a white, pink and turquoise terrace with wooden floorboards and a friendly tree growing through it. The food is Argentinian and new Caribbean in style, so as well as a 14oz steak with chimi-churri sauce, you can expect Cuban citrus chicken and spicy voodoo snapper. There is a long cocktail menu for before dinner, and in season it is worth reserving. The **Paradiso** restaurant (℃ 776 8806) is in the Mongoose Junction II shopping centre. Hardwood and imitation marble, pastel colours and Italian fare—try the seafood *puttanesca* with shrimp scallops and olives or the chicken *piccante* (spicy). **Café Roma** (℃ 776 6524) also serves Italian food in a pretty tropical dining room upstairs on Main Street in Cruz Bay: Venetian shrimp in lemon and garlic and a multiplicity of pastas and pizzas. You will find West Indian fare at the **Old Gallery** (℃ 776 7544), which is set in a classic West Indian town house with pink-shuttered doors and grey and white walls. You can sit on the veranda above the street, or inside. Rice 'n' peas with a fillet of snapper stuffed with crab, as well as steaks and pizzas.

There are some fun places to get a meal at the other end of the island, around **Coral Bay**. **Shipwreck Landing** (℃ 776 8640) has a comfortable air; you eat on a wooden deck overhung by palms and bougainvillea, right across from the sea. Barbecued chicken, lime butter mahi-mahi or burgers and sandwiches. Close by is **Miss Lucy's** restaurant, dressed up in pink right on the waterfront, which also serves good fish or American fare. **Don Carlos** is a cool and easy Mexican restaurant; hip waitresses, fluorescent lights and Latin music over a burrito or a marinaded *ceviche*.

You can get a good meal at the **Lime Inn** and **Fred's** restaurant: both serve wholesome American and Caribbean fare; chicken or fish, or a goat stew. The **Dockside Pub** near the ferry departure point will fix you bratwurst or a sub. To round off an evening, drop in to the **Garden of Luscious Licks** on Main Street, where you will find health foods and ice-creams. Fresh salads, veggieburgers, freshly squeezed juices, brownie bars and peace pops. 'Positive vibes—and hugs—the kind of hangout place that nourishes the body and the soul!', if you like that sort of thing.

Bars

 St John can get surprisingly lively and at the weekend you will find Cruz Bay buzzing past midnight. Some of the bars put on bands. Wharfside Village, the downtown mall, is the busiest area, where **Beni Iguana** is ever popular and has entertainment and a raucous crowd at the weekends. The **Pusser's Pub** is done up in the brass and polished wood of mock nauticalia—there is an oyster bar in the **Crow's Nest** with a good view of the harbour. **Larry's Landing** is all about beer, television and pool. And on Kongens Gade you will find **Grumpys' almost by the Sea**—'where hurricanes and hang-overs make the only difference, 2000 miles away from self-importance'—an upstairs deck where you sit under parasols and the branches of a tree, good for a beer and a bit of amateur philosophy if you're up to it. **Fred's** next door can be quite lively and has a band a couple of times a week, as can the **Lime Inn**. St John's discotheque is the **Boom Boom Room**, just up the hill in town. In **Coral Bay** try **Don Carlos** for a lively drinking crowd and **Skinny Legs** for television and beer. **Sea Breeze** sees a rum-bustious crowd from time to time.

St Croix

St Croix (pronounced St Croy) is the largest of the Virgin Islands. Unlike the hillier islands of St Thomas and St John, St Croix has stretches of flat and fertile land between its hills and so it has traditionally been agricultural. Once, its 84 square miles were divided up into about a hundred sugar plantations. But now agriculture is in decline and has been overtaken by tourism as the main industry and source of revenue. But tourism is not as intensive in St Croix and you can still find deserted beaches on the island. The streets of Christiansted simply do not have the pressure-cooker effect of Charlotte Amalie. Things are more low key here, but you will find some surprisingly good places to stay and eat. Like so much of the Caribbean,

St Croix feels a little haphazard. The island's name is French (a straight translation of Columbus's original name for it, Santa Cruz), but this is one of the few legacies of the short French ownership in the 17th century. The island was bought by the Danes in 1733 after they had established themselves in St Thomas.

From time to time, St Croix has been the senior island of the three US Virgin Islands, because of its successful plantation economy and because it had the largest population (presently about 55,000). The Governor resided here in the 19th century and it was in Frederiksted on St Croix that he declared that the slaves should be freed in 1848. Earlier this century the island's importance declined with the failure of agriculture, while St Thomas became an important naval base and then boomed with the tourist industry. Only recently have the Cruzians started to catch up with their neighbours.

St Croix has a mixed community—as well as the original Cruzians, who are mainly of African descent, a large number of Puerto Ricans have made their way on to the island over the last hundred years, escaping the poverty of the larger island. There are also many 'down-islanders' and there is even a small community of Danes, the strongest remnant of the colonial legacy. It is not very strong, but one commentator claimed that a week among the Cruzians was like a tropical version of a tortured Ibsen play! Generally the Cruzians are slow and polite.

It is not entirely a happy community, as shown by the looting and racial problems that followed Hurricane Hugo's extraordinarily destructive passage in 1989, when 90 per cent of the Cruzians were left homeless. About 20 per cent of the population moved off the island after the hurricane and some have returned since. On a lighter note, there is little love lost between the St Thomians and the Cruzians, who consider St Thomas over-developed and rather stressful.

Christiansted, the capital, and Frederiksted (once the more important town because of its better harbour) are traditional West Indian waterfront towns, where the arched walkways can transport you back to the days of clippers and ocean-going trading ships and wharves heaving with barrels and tea-chests. They have been well restored.

© (809)– **Getting There**

A number of hopper airlines fly into St Croix from both directions along the island chain, from Puerto Rico and down to Sint Maarten and Antigua. In addition there are endless links to St Thomas: **Island Air Shuttle** (local © 778 2939), **Vieques Air Link** (© 778 9858), **Air Anguilla** (© 778 1880) and **Sunaire Express** (© 778 9300). A charter jet can be hired through **Bohlke International Airways** (© 778 9177, fax 772 5932).

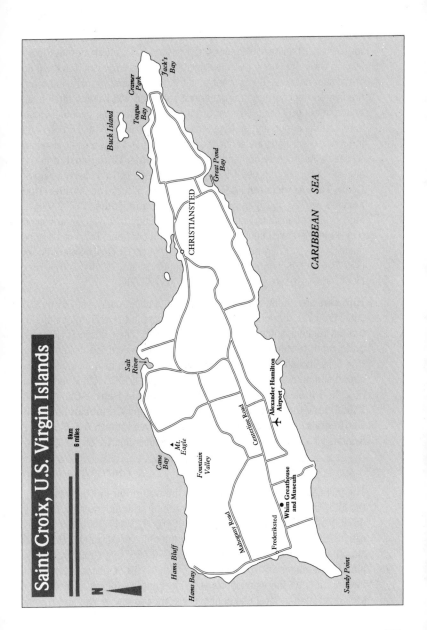

Saint Croix, U.S. Virgin Islands

Getting Around

There are no public **buses** on St Croix, but share-taxis run the principal routes (Christiansted to Frederiksted costs $1.50, other journeys less), leaving when they are full or the driver has the urge. You can pick them up at the supermarkets. If you want to get to the east end of the island or off the beaten track (around the rainforest area) you will have to hitch-hike, which does not work brilliantly, or take a **taxi**. These can be found at the hotels, at the airport and on King Street in Christiansted or by Fort Frederik in Frederiksted. Rates are set by the government and cabs are not metered, so check the price beforehand. Typical fares: from **Christiansted** to the airport—$10, Frederiksted—$20, north coast—$16. Taxi operators are **St Croix Taxi Association** (✆ 778 1088) at the airport, and **Antilles Taxi Service** (✆ 773 5020) and **Caribbean Taxi and Tours** (✆ 773 9799), both in Christiansted. Taxi drivers will willingly take you on an island tour—many are well informed—for about $30 per hour. Tours can also be made in tourist safari buses (about $20). Contact **St Croix Safari Tours** (✆ 773 6700), departure about 10am from Christiansted. Alternatively try a bit of aerial sight-seeing: St Croix Aviation (✆ 778 0090).

Hire cars are readily available, but come at a price, starting at $45 or $50 a day (you can sometimes find reduction offers in the promotional literature). Most companies will deliver the car to you. The roads in St Croix are quite good, certainly when compared with elsewhere in the Caribbean. Hire firms include the international companies, which have an office at the airport and in town: **Avis** (✆ 778 9355), **Budget** (✆ 773 2285) and **Hertz** (✆ 778 1402), and local firms such as **Olympic Rent-A-Car** (✆ 773 2208) in the Caravelle Arcade in Christiansted and **Caribbean Jeep and Car Rentals** (✆ 773 4399). **Scooters** can be hired through **A & B Scooter Rentals** (✆ 778 8567) in Christiansted. Remember to drive on the left.

Tourist Information

The main St Croix Tourist Board is on the waterfront in Christiansted in the Old Scale House (with weighing machine still underneath), PO Box 4538, Virgin Islands 00822 (✆ 773 0495, fax 773 0495). Tourist arrivals can also check details with the information office at Alexander Hamilton airport and in Frederiksted on the pier (✆ 772 0357). St Croix produces a pink island guide, *St Croix This Week*, with details of current events and helpful hints on the watersports and shops and even how to invest in a dream vacation or local real estate. There are also one or two advertising-led dining guides.

In a **medical** emergency, go to St Croix Hospital and Community Health Centre in Christiansted (✆ 778 6311). **Ambulance ✆ 922, police ✆ 915**.

Beaches

There are some excellent beaches in St Croix. The main ones will usually have some development, but there are many charming and isolated coves in between them, so if you want to find a secluded spot to yourself, it is worth asking around or simply taking side-roads and tracks down to the sea. The snorkelling is good and many reefs are close to shore. All beaches are public, though if you want to use a hotel's deck chairs or changing facilities, you may well be charged (*up to $5*). Most watersports are available.

St Croix's best beach is on **Buck Island**, a couple of miles off-shore at the east end. The Buck Island underwater life is particularly good—there is an enormous reef of seafans, and antlers of staghorns teem with angelfish in shimmering yellow, blue and green. A very good snorkelling trail guides you through all of this. The island is a National Park. Many boats make the tour out there, about an hour's sail, for the day or half a day (*about $25 for a half-day, $40 a full day*).

The closest beach to downtown Christiansted is on **Protestant Cay**—the small island about two minutes' swim off the waterfront, *or an expensive $3 ferry ride*. Watersports equipment is available here. East of town is the small, palm-backed strand at the **Buccaneer Hotel**, where there are chairs and facilities (*$4 fee*) as well as a beach bar. And just east of here is the perfect half-moon curve of luscious sand at **Shoy Beach**; there are no facilities and you have to find your way down through the trees, but it is a superb and quiet suntrap. The calm shallow water at **Chenay Bay** is good for children, and also has facilities and watersports.

Cramer Park (at the eastern tip of the island on the north side) is popular with Cruzians so it fills up at weekends. There is a changing room, but take drinks, a picnic and snorkelling gear to see the underwater life. On the other side of the point and even more isolated is **Isaac's Bay**, where the snorkelling is even better. The best way to get to this beach is from the eastern end of Jack's Bay, though you must walk down there. **Grapetree Bay**, on the south shore at the eastern end, is a secluded strip of sand where the waves get up sometimes.

The sand comes ashore in mounds at the southwestern tip of St Croix at **Sandy Point**. It is quite isolated here, and you are advised to be careful about locking your car and leaving belongings unattended. Take food and drinks. In season (May to July), leatherback turtles make their way up the beach here at night to lay their eggs. Cut into the cliffs of the north coast are a number of coves, of which the best is **Cane Bay**, where the palm-backed sand comes and goes, but the reef remains, giving superb snorkelling. Jewel fish glint among the coral heads and striped sergeant majors cruise around on patrol. There is also a good strip of sand at the Carambola Hotel.

Beach Bars

There is a popular haunt at **Chenay Beach**, a simple, open-sided bar where you can retreat for a beer and a snack after a sailboard trip taming the waves or re-hydrate after lying in the sun. Set on a pretty, covered veranda, **Duggan's Reef** is a little more formal, though you can watch the windsurfers at work here as well. Burgers, salads and island-fare (moderate prices). On the western side of town, fol-lowing the northern shore, there are two pleasant stopovers—**Columbus Cove**, where you will find simple fare to go with a view of the yacht on the lagoon, and the **No Name Bar** at the Cane Bay Reef Club. And for a more formal meal on a wild waterfront you can try **Picnic in Paradise** (© 778 1212). You approach on a wooden walkway through the seagrape and sit on a waterfront deck shaded by a sea almond tree. Delicious salads by day, more formal meals by night.

But the western end of the island is the place to head for a lazy day and a sunset view over the sea. The **Sand Bar** is rustic but gets quite active with live music a couple of days a week and the **La Grange Beach Club**, *adm*, is a little more formal—on the terrace you can order sandwiches and salads (cheap). The **West End Beach Club**, set on the best stretch of sand, is probably the liveliest, with vol-leyball and crowds at the weekend. It serves salads and burgers (cheap).

Sailing

So remote from the rest of the Virgins, St Croix does not see the yachting traffic of the other islands, but there are some good anchor-ages around the island if you stop over there. The main service area, and a very picturesque port, is Christiansted, where you can anchor in the lee of Protestant Cay and be within a short dinghy ride of the downtown activity. There are plenty of places to provision and you can take on fuel, ice and water at St Croix Marine. The most popular sailing grounds are to the east of Christiansted, towards Buck Island, where there is an excellent daytime stopover (there are mooring buoys). There is a full service marina opposite Green Cay. West of Christiansted you will find a small marina at Salt River with a bar. It is quite hard to get into, but well protected once you have made it. There is a port of entry in Christiansted. For supplies and technical assistance you can contact the marinas: try **St Croix Marine** (© 773 0289).

Watersports

Most watersports can be arranged through the hotel and independent operators around the island—wetbikes are for hire if you want to scoot around among the

yachts at anchor and **waterskiing** is also
easily arranged: Most resort hotels
have watersports equipment too.
If you wish to go **parasailing**,
you can get airborne in Christiansted
practically without wetting your feet.
Contact **St Croix Water Sports
Centre** (✆ 773 7060) at the Hotel on
the Cay (a general watersports operator).

Windsurfing is well served on the island. The winds are good at the eastern end,
off Chenay Bay and Teague Bay. **Mistral** has a concession at the Chenay Beach
Resort. Hotels usually have small sailing boats, sunfish and hobie cats available to
their guests. If you want to go out on a larger yacht for a **day's sail**, there are
plenty of organized cruises which are quite fun (many go to Buck Island). You can
try **Mile Mark Charters** (✆ 773 2285), who arrange trips out of Christiansted,
Captain Big Beard's Adventure Tours on the catamaran *Renegade* (✆ 773
7977) or **Llewelyn's Charters** (773 9027) for a trimaran trip. *Diva* (✆ 778 4675)
takes more personalized trips with a maximum of six and *Junie Bomba* (✆ 772
2482) departs for day and sunset tours from Frederiksted.

Deep-sea fishing is well organized in St Croix, with fleets of sleek cruisers in
which to ply the deep for 6ft marlin, sailfish and wahoo. *A full day can cost from
around $600 and a half-day from $400.* Try *Ruffian* (✆ 773 6011), which leaves
from the King's Alley Wharf.

The best **snorkelling** grounds are listed in the beaches section, but the reefs also
offer good **scuba diving**. The island is almost completely ringed by barrier reefs
and there are endless dive-sites, some of which drop off just a few hundred yards
off-shore. It is particularly good for its soft-coral life. There is a wall off the north
coast between Christiansted and Hams Bay in the west: the Salt River drop-off
starts in 20ft of water, dropping to thousands, as with the Cane Bay drop-off (from
35ft). Frederiksted has good corals and off-shore at Buck Island is a popular spot.

Many of the hotels offer dive-packages and it is also easy to fix up lessons if you
wish to learn. *A single-tank dive costs from $45.* Outside operators include **V.I.
Divers** (✆ 773 6045) or **Dive Experience** (✆ 773 3307) in Christiansted, the
Cane Bay Dive Shop (✆ 773 9913) on the north shore and **Cruzian Divers**
(✆ 772 3701) in Frederiksted.

Other Sports

There are two 18-hole **golf** courses on the island, the Carambola (✆ 778 5638) on
the northern shore and at the Buccaneer Hotel, east of Christiansted (✆ 773

2100). *Green fees are $20–30*. The Reef is a 9-hole course in the eastern Teague Bay area (© 773 8844), *fee comparable for nine holes*. **Horse riding** can be fixed up through **Paul and Jill's Equestrian Stable** at Sprat Hall Estate in Frederiksted (© 772 2880), for a ride through the diminutive rainforest or around old-time St Croix, the land of the windmills. **Tennis** courts are available in practically every hotel on the island, and some have a tennis professional who can give lessons.

Christiansted

With its waterfront walkways and arched Danish storage houses, Christiansted is an alluring harbour town that rings with echoes of another age. The inevitable invasion of air-conditioned boutiques and fast-food halls that makes it a 20th-century trading town have been kept out of sight—neon signs must not protrude beyond the original façades—and so you have the impression that a colonial official in serge with gold epaulettes might round the corner at any minute. But instead of clippers at anchor, the harbour is ranged with yachts and from time to time the seaplane belly-flops into the bay.

The town was laid out by the Danes when they arrived in 1733 and is named in honour of King Christian VI. It is protected by a large barrier reef, on which the waves break a few hundred yards out from the shore. Any potential invading force would have had to negotiate the reef and then face unformidable **Fort Christiansvaern**, *open weekdays 8–5 and weekends 9–5, adm (which also admits you to the Steeple Building across the way)*. Nobody did and so the yellow fort never saw action, but it is pleasant to visit (it seems that the walls were used mainly to lock the soldiers in at night rather than keep invaders out). It was started in 1733, with stones brought from Denmark as ballast, and since 1878, when it was abandoned by the military, it has functioned variously as a police station and courthouse. The fort's guns have a a good view over **Protestant Cay**, an island-hotel just a few minutes' swim out to sea. It takes its name from the French era when only Catholics could be buried on the mainland, and so Protestants were buried here. It is mostly referred to as the Hotel on the Cay, and is supposed to be the setting for Herman Wouk's classic novel about the nightmarish life of a Caribbean hotelier, *Don't Stop the Carnival*, (*see* p.237).

Back on the mainland, newly arrived captains would first check in to the **Old Danish Customs House** before unloading. It was built in the 1750s, and the staircase, a suitably imposing entrance for the captains, was added later. Next stop was the **Old Scale House** (weighing scales still in place) which would measure their cargo. The building also contains the Tourist Information office. Beyond the **Old Danish West India and Guinea Company Warehouse**, which the company used as its headquarters from 1749 (now the post office), is the **Steeple Building**, a Lutheran Church constructed in 1735 (the steeple itself was added in 1794). Today it houses the **National Park Museum**, *open Mon–Fri, 9am–4pm, adm (with fort)*, where you can see exhibits of Indian calabashes, maps of Danish St Croix and diagrams of rum production.

On King Street (Kongens Tvaergade), you will find **Government House**, with its arched veranda and red pillar boxes. It is two private homes set around a garden, joined together when Governor van Scholten bought them in 1830s. The staircase at the entrance leads to the main hall, now redecorated with chandeliers and mirrors like those under which the islanders danced a hundred years ago (the Danes took the originals with them when they left in 1917, but gave some others back to the islands in 1966). Today the buildings house the court and government offices.

Those looking to score a few duty-free bargains will find the main shopping streets just behind the waterfront around King Street and King's Alley, in the old trading houses. Another echo of the old West Indies (from before the age of the supermarket) can still be seen in the covered **market** (*weekdays and Saturdays*), which has been there in one form or other since 1735. A few Cruzians have stalls selling ground provisions to other islanders.

Around the Island

St Croix's 84 square miles were once divided into about a hundred sugar plantations and the windmills once used to crush the cane (without sails and growing steadily more dilapidated) seem to be on every hilltop. From them there are splendid views across the island and often as far north as the other Virgin Islands, grey stains on the horizon 40 miles to the north.

Travelling west from Christiansted on the north shore road you pass **Salt River**, a mangrove bay where Columbus put in for water in 1493, and then eventually you come to Cane Bay, where the road twists and drops into small coves forested with palm trees that are cut into the northern cliffs. The views are spectacular. Finally the road turns inland past Fountain Valley to the Centerline road.

The **Centerline Road** runs west from Christiansted to the town of Frederiksted, mostly in a direct straight line in the centre of the island. As it leaves Christiansted it passes close to St Croix's small industrial area, where you will find the Hess Oil Refinery on the south coast, now running at a reduced capacity, and the aluminium plant. The road eventually passes the Alexander Hamilton airport. (Alexander Hamilton came to St Croix from Nevis as a boy and grew up in Christiansted before leaving for North America in the 1760s.)

Across the road you come to the **St George Village Botanical Gardens**, *open daily, guided tours, 9–4, adm,*

laid out over a 16-acre site that was a plantation estate and before that an Arawak village. Some buildings around the great house have been restored and on the various trails you will find many Caribbean favourites including the bulbous sandbox tree (the pods of this spiky-barked tree were used to hold sand that was then sprinkled on ink to stop it smudging), the autograph tree (you can write on its leaves) and the dildo cactus, named for its shape. The garden is making a collection of all the plants in St Croix that are endangered.

Sugar-cane was the source of St Croix's wealth for many years and the crop blanketed the land as late as 1966. It is gone now, but the distillation of rum has continued, with imported molasses, at the **Cruzian Rum Distillery** (© 772 0799), just off Centerline Road to the south. A half-hour guided tour will lead you among the vats of distilling molasses, where the smell will have you teetering on the walkways. Some rum is bottled here for sale in the USVI, but most is exported. *Tours finish with a snifter in the bar, 9–11.30 and 1–4.15, adm free.* A couple of miles farther along the road is the **Whim Greathouse and Museum**, *open Mon–Sat, 10–3, adm expensive*, which will cast you back to the days of plantation glory, when planter Mr McEvoy lived in this house with the air of a church, surrounded by a moat. It has been restored by volunteers and refitted with period furniture. In the dungeon-like outhouses you can see the tools of all the artisans—cooper (barrel-maker), logger, wheelwright, joiner and blacksmith.

Frederiksted

St Croix's second town is Frederiksted, set on the west coast, 17 miles west of Christiansted. Founded in 1751, Frederiksted has always been important because it has a better harbour than Christiansted, and large ships were able to dock there. Nowadays the traffic is mostly cruise ships, but even a hundred years ago liners were passing by; in 1887 Lafcadio Hearn stopped off in the town *en route* for Martinique, describing it in his *Two Years in the West Indies*. To him the town had 'the appearance of a beautiful Spanish town, with its Romanesque piazzas, churches, many-arched buildings peeping through breaks in a line of mahogany, bread-fruit, mango, tamarind and palm trees'. The town, much of which was rebuilt after it was burned in a riot in 1878, was well known for its elaborate West Indian gingerbread architecture. The pretty arches are still along the waterfront, but the feel of the Spanish town has gone.

As usual, the harbour is watched over by a fortress, **Fort Frederik**, now run down. Constructed in 1752, it was here that Governor van Scholten made his announcement that he was abolishing slavery in the Danish islands in 1848, against the orders of his king. Close by is the **Old Customs House**, where the duty would be paid on the incoming and outgoing cargo. From here, Strand Gade runs past a line of old stone warehouses with arched walkways above the pavement.

Well worth a visit is the **St Croix Aquarium and Marine Education Centre** on Strand Gade, which has a series of small aquaria. They are brought alive by Lonnie Kaczmarsky, who will tell you stories of the dentist shrimp (which cleans the teeth of other fish without them eating him), sponge crabs who disguise themselves with sponges and then eat them if they cannot find a meal, and the triangular arrow crab who looks like a cartoon character. He takes guided snorkelling tours.

The Rainforest

A mile out of Frederiksted, towards the north coast of the island, is St Croix's miniature 'rainforest'. It does not receive enough rain to be a real rainforest, but the vegetation is different from the rest of the island and as you drive along **Mahogany Road**, the creepers and lianas will reach down to grapple with you. Orchids perch and ferns explode in the upper branches, just beneath the 100ft canopy, and you may see a hummingbird flit by. There are a number of roads leading from the top of West End Road into the forest (many are unpaved and so it's best to go by jeep), and there are footpaths if you wish to walk. In the forest you will find **St Croix LEAP** (from Life Experience Achievement Programme), which has a wood mill and craft shop selling products from local timber.

The East

The eastern end of St Croix is drier and less lush than the west. It is becoming steadily built up with housing estates and holiday condominium complexes and there are some fun restaurants and bars. The beaches are worth a visit (some active, others reclusive), but all you will see among the windmill cones and the modern villas are a few goats and the dildo cactus. Point Udall is the easternmost point in the United States.

© (809)–   ***Where to Stay***

Like St Thomas, St Croix has a variety of hotels with beach-front resorts and some smaller hotels with antique (and mock-antique) charm, set in the older Danish buildings. There are very few cheap places to stay. **Villa rental** can be arranged through **Island Villas**, 14A Caravelle Arcade, Christiansted (© 773 8821, fax 773 8823, US © 800 626 4512) or **Tropic Retreats in Paradise**, PO Box 5219, Christiansted (© 778 7550, US © 800 233 7944). USVI government tax of 8% is levied on all hotel bills.

The **Cormorant Beach Club**, 4126 La Grande Princesse (℗ 778 8920, fax 778 9218, US ℗ 800 372 1323), is a very elegant small retreat with modern Caribbean comfort. It has everything for the luxurious escape— sumptuous high-pastel rooms with their own balconies and a view of the ocean, afternoon tea and no telephones. And when you feel like emerging from your seclusion, there are watersports on the windy beach right out- side and for the evenings a charming restaurant looking out through the palms. Just 37 double rooms, expensive. The **Buccaneer Hotel**, PO Box 25200 (℗ 773 2100, fax 778 8215, US ℗ 800 223 1108), just outside Christiansted, is set in 300 acres of rolling grounds that descend to a string of private beaches. It is large, with 150 rooms around the central estate house of coral rock, but elegant and comfortable in an older Caribbean style. High on a hill further east you will find a luxurious enclave at the **Villa Madeleine**, PO Box 24190 (℗ 773 8141, fax 773 7518, US ℗ 800 548 4461). Built in the formal style of a plantation house, the villa itself is new, but it has a comfortable ambience with billiard room and piano bar. The 43 villas each have their own pool and a view, and are sumptuous and very neat—bamboo four-posters and wicker furniture—and have all the necessities for 20th-century comfort including cable television and video recorder. Very expensive. A comfortable beach hotel on a quiet beach is the **Chenay Bay Beach Resort**, PO Box 24600, St Croix 00824 (℗ 773 2918, fax 773 2918, US ℗ 800 548 4457). There are 50 prettily decorated rooms in quite simple cottages set in a horseshoe around a grassy garden above a small, calm beach. Air-conditioning, television, telephone, kitch- enettes and balconies; expensive. At the other end of the island you will find an extremely fine setting at the **Sprat Hall Plantation**, PO Box 695 (℗ 772 0305, US ℗ 800 843 3584), a couple of miles north of Frederik- sted. The estate house, in which three rooms are decorated with period furniture, including four-posters, dates from the late 1600s. Sprat Hall stands in open grounds just in from the coast, where there is a private beach. Small but friendly, just 18 rooms, some with kitchens, but a fine antique dining room with home cooking. Moderate to expensive.

moderate

St Croix has a number of small hotels and inns with great charm, many of them set among the old buildings of Christiansted. In town, the **Pink Fancy**, at 27 Prince Street, a little way from the centre (℗ 773 8460, US ℗ 800 524 2045), has just 10 rooms, set in a old town house with arched brick foundations and a clapboard upper, with louvred windows and shutters. As the name suggests, it is painted pink, but the rooms are decorated with Brazil wood in keeping with the antique style. An echo from St Croix's illustrious past, it serves breakfast, but has no restaurant. **Hilty House**, PO Box 26077, St Croix, USVI 00824 (℃/fax 773 2594) has just five rooms set in a private house on the hill behind Christiansted. Very elegant and stylish ambience, with hand-painted tile floors and stucco walls, and a gracious welcome and personal attention from the English owners. Pool and sunning deck, bed and breakfast plan. It's a good idea to have a car. There is a clutch of other small hotels in Christiansted, set in the trading streets and converted warehouses along the waterfront. **Club Comanche**, 1 Strand Street (℃ 773 0210, US ℃ 800 524 2066), is in the thick of it in the centre of town. The 40 rooms are reached via a network of stairs, walkways and balconies from the old wooden main house. Rooms are air-conditioned with cable television and some have kitchens. For marginally less you can stay at the **Danish Manor Hotel**, 2 Company Street (℃ 773 1377, fax 773 1913, US ℃ 800 524 2069), where the 14 rooms give on to the brick courtyard with pool and explosive greenery.

There are a few places to stay around Frederiksted. In town, try the **Antilles Frederiksted Hotel**, 20 Strand Street (℃ 773 0500, US ℃ 800 524 2025), a comfortable hotel with a small courtyard. There are not many cheap places to stay in St Croix. The least expensive is **Paradise Sunset Beach Hotel**, PO Box 1788, St Croix 00840 (℃ 772 2499, fax 772 0001), near the northwestern tip of the island. Quite a simple set-up, with rooms in a block that stands above a pool. Fine view of the sunset and sand close by.

℃ (809)–   **Eating Out**

Christiansted

Like the hotels, many of Christiansted's restaurants and bars are set in pretty town houses and along the waterfront. If you are staying at the eastern end of the island it's worth making the effort to get to Frederiksted for a cocktail and dinner. Restaurants accept credit cards and most charge service at 10%. Categories are arranged according to the price of a main dish: *expensive*—US$20 and above; *moderate*—US$10–$20; *cheap*—US$10 and below.

expensive

At **Kendrick's** (℃ 773 9199) on King Street, you climb stone stairs to reach a subdued and intimate antique drawing room where bow-tied waiters ply back and forth to multiple dining rooms in smaller annexes. Start with the rum punch and follow with baked artichoke heart with seared scallops, shallots and lemon cream, then grilled shrimp with spicy gazpacho butter sauce and finish with an exotic coffee. Mainly French in inspiration, and nouvelle in presentation, moderate to expensive, reserve in season. The **Top Hat** restaurant (© 773 2346) on Company Street is run by Danes and retains some Danish elements in its menu. There is a lively bar where you can linger before moving in to the wooden-walled dining room with its tray roof and network of supporting beams. Home-made sausages followed by *flikadeller* (meatballs) with red cabbage and mashed potato, or Copenhagen steak. **Picnic in Paradise** (© 778 1212) has a charming setting on a waterfront deck and an airy dining room, on the north shore near the Carambola Hotel. Innovative international cuisine.

moderate

At the **Tivoli Gardens** (© 773 6782) you eat on a veranda hung with greenery. Try chicken tivolese, in tomato sour-cream sauce, or snapper Marrakech in orange, cumin and coriander sauce. Named after the proto-continent of the Mesozoic era (180 million years ago), **Pangaea** (© 773 7743) is set in a pretty creole town house with a balcony where you dine while watching the street go by. Intimate air and African decor in the shields and patterned table-cloths, mainly Caribbean fare—spiced red snapper with tamarind and coconut or boneless breast of chicken with Haiti Mamba. **Kim's** restaurant (© 773 3377) is a small and charming spot, over-brightly dressed in pink and painted flowers. Local food and some international dishes, menu on a clipboard, very friendly service. Great ice-creams. The curiously named **Anabelle's Tea Room** (© 773 3990) uses the best of its setting in a courtyard, where you dine under trees. Spanish, Cuban and general West Indian fare. **Luncheria** (© 773 4247) is also in a pretty court-yard on Company Street in town. Mexican food; *enchiladas*, *burritos* and *tostadas*. **Duggan's Reef** (© 773 9800) looks over the waterfront to Buck Island, and is a fun place for dinner, with international fare.

cheap

For something a little more local, try **Harvey's** on Company Street, which has a classic West Indian setting, complete with plastic tablecloths and fold-away chairs. No written menu—chat with Sarah through the stable door. Try callaloo followed by conch in butter sauce, or chicken or goat (curried or stewed). It comes with a tonnage of ground provisions—sweet potato, plantain and yam. Another option is **Junie's**, near the 7th Day Adventist Church and the Hess Oil Refinery. Plastic table-cloths, huge anthuriums and loud music; stew fish, chicken or curried shrimp with more ground provisions. For an international style snack-bar try **Cheeseburgers in**

Paradise, set in a pretty tin-roofed shack by the roadside heading east from town. Excellent cheeseburgers, sandwiches and salads, popular with a local white crowd. For the best roti and take-away chicken, try **Singh's Fast Food** restaurant at the top end of King Street by the Anglican Church in town. If you are in need of a strong cup of coffee for breakfast, a popular place is **Morning Glory** in Gallow's Bay, opposite the main post office.

Frederiksted

Le St Tropez (© 772 3000) stands in the centre of town on King Street, its dining room walls hung with memorabilia, and palms in the courtyard garden. The cuisine is French—even *cuisses de grenouille persillées* (frogs' legs) as a starter, followed by *magret de canard aux baies roses*, moderate. The **Café du Soleil** (© 772 5400) has a very attractive setting with pink decor and trelliswork on an upstairs deck, looking through lit trees to the sea. The menu is French and international. Start with a *panache* of seafood in saffron broth, with leeks and tomatoes; follow with chicken breast in a marsala or tricolor salsa. Moderate, closed Thurs. The **Blue Moon** (© 772 2222) is set in the vaulted interior of an old trading house on Strand Gade. Cajun barbecue shrimp, or Florida-raised, pan-seared catfish, followed by hot fudge rum cake. Live jazz on Fridays; Sunday brunch is also a favourite gathering time. **Pier 69** is ever popular, a courtyard with parasols and a bar-boat set inside, with music at the weekends. For something a little more West Indian try **Stars of the West**, in one of the old warehouses on Strand Gade; bake chicken or conch, steam fish, cheap.

Bars and Nightlife

Many of the restaurants listed above and the beach bars double as bars in the evening. There are some fun bars on the waterfront in Christiansted, where the yachties crawl ashore for a beer. You can start an evening at **Stixx Hurricane Bar** or the bar at the Comanche Hotel, which is good for an early evening drink listening to the piano player. **Cocktails** on Kongens Gade is a loud and lively video bar, and **Spinnaker's Grille**, in the Gallow's Bay area, is an American-style sports bar with a weekend karaoke session. The beach bars north of **Frederiksted** are ideal for a cocktail while you watch the sunset. Or you can catch a beer and a game of darts at the **Brandy Snifter** on King Street.

Some hotels stage steel band shows and live jazz: ask around. There are two discotheques on the island: **Two plus Two** on the Northside Road just west of town, and **Calabash**, open mainly at the weekends.

Note: page numbers in *italics* indicate maps. **Bold** entries indicate main references.

Index